GUNSLINGERS

Allied Fighter Boys of WWII

JAMES P. BUSHA

LYONS
PRESS

Guilford, Connecticut

An imprint of Globe Pequot, the trade division of
The Rowman & Littlefield Publishing Group, Inc.
4501 Forbes Blvd., Ste. 200
Lanham, MD 20706
www.rowman.com

Distributed by NATIONAL BOOK NETWORK

British Library Cataloguing in Publication Information available

Library of Congress Cataloging-in-Publication Data
Names: Busha, James P., author.
Title: Gunslingers : Allied fighter boys of WWII / James P. Busha.
Other titles: Allied fighter boys of WWII
Description: Guilford, Connecticut : Lyons Press, [2022] | Includes index. | Summary: "This book focuses on the young men who answered the call to duty and were transformed from "farm boys to fighter pilots." It offers a rare glimpse of what it was like to fly a variety of frontline fighters in World War II, including P-39 Airacobras, P-40 Warhawks, P-38 Lightnings, P-47 Thunderbolts, and P-51 Mustangs, among many others"— Provided by publisher.
Identifiers: LCCN 2021043283 (print) | LCCN 2021043284 (ebook) | ISBN 9781493063697 (hardcover) | ISBN 9781493063703 (epub)
Subjects: LCSH: United States. Army Air Forces—Biography. | Fighter pilots—United States—Interviews. | Fighter pilots—Great Britain—Interviews. | Fighter planes—United States—History—20th century—Anecdotes. | Fighter planes—Great Britain—History—20th century—Anecdotes. | Great Britain. Royal Air Force—Biography. | World War, 1939-1945—Aerial operations, American. | World War, 1939-1945—Aerial operations, British. | World War, 1939-1945—Personal narratives, American. | World War, 1939-1945—Personal narratives, British.
Classification: LCC D790.2 .B87 2022 (print) | LCC D790.2 (ebook) | DDC 940.54/490922 [B]—dc23/eng/20211012
LC record available at https://lccn.loc.gov/2021043283
LC ebook record available at https://lccn.loc.gov/2021043284

♾️™ The paper used in this publication meets the minimum requirements of American National Standard for Information Sciences—Permanence of Paper for Printed Library Materials, ANSI/NISO Z39.48-1992.

CONTENTS

CONTENTS

Introduction

Just Doing My Job

When I began interviewing pilots from World War II in 1999, I always ended the conversation with, "I wish I would have called you twenty years earlier." There was always a long pause, and the gentleman I had just spent the last several hours with would say, "I wouldn't have talked to you then. The only reason I'm telling you all of this now is so my grandchildren, or great-grandchildren, know what their grandfather did in the war."

Each of the more than 350 pilots I interviewed, from all branches of the service, made one fact very clear: They were not the heroes. In their minds, they had simply answered their country's call of duty and service. They were "just doing their jobs" to preserve freedom for the entire world. To them, the real heroes were the guys who gave the ultimate sacrifice and didn't make it back. These combat veterans all have a common bond, as they all flew and fought in World War II as fighter pilots. Their stories give you the unique perspective seldom heard as they place you center stage inside the various cockpits with the brave airmen who flew these harrowing missions. Their fears, humor, and sadness will help you understand what it must have been like living on a razor's edge during aerial combat.

Unfortunately, the era of the World War II generation is drawing to a close. Almost every pilot depicted in this book has since "Gone West." Remember this when you read about their exploits, the dangers they faced, and the sacrifices they made as they laid their lives on the line so future generations could enjoy the freedoms we share today. Tell others about this book, and books like it, for we shall be indebted to these brave men forever. We must never, ever forget what our brave soldiers, past and present, have done for our countries. They did more than their fair share. In my mind, they are all heroes.

—Jim Busha, 2020

PART I

BACKS AGAINST THE WALL: 1940–1943

Their Finest Hour: RAF Spitfire

To the neutral observer in 1940—especially those individuals living comfortably and relatively free thousands of miles away inside the safe confines of the United States of America—the war in Europe resembled a rather large chess game played out on a much grander scale. The black king, queen, rooks, knights, bishops, and pawns—also known as the Nazis—were having a field day as they blitzkrieged across Poland, Denmark, Norway, Belgium, Holland, Luxembourg, and, finally, France. It seemed that no country—no army, air force, or navy—could stop the German war machine as it set its sights on the island nation of Great Britain.

By all accounts, the lone "white knight" known as England stood firm and stoic as the early summer of 1940 brought with it much uncertainty and growing apprehension. The situation looked rather grim, with the capture and occupation of the country seemingly inevitable. The German High Command with its well-trained Luftwaffe, held at bay on a very short leash, were watching from across the English Channel. They enjoyed the spoils of French cuisine and wine as they waited for England to drop to her knees and beg for mercy.

But the Germans in their infinite ignorance failed to take into account the undying spirit and never-ending will of the free people living and breathing just a stone's throw away across the Channel, resolved to fight to the last man.

The final stage had been set as the curtain slowly opened on the greatest air battle known to man. The Battle of Britain was about to take place between the highly trained Luftwaffe fighters and bombers and the vastly outnumbered but equally nimble Hurricane and Spitfire fighters of the Royal Air Force (RAF).

When German commander Hermann Göring finally unleashed his "hounds of the Luftwaffe" in July of 1940, he had at his disposal over 1,200 bombers, 300 dive-bombers, and almost 1,100 fighters ready to swarm over England at will and annihilate the British aircraft industry and massive ground infrastructure. Göring, along with his superior, Adolf Hitler, believed that if they caused a panic among the British people through intimidation and terror, they would be able to force England into an unconditional surrender. What Hitler and his cohorts didn't count on was the 2,440 British RAF and more than 500 pilots from various free and occupied countries joining together as one to form an impenetrable wall of RAF fighter aircraft.

As the rest of the free world watched and held out hope, praying for the island nation, swirling dogfights between Spitfires, Hurricanes, and Bf 109s took place in the skies over England as wretched black contrails poured from the burning, twisted aircraft. Fighters and bombers fell from the English sky in great numbers as losses of men and aircraft on both sides began to mount. In a speech given during the height of the battle, in August of 1940, Prime Minister Winston Churchill famously said of these brave men, "Never in the field of human conflict was so much owed by so many to so few."

Here are stories from some of these courageous few who fought over the fields of England and Australia, far away from their homelands, sacrificing personal dreams, hopes, and aspirations, all in the name of freedom.

SPITFIRE MK I
Pilot/Officer Ludwig Martel
603 Squadron RAF

My early fighter training was performed in my home country of Poland during the spring of 1939. I was flying P-7 open-cockpit, high-wing, fixed-landing-gear fighters. I only flew the P-7 for a short time, though, because I had to flee my country from the blitzkrieging Nazis. I focused all my attention on fighting the "bloody German bastards" and flying for the RAF.

I eventually made it to England where I was welcomed with open arms and accepted into the RAF. I received 20 hours of flight training in the Spitfire Mk I and felt that it was the most wonderful aircraft I had ever flown. I learned the English language and the English way of flying in an operational training unit and found it to be a very pleasant experience. That is, until I went into combat.

The early fighter tactics of the RAF were about the only thing I disagreed with. We had been taught to fly in a very close, tight formation. With twelve Spitfires flying that close, it was difficult to look around for the Luftwaffe, let alone to keep an eye on our leader. The Germans called our V-shaped formations *idiotenreihen*, which means "rows of idiots." I certainly felt like one when I got shot down in my Spitfire on October 25, 1940, as I stayed in formation while the German Bf 109s attacked from above. It was quite apparent that the Germans had a different philosophy in fighter tactics, and eventually the RAF saw the light and changed theirs, too.

Pilot/Officer Ludwig Martel COURTESY OF LUDWIG MARTEL/JAMES BUSHA

ME 110 SANDWICH
Pilot/Officer Al Deere
54 Squadron RAF

On May 26, 1940, approaching Gravelines at 17,000 feet, two enemy aircraft were sighted. Red Leader and I gave chase using 12 boost. These aircraft were identified as Me 110s. Red Leader shot one down in flames. On returning to Grave we saw enemy bombers attacking destroyers off Calais. Ongoing into the attack we were in turn attacked by Me 110s. I shot one Me 110 down in flames after three bursts and immediately became sandwiched between two more Me 110s experiencing considerable fire. I steep-turned and got on the tail of one Me 110, and after three short bursts both engines commenced smoking. The enemy, rapidly losing height, prepared to land north of Calais. I then returned to base as my port wing was badly shot away.

HELL'S BELLES
Flight Lt. B. Lane
19 Squadron RAF

I was on patrol on May 26, 1940, leading Yellow Section with 19 Squadron. We were at approximately 10,000 feet over Calais when we sighted twenty-one Ju 87s proceeding out to sea. I was astern of Red Section, who attacked the starboard rear section on E/A (enemy aircraft), Blue Section attacking a section on the port side of the formation. I attacked as soon as I could, selecting an E/A to starboard of the formation, as it turned left.

I fired one burst at approximately 400 yards from below and astern. Tracers appeared to enter E/A, which climbed and stalled. I fired again

Mk II Supermarine Spitfires prepare to launch from an English base. COURTESY OF BOB LARGE/JAMES BUSHA

from about 200 yards and E/A went into a dive. The escorting Me 109s were by this time attacking and I was forced to break away, but sighted a Ju 87 diving toward the sea.

No fire was experienced from the rear gun, and E/A appeared to be out of control. I looked around and observed an Me 109 attacking a Spitfire, which was almost immediately hit forward of the cockpit by a shell from the E/A. The Spitfire went into a steep dive and I subsequently observed a parachute in the sea about a mile off Calais.

A dogfight now ensued, and I fired a burst at several E/A, mostly deflection shots. Three E/A attached themselves to my tail, two doing astern attacks while the third attacked from the beam. I managed to turn toward this E/A and fired a good burst in a front-quarter deflection attack. The E/A then disappeared and was probably shot down.

By this time I was down to sea level, and made for the English coast, taking violent evasive action. I gradually drew away from the E/A using 12-pound boost, which gave me an airspeed of 300 mph.

SPITFIRE MK I
Pilot/Officer Robert "Bob" Large
Operational Training Unit, Scotland

During the summer of 1940, when the great air battles between the RAF and Luftwaffe took place high over England, I was stuck in Scotland having just completed my checkout in the Harvard. Having survived training thus far, the RAF instructors had no other choice but to turn me loose on the Spitfire Mk I. Like everyone else before me, it was a wonderful experience. There were no dual controls and no instructor screaming at me in the back to "put in more rudder, watch your airspeed!" I was alone and relied on my training and luck.

The very first time I took off in the Spitfire Mk I was the most exhilarating experience I had ever had thus far. The power was enormous compared to the previous aircraft I had flown. I remember flying in the Spit I. As you selected your undercarriage up with your right hand and then with your left hand, you pumped a large handle up and down to manually bring your gear up. It was an extraordinary thing as I went roaring into

Pilot/Officer Robert "Bob" Large COURTESY OF BOB LARGE

the sky, working this handle backward and forward, causing my stick to move in the opposite direction each time I pumped the handle. The Spitfire flew up and down with each rhythm of my pumping.

What a sight it must have been for my poor instructor on the ground, seeing me on the verge of destroying an RAF aircraft. To make matters worse, I had left the hood open on takeoff and my scarf began to billow and unravel from around my neck. The scarf flew out and twisted my helmet and oxygen mask around my face until I couldn't see anything at all.

But that was how we learned. We were young and quickly sorted these things out. If we didn't, then we were dead!

DOUBLE TROUBLE
Sgt. P. Else
610 Squadron RAF

On July 25, 1940, I was flying No. 2 position in Blue Section when we sighted about twenty or more Me 109s above twelve Ju 87s. We climbed in line astern to attack the 109s and fired at one with considerable deflection, with no results. I then had to shake one Me 109 off my tail, which I did with comparative ease with a tight diving turn. I then found myself on the edge of the melee and slightly on the starboard rear beam of two Me 109s flying in line astern.

I attacked the rear machine from the quarter closing to astern, opening fire at 200 yards and closing at about 25 yards. I could see the explosive bullets from my guns hitting him in the rear of the fuselage and the tail unit. As I broke off the attack—owing to the danger of hitting him—he fell on one side, evidently from the attitude the machine had adopted, out of control. Both Me 109s took no evasive action at all, as I caught them both by surprise. The Me 109s were definitely working in pairs.

BLOODY WELL DONE!
Pilot/Officer R. Wallens
41 Squadron RAF

I was Green Leader during a squadron patrol on August 8, 1940, when over Manston at 25,000 feet I sighted below me at 12,000 feet about six aircraft. I detached my section to investigate and found that the aircraft in question were Me 109s, seven in number in two straggling vics of three and four. My number 3 attacked the rear of the latter formation, and I attacked from astern using only a very short burst when he broke away. E/A must have been hit in the petrol tanks, as white and blue smoke poured forth and the E/A went straight into the sea.

On coming up from this attack I found myself on the tail of another Me 109. A short burst from the quarter using deflection was sufficient to send this aircraft into the sea off Dover. I engaged a third Me 109, and a short burst from close range sent it straight into the sea off Goodwin Sands. I pursued E/A across the Channel and had to use evasive action myself. When just off Calais (3,000 feet), I saw a fourth Me 109 flying at sea level. I did a diving quarter attack giving only a very short burst and this E/A toppled straight into the sea.

On my return to England a torpedo motorboat that must have left Calais Harbour loomed up in front of me and I fired a short burst in passing. I saw a number of the crew enter the sea rapidly as a result of this attack!

It is difficult to estimate the height at which each combat took place, but the running fight was between sea level and 12,000 feet. Much use was made by E/A of the cloud banks between 3,000 and 8,000 feet and the haze over the sea. On this occasion the enemy was prepared to fight, but he wanted to carry it across to the French coast.

I had no difficulty in overtaking the Me 109s either diving or in level flight. They were silver all over with the usual black crosses and seemed by their appearance to be new machines.

Running Late
Sgt. J. Stokoe
603 Squadron RAF

On August 31, 1940, we were ordered to patrol base at 12,000 feet. As I was rather late, the formation took off without me. I took off alone, climbed into the sun, and rejoined the formation, which was circling at about 28,000 feet. I observed two Me 109s above and climbed after them in full-fire pitch.

The Me 109s kept close together in a steep spiral climb toward the sun. I pumped several bursts at the outside one from about 200 yards with little effect. I closed to about 50 yards and fired two more long bursts. Black smoke poured from his engine, which appeared to catch fire, and eight to nine huge pieces of his fuselage were shot away. He spun steeply away and crashed inside the balloon barrage.

I continued climbing after the other Me 109 and fired two long bursts from about 150 yards. White smoke came from his aircraft, and he spiraled gently downward. I broke away as I was out of ammunition, and failed to see what happened to him.

Tally Ho!
Pilot/Officer N. Agazarian
609 Squadron RAF

We were patrolling Bournemouth at 18,000 feet on September 26, 1940, when we saw a formation of about sixty bombers approaching the Isle of Wight. We went to intercept them and were just about to attack when Me 109s flew over our heads and proceeded to get behind us.

My leader started taking evasive action and I followed as long as possible. Finding that I couldn't, I decided to attack the bombers, and went in to the leader from the beam. I opened fire at about 300 yards and gave him a two-second burst. As I broke away I saw glycol streaming from his port engine. I decided to try an attack from dead ahead. The bombers were turning south; I couldn't get my lights on, so I did not fire, and narrowly escaped collision.

I climbed up on their starboard side—they were crossing the Isle of Wight on their way home—and attacked the last E/A from the beam, following up with the quarter, and saw black smoke streaming from his starboard engine. This may have been an He 111. I opened fire at 300 yards and gave in all about five seconds. I think I gave another attack on the bomber but can remember nothing about it.

I then climbed up to attack an Me 109. When I saw another diving past me, I turned and dived after it. It zoomed and I followed, getting in a short burst from about 400 yards. I then gave my machine full throttle and rev and caught up with the 109 hand over fist. When about 50 yards away and directly behind, I gave him the rest of my ammunition. He went onto his back and spun down. I followed him down, and the spin straightened out into a vertical dive so that I could not keep up with him. I lost interest and climbed up to about 3,000 feet and went home.

SUPERMARINE SPITFIRE MK V
Pilot Robert W. "Bob" Foster
1 Wing RAAF 54 Squadron, Darwin, Australia

It had been Prime Minister Winston Churchill's idea to send us to Australia in late 1942. I think it was more of a political goodwill gesture on his behalf as a return on a favor for sending Australians to the deserts of North Africa. Whatever the case, we were all allies joined together to fight the Axis.

I had originally flown Hawker Hurricanes during the Battle of Britain and in turn trained over one hundred fellow pilots in Hurricane flying before I was sent to Australia in the summer of 1942. My beloved Hurricane was left behind in England and was exchanged for the Spitfire Mk V. I found the Spitfire to be a good airplane to fly, but when it came to mixing it up with the Zeros, it lacked the maneuverability to stay with them.

The fighter tactics in the South Pacific were much different compared to what I had been used to back in England. When we tangled with the German 109s, we could mix it up and stay with them, but out here in the "bush" against a Zero, things were much different. The Spitfire

RAF pilot Robert W.
"Bob" Foster COURTESY OF
ROBERT FOSTER

had the height and speed advantage, but the Zero reigned supreme when it came to turning. If one had any sense or a desire to stay alive, you didn't try to mix with a Zero at all costs. Most of our time was spent sitting on the ground until we were scrambled to intercept the inbound Japanese bombers. Our role was purely defensive, because the Spitfires we flew did not have the range to escort the Allied bombers to their targets.

On February 6, 1943, I was part of a flight of two Spitfires, scrambled from our base at Darwin to intercept an incoming Japanese reconnaissance Mitsubishi Dinah aircraft. The Dinah was very lightweight and very fast, and it gave the Australian P-40 Kittyhawks fits because they could never catch it. Things were about to change as we climbed to intercept this one. Our Spits were just as fast as the Dinah, and I think we surprised them when we came in from behind, high and fast, shooting it down. It was the first aerial victory for the squadron and the first victory for me in a Spitfire.

By the end of July 1943, I had shot down four more Japanese airplanes, all Betty bombers, as they made their raids into Australia. The tide had turned, as the Japanese bombing raids became few and far between, the last one occurring in late July.

I finally was sent back home to England, as my time had expired. I had been going at it since the summer of 1940. At times, it seemed as if this war would never end.

2

Bloody Good Show: P-40

ADVENTURES IN THE "WAIRARAPA WILDCAT"
Flight Officer Geoffrey B. Fisken
Royal New Zealand Air Force (RNZAF)

Buffalo Rider

In February 1942, while the Japanese army closed in on the besieged city of Singapore, the Commonwealth Forces found themselves with their backs up against the wall. They desperately tried to slow the advance. If the Japanese could be stalled for even a short period of time, it meant that the Commonwealth Forces could "advance to the rear" and fight another day.

Coordinated attacks by Japanese air and ground forces coupled with superior modern equipment gave little hope to the retreating Allies. A decimated RAF tried in vain to halt the aerial onslaught. Outnumbered and outgunned, sixteen to one, pilots of the RAF and the RNZAF continued to slug it out with the Japanese Zeros.

Most of the "slugging" was done by the Zeros. The outdated and underpowered F2A Brewster Buffalos flown by Commonwealth pilots were no match for the tight-turning, agile Zero. However, in the right hands, whether flying a Buffalo or a Kittyhawk, one Allied pilot exploited a weakness in Japanese aerial tactics. He noted, "In order to be successful against the Japanese, especially the Zero, one had to have an altitude and attitude advantage. I thought the Buffalo was a delight to fly. A beautiful airplane but a bit underpowered. The Zeros were too fast and they could

RAF and RNZAF Brewster Buffalos line up for inspection near Singapore.

turn inside of us. If you wanted to dogfight them, you simply committed suicide."

Being young and somewhat foolhardy, I still had aspirations of growing old back in New Zealand. When we saw a flight of Japanese fighters coming in, we climbed as high as we could above them. As they drew closer, we pushed the old Buffalo over, throttles to the stops, and went screaming down, firing through them. We were always outnumbered, which to me was an advantage, as I had more targets to pick from!

On February 1, 1942, it was no different. I already had five victories against various Japanese aircraft. Little did I know that this would be my last flight in the Buffalo. Pushing the nose over and picking up speed, I hurtled myself at the swarm of Zeros below. I picked one out and gave him a three-second burst. With no protective armor, it burst into flames and cartwheeled down.

Two of his friends latched on to me as I tried to shake them. I got a bit of a cannon shell in the leg and a bullet in the arm. The Buffalo was chewed to pieces as I dove for the deck. My undercarriage was shot out. My engine was coughing and smoking as my prop stopped. I managed to bring it in to Kallang Aerodrome and crash-landed it there. In the process, I busted up my knee, but other than that, I was all right!

Big Bad Kitty

With my arm in plaster and me walking on a stick, I wasn't much use to the RNZAF. On February 12, 1942, along with some others, I was loaded on a sampan and delivered to a larger ship that took us to New Zealand. Sadly, 130,000 of my fellow Allied countrymen weren't so lucky. If only I'd had an airplane with more horsepower, then maybe I could have done some good.

My wish was granted when I returned to New Zealand, posted with the newly formed 14 Squadron, which contained remnants of 488 Squadron NZ and the remains of the RAF. We were introduced to our new machines. P-40 Kittyhawks given to us by the Yanks lined our field. I quickly checked out in the P-40 and found it a delight to fly.

The transition was easy and straightforward. The P-40 was much faster, more responsive, and enjoyable to fly. It had no bad habits to speak of. But then again I had been so accustomed to so many bad habits in the Buffalo that flying the P-40 was a "piece of cake"!

We stayed in New Zealand for the next nine months and trained with our new planes. A lovely Allison motor powered the P-40s. It carried a total of six .50 caliber machine guns, three in each wing, with a fixed steel ring gunsight out ahead of me to make sure I hit what I aimed at.

I began to work with my armor on how I wanted my bullets loaded. With a series of ball, armor-piercing, explosive, and tracer rounds, we came up with a deadly combination. I also sighted my own guns in. I had them sighted into an area of about 15 square feet. This was a very tight firing area, as I wanted to make sure that whatever flew through this "cone of death" didn't survive.

As I got squared away on my own P-40, I tried to help some of the newer fellows with defensive tactics. A lot of instrument training by flying into clouds would be a lifesaver in combat. Many times, when I had a Zero or two on my tail, I would pop into a cloud and escape. The Zero would not follow but would stay on the outside, waiting. After a while they got sick and tired of waiting for me to come out and flew away.

New Tactics and Plenty of Targets

I was promoted to flight officer and given my own section to lead. Our training and tactics were quite similar to when I flew the Buffalos. When the Japanese were spotted, we would climb as fast as we could above them. Calling the bounce, we pushed the Kittyhawks over and picked out a red circle painted on their wings. As long as you stayed focused on a single target and didn't try to "flock shoot," you would do all right.

Rocketing downward at well over 400 miles an hour in this hit-and-run road made the Japanese mad as hell! There was no way their planes could survive our high-speed dive. Using our newly gained energy, we simply pulled out of the dive and screamed back up to give it another go. In a very short time, we proved just how successful these tactics were.

In mid-1943, the Yanks invited us to a place called Guadalcanal. We were given new P-40Ms and asked to join the show. The P-40 I got had a big menacing black cat painted on the nose. My wife, along with most of my crew, was from Wairarapa, New Zealand. So the name "Wairarapa Wildcat" was added to the cowling. Now it was time to go "claw up" some Zeros!

As we began to fly combat patrols around the Solomons, a "new threat" emerged, even more menacing than the Japanese: trigger-happy Yanks! I would be stooging along on patrol, half-asleep, when I was awakened by the sound of machine-gun fire. Looking back in the rearview mirror, there were Airacobras on my tail, shooting at me! I knew the Yanks were eager for combat, but I was on their side!

Eventually a circular went around to all the bases showing drawings of what a New Zealand P-40 looked like. It was also decided at that time to add a set of "starburst" white stripes on the wings and fuselage and a white spinner for the nose. It seemed to work, as the Yanks stopped firing at us. Later, they got bad again, so we had to paint our tails white! They used to fire at anything and everything! I can laugh now, but it wasn't very funny back then.

On June 12, 1943, we had received word from our coast-watchers that the Japanese were on their way down with a large force of fighters. Climbing through 20,000 feet, I could see them coming. I saw about twenty-five Zeros trying to circle around behind us. They still had the

Flight Officer Geoffrey B. Fisken, RNZAF

altitude on us as they came closer. The lead Zero went right through our flight of twelve P-40s, firing his cannons and machine guns at us, when suddenly he pulled up right in front of our flight to do a split turn. He never had a chance.

The Zero was about 250 yards out ahead of me as I concentrated on that big, red circle—a very nice target. I gave him a five-second burst and saw hits just below the cockpit and at the wing root. He immediately burst into flame and went over. I glanced in my mirror and saw a few of the buggers shooting at me.

I pushed the throttle through the gate, rolled her on over, and dove out of there. As I pulled back up with plenty of energy, I saw three more Zeros above me. I picked one out and gave him a couple of three-second bursts, hitting him. The smoke turned to flame as he crashed below. The other two joined with some more Zeros. Ganging up on me, they tried to tear me apart. I did the only thing I knew how to do: dive and get the hell out of there as fast as I could!

Diving downward, I saw another threesome of Zeros at 3,000 feet. I had a shot at one of them, poor at best. I gave him a good burst as the deflection increased. The tracers were loopy as hell, but I saw hits and part of his wing tear away and fall off. After that, the Zeros just disappeared and left. Running low on ammo, I did the same and returned to Henderson Field.

We flew almost daily in search of the Japanese. We never really had to look that hard, as they always seemed to be around. On one flight I got tangled up with a lone Zero. Instead of diving away, I stayed in there to see what the P-40 could do. As I began to turn with the Zero, I put my feet on the dashboard and hung on to the stick as hard as I could. I tried to pull her around but had no luck. The Zero was turning inside of me so I gave it up and got out of there. That was the only time I was foolish enough to try that "bad job."

In July of 1943, I was a newly promoted flight lieutenant with a mild case of malaria. There were two kinds of pilots I flew with: ones with malaria and ones that were going to get malaria. It was just something you lived with and hoped you didn't get an attack in the air.

Increasing Odds

All in all, morale was quite good as the Allies made a stand at Guadalcanal, stopping the Japanese advance. If it hadn't been for the Yanks and their machines they gave us, I fear New Zealand would have been occupied. It also became apparent that their numbers were decreasing. Instead of sixteen Zeros to one P-40, it was now down to ten to one!

On July 4, 1943, a flight of twelve RNZAF P-40s took off and headed for the New Georgia area. It seemed that the Japanese had torpedoed some of our Allied ships as they were coming down the straits. We had radio contact with the destroyers in the area as we approached our top cover assignment. Originally, three flights of four P-40s would provide top cover for the disabled ships.

Just before we got there, one of the ships below called "Two inbound bogeys at 3,000 feet." A section leader senior to me left with four P-40s to investigate. It turned out to be a costly mistake, for both of us.

A third of our flight had just left when I spotted trouble ahead. Forty Zeros escorting half as many twin-engine Bettys were on their way to finish off the ships. The only thing standing in their way was a bunch of

New Zealand "cowboys" itching for a fight. For some unknown reason, my armorer had loaded my P-40 up with more explosive ammo than usual. Bless his heart!

Flying at 20,000 the Zeros saw us at the exact same time. They were flying top cover for the Bettys that were below us at 10,000 feet. The Zeros turned into us as we began to go around in a large circle, each trying to gain the advantage. They turned into us and made a head-on pass. I got one Zero right away with a full deflection shot. The explosive ammo lit him up as his fireball fell back to earth. I argued with another Zero as we scissored back and forth. He crossed into my firing cone just long enough. He too fell earthward. My mirror was full of Zeros as I pushed it on over and dove for the deck.

On my way down I saw the flight of Bettys heading for the ships. I pulled out of my dive and got behind the upside Betty. I was a bit higher than he was as I centered the gunsight. The Betty took some evasive action as it began its own dive to escape me. At 300 yards I began to fire at the Betty. I could see muzzle flashes from the rear guns as he tried to knock me down. The gunner failed to compensate enough, as his shells missed me. At 250 yards his guns were silenced as I belted him.

Instead of aiming for the engines or wings, I aimed for the cockpit. I figured if I could concentrate my fire in that area, then that's where the most damage would be done. The Betty began to smoke and wing over as I closed on her, still firing.

The fireball was intense as the Betty blew up right in front of me. I flew through the orange ball of fire as pieces of the Betty struck my plane. My P-40 whistled on through, the Allison never missing a beat. I was completely out of ammo as I dove to the water below. The sea below was full of aircraft pieces and roundels of water where airplanes had crashed. I headed for home alone, wondering how the other chaps had fared.

My number two did not make it. He got tangled up with some Zeros and bailed out. I found out later that the Japanese killed him on the ground. I had some words with the section leader that was senior to me. I told him if he ever left me again to look for bogeys, he wouldn't have to worry about the Japanese getting him, as I would shoot him myself, right between the eyes!

Shortly thereafter, with only one week of flight lieutenant experience under my belt, I was demoted back to flight officer. At least the pay was good while it lasted! The scrapes with the Japanese soon tapered off, too. The tables were turned and it was now our turn to be on the offensive.

The Allied momentum increased at a very rapid rate as the Japanese began to get pushed back. Most of my P-40 flying was now in a dive-bomber role, supporting troops on the ground. A few bomber escorts with the hopes of tangling with a Zero or two never materialized.

In late 1943, the injuries that I received in Singapore began to catch up with my body. Reluctantly, I was invalided out of the war and returned to New Zealand. I picked up where I left off, working as a shepherd on one of my family's stations (farms). Although I now slogged through sheep manure, I couldn't have survived without the P-40!

(FO Geoff Fisken finished the war with eleven aerial victories and became one of the RNZAF's highest-ranking aces.)

3

Over the Blue: Yanks in Spitfires over the Mediterranean

Although the United States supplied many different types of airplanes to its Allies during World War II, there was one particular "Reverse Lend-Lease" aircraft the British most enjoyed sharing with her friends: the Supermarine Spitfire. Whether utilized as a ground strafer, a bomber escort, or a photoreconnaissance platform, the British-built Spit was considered a dream to fly by most Yank fighter pilots. Although it had been deployed to different locations all over the world and proved its worth tenfold, it was over the deserts of North Africa and the Mediterranean Theater of Operations (MTO) that it held the line with the fledgling US Army Air Force.

Follow along as three American pilots share their insights into what it was like to fly the legendary Spitfire.

COMPARING THE SPITFIRE MK V TO THE EARLY AMERICAN FIGHTERS
Lt. Col. Robert J. Gobel, USAF
31st Fighter Group, 308th Fighter Squadron, 12th Air Force

By the time I arrived in the MTO, I had over 240 hours of fighter time in Curtiss P-40 Warhawks and Bell P-39 Airacobras. I had dueled fellow squadron mates over the well-protected and Axis-absent skies above Panama. I thought the P-40 was a great block of concrete with wings on

Mk V Spitfire in American markings

it, but given a little time and opportunity, I thought I could do all right with it. The Airacobra was another story.

I was young and naive and christened with the title "fighter pilot." I thought the P-39 was a good plane, but at the time I just didn't know any better. It had some very tricky flight characteristics to it and you had to honor those if you wanted to stay alive. In retrospect, I was glad I didn't have to go up against the highly maneuverable Bf 109 with it. Actually, it was a greater danger to American pilots than it was to the Germans. In fact, years after the war, I had mentioned to Luftwaffe ace Gunther Rall about my flying the P-39 in training. Gunther smiled at me and said, "We [the Luftwaffe] were very familiar with the P-39; we loved them!"

When I was deemed combat-ready, with no actual combat, I was shipped overseas. Shoehorned aboard a Liberty ship full of other combat-bound servicemen for twenty-one days, we bobbed on the Atlantic Ocean, dodging U-boats, until I finally arrived in Oran, Algeria, in early 1944. From there I was sent to the 12th Air Force fighter training center at Telergma, which was the former home of a French Foreign Legion outpost.

Unfortunately, we were not living the comfortable high life as our brother pilots were in the European Theater of Operations (ETO). About the only thing we did have in common was our great affection for flying the Spitfire.

I had just been assigned to the 31st Fighter Group, 308th Fighter Squadron of the 12th Air Force. Our group along with the 52nd Fighter Group was to receive training in the Spitfire Mk V in preparation for our role as a close air support unit flying Spitfire Mk VIIIs and IXs. The Spitfire was a recognized front-line fighter and a proven combat veteran. For me the Spit was a true joy to fly—light on the controls, very nimble, and highly maneuverable—very different from anything else I had flown previously. It turned on a dime, and it was easy to see why the Brits loved it.

The only issue I had with them was that they had short legs: We couldn't carry enough fuel to carry the attack long distances. Although the cockpit was snug, I felt as though I was an extension of the airplane. Inside the cockpit the layout was a little different than the American fighters I had flown. Instead of a straight stick, the Spit had a lovely loop control that took no time getting used to. I was elated at flying the Spitfire and looked forward to the day I would fly it in combat.

Unfortunately, that day never came. After receiving 20 to 25 hours of familiarization time, our group of recently trained Spitfire pilots was moved to the home of the 31st Fighter Group at Castel Volturno. It was a very short stay. Without warning, we were removed from operational flying, told to turn in our Spitfires, and transferred to the 306th Fighter Wing of the 15th Air Force. We were also told that our new combat assignment would now be bomber escort, and we would be flying an airplane that was a cousin to the Spitfire called the P-51 Mustang. Although the Mustang was faster than the Spitfire, it was not quite as nimble.

It was fun to fly while it lasted, and I will always have fond memories of the Supermarine Spitfire.

SPITFIRE MK IX
Lt. J. D. "Jerry" Collinsworth
31st Fighter Group, 307th Fighter Squadron, 12th Air Force
Tunis, Algeria

When the group switched over to the Spitfire Mk IX from the war-weary Mk V, it changed our squadron's whole outlook on life. The new and improved Spitfire made me turn from a defensive mind-set to an offensive one. The Spitfire Mk IX could still out-turn the Fw 190, and in some cases we could still outclimb and outrun them as well.

Most of the time, though, it was the Germans who were on the run! I went from horrifying and scary looks in the cockpit to beating and thumping my chest in triumph as we tangled with the Luftwaffe over the deserts of North Africa.

On May 6, 1943, I was in a flight of four Spitfire Mk IXs cruising over Tunis, Algeria, at 10,000 feet. Leading our finger-four formation was our squadron commander, Maj. George LaBresche. I had flown a Spitfire Mk V with Major LaBresche on one of the missions over Dieppe, France, in August of 1942, where we both barely survived by the skin of our teeth.

Times had changed and we were now itching to fight. It didn't take long to find a scrap to get into as my wingman, Johnny White, spotted a pair of Fw 190s above us. After receiving the okay from the major to attack them, Johnny and I pointed the noses of our Spitfires skyward and went tearing after them.

Johnny and I were a great team, and we always knew what the other was thinking as we closed in to attack. I got behind the number-two Fw 190 and gave him a short squirt of machine-gun and cannon fire, until I saw his canopy come off, and then I stopped firing and watched him bail out. I broke to the right to clear my tail and continued through a full 360-degree turn. I looked for Johnny but I couldn't find him anywhere, as the sky was empty except for the billowing white parachute a quarter-mile away.

Seeing no other German airplanes in the area, I decided to go back and give this guy in the parachute the once-over. As I closed in on him, hanging in his straps, I pulled some power back on the Spitfire and stared

Lt. J. D. "Jerry" Collinsworth, USAAC, poses in his Spitfire.

at him through my open canopy. This guy had just made me one step closer to becoming an ace, so I wanted to thank him. I placed my thumb on my nose and moved my fingers back and forth, waving at him. It was a hell of an insult to him, but I'm sure he was glad I wasn't shooting at him as he hung helpless in that parachute.

After I had my fun, I split-S'ed out of there and headed for home.

IVY LEAGUE FLYER
Pilot/Officer John Keller
680 Squadron RCAF
PRU Spitfire Mk XI

Joining the Fight
I had great sympathy for the poor British during the dark days known as the Battle of Britain. Reading about their plight I wished that I could do something good to help instead of attending those lavish parties that they were giving at Harvard while I was there as a senior. I had taken a short course in something called the Civilian Pilot Training Program in

1940 and became immediately interested in flying while at the controls of a J-3 Cub.

Although I was desperate to join the fight, I knew I didn't have enough money to get to England. I did have enough to get to Canada, however, which was only a hop, skip, and a jump for me. I dropped out of Harvard in late 1941, ran to Canada, and joined the Royal Canadian Air Force (RCAF), training with them for ten months. One of the airplanes I trained in was ironically called the Harvard, the Canadian version of the AT-6. In November of 1941 I got married, and then two weeks later I was on a troopship bound for England.

When I arrived in England I was told there were no aircraft for us; they were all in the air currently defending the British Isles. We were "volunteered" to go to the Middle East, where allegedly aircraft would be readily available. I embarked on a long two-month trip that took us around the Cape of Good Hope up to Egypt. From there I was sent out to Libya to an advanced landing ground. My further flight training became all fouled up due to one Desert Fox—Gen. Erwin Rommel and his Afrika Korps, as they pushed us backward for two months, losing one airfield after another.

Although I had earned my wings and was deemed a fighter pilot, I was stuck shepherding a petrol bowser to the Nile Delta. From there I was shipped up to Syria and met a delightful chap named Geoffrey Morley-Mower who became my instructor as I acquainted myself with the Hawker Hurricane.

I really thought the Hurricane was a dog. It was very clumsy and very difficult to fly, but it won the Battle of Britain. The Spitfire had a much better public relations team and received all the credit for saving Old Blighty, but it was in fact the Hurricane that saved the day. I never flew the Hurricane all that well even though I was offered a choice when I completed my training: fly a Hurricane on the deck with 40mm cannons sticking out of the wings, or fly as high as I could up at altitude with nothing in the wings for protection and only a couple of cameras stuffed inside the fuselage as part of the photoreconnaissance unit (PRU). I chose to be on the deck, but my instructors must have seen how I handled a Hurricane, so they sent me up high, unarmed and very afraid.

Spitfire Love Affair

I joined 680 Squadron and stayed with them for the rest of the war. I was introduced to the Spitfire Mk I and II, which I thought were beautiful airplanes, one in which I thought I could cope, and manage quite well. Sitting in the cockpit, your shoulders were only about an inch away from both sides, and it felt like you were part of the airplane—an integral part, if you will. In the air it was a delight to fly. It had a lot of power, even though it was the same Merlin engine that was in the Hurricane: a 1,655hp Rolls-Royce. The "poor" bloody British had no extra money for joyrides or extra engine hours, so I really didn't get much time flying for the fun of it.

Our training field in Beirut was interesting, to say the least. We had two runways that formed a big X. One was concave and the other convex, which made for some very interesting landings on my part—but I survived. Every hour was mainly spent flying over occupied Europe. In reality, I only had 15 to 20 hours of Spit time before I was sent out on missions over Europe doing photographic reconnaissance.

Most of my flights departed from Libya, flying over the north coast of Africa out over the Mediterranean and then photographing the airfields, marshaling yards, and harbors of Greece and the surrounding islands. For almost all of my PRU flights, I was operating at between 25,000 and 30,000 feet or above, unpressurized, unarmed, and shit-scared!

We started out with the Mk I Spits and ended up with the Mk XI. The Mk XI was my favorite, of course; it was a pure delight to fly, as it had a retractable tail wheel and it was supercharged. You would be happily cruising along at 12,000 or 13,000 feet and the supercharger would kick in and give you a great big boost in the tail as you slammed back in your seat while your airspeed jumped another 20 to 25 miles per hour.

Our 680 Squadron was a wonderful outfit, full of nice guys, made up of all kinds of nationalities, including Tasmanians, Australians, Canadians, and this one lone American—me! Our Spitfires matched our pilots in the unit: We were not a very pretty bunch. Both men and airplanes were downright filthy-looking. Below all the dust and dirt was a dark blue fuselage that was chipped and dented. Our Spitfires weren't fancy-looking, but they sure could go high!

PRU Missions

Thankfully we had nice long runways both in Cyprus and Libya as our Spits operated from Lancaster bomber bases, and it felt like extra security to land and take off from these. We carried two F24 Fairchild cameras weighing 21 pounds apiece that were behind the cockpit, embedded in the fuselage. To operate them we had one little control on the dashboard where you could turn the camera on and vary the interval between each picture, so almost every spot on the ground was taken twice from a different angle. That way the analyzers could do stereoscopic views of the ground.

The interpreters used to work far into the night interpreting our images and gleaning wonderful amounts of information about the ships being loaded, how many fighters and bombers the Germans had on a particular airfield, or what kind of supplies were in the marshaling yards. This intelligence proved invaluable to mission planners, as our bombers would return to where our lone Spits had once been.

In all of my eighty-one missions I was only shot at twice over Crete when the German flak guns targeted me. The scary part is, when you are all alone you know exactly who they are firing at!

On another trip when I was returning from a recon over Europe, the engine suddenly began to run rough. It felt as if it was shaking the Spitfire apart and I could barely maintain my altitude. I was concerned that I was going to have to set in down in the drink with a swim in the Mediterranean. Thankfully the northern coast of Libya was now underneath me, so I switched off the engine and was shocked to see what was staring at me from out in front of my nose. Lo and behold, there was one foot missing off one of my wooden prop blades and two feet off another blade. I didn't recall being shot at, and the only way I can account for the damaged blades was because of icing—or gremlins!

Cold temperatures were always an issue, and one of the problems with carrying these bloody cameras up so high was that half of our heat had to be pumped in the back to keep the camera toasty warm while we as the pilots were freezing!

Most of my flights were 3.75 hours, and that was about the duration. With only 270 imperial gallons of fuel in the wings, we couldn't fly much longer than that. On one trip I clocked 400 mph coming out and 400 mph coming back—a tailwind each way. Who could ask for anything better!

The only defensive weapon I carried was a Very pistol to shoot flares up if we had to bail out over the Med and paddle around in my dinghy. When I flew my missions I usually wore a bright red shirt, for a couple of reasons: One was as a good luck charm, and the other, more important reason was the fact that if I ever went down in the sea, I was hopeful the air-sea rescue chaps would spot me a mile away—and that the Germans were color-blind!

The only German aircraft I had encountered were below me, as I took photos of them at their bases. Thankfully they didn't have good radar; otherwise, they would have been up there waiting for us and we would have been as helpless as church mice surrounded by a bunch of ravenous alley cats. The Me 109 was a fearsome opponent and quite deadly for any PRU pilot.

I had the opportunity to transfer into the United States Army Air Forces (USAAF) and wind up who knows where and flying who knows what. I had been flying high over Europe every two or three days, in an airplane that I thoroughly enjoyed, and was with a group of men that were a delight to be with on a daily basis. Needless to say, I never made any application and let the deadline lapse.

After the war, as a reward for serving with the RCAF, they sent me a check once a month so I could apply it to my schooling back at Harvard. But my personal reward had been even greater: being allowed to fly a Spitfire.

4

Iron Dog: P-39

Although the Bell P-39 Airacobra was designed as a front-line fighter, one loaded with a lethal combination of both cannon and machine guns, its high-altitude dueling attributes were nonexistent. The original design called for a turbo-supercharger that would have taken the P-39 to new heights, but to save weight, Bell decided to take it out. There were only two types of P-39 pilots: those that loved the P-39 and those that despised it.

Follow along with pilots on both sides of the fence as they share their experiences flying the "Iron Dog."

SNAKE ATTACK
Lt. Col. Doug S. Canning Jr.
347th Fighter Group, 70th Fighter Squadron
"Cactus Air Force," Henderson Field, Guadalcanal

I had just finished getting checked out in a P-36 back in the States when the war broke out. Most of us thought we would make the next leap into combat at the controls of a P-40 Warhawk when we arrived at our unknown destination somewhere in the Pacific. But when we finally set foot at our new base in early 1942, most of us in the squadron were absolutely dumbfounded for a couple of reasons. The first was because we had been offloaded on the exotic island of Fiji, more of a tourist destination than a front-line fighter base. But the bigger concern was that there wasn't a Warhawk around, just a bunch of wooden crates containing Bell P-39 Airacobras.

To me the P-39 was a super airplane, but not for dogfighting. It couldn't turn quick enough, it couldn't climb fast enough, and it was definitely afraid of heights. The Allison engine could barely provide enough power to get us above 14,000 feet. The P-39 was also heavy and slow; no one ever referred to it as "agile." But when we took it off its leash down low, the P-39 received high marks for its strafing ability. With a mixture of cannon and machine guns, the P-39 was an excellent gun platform.

While the life of a fighter pilot on Fiji was comfortable, it also gave us plenty of time to practice our combat tactics. Unfortunately, some of the other squadrons got thrown in the mess quicker than we did.

It seemed that not much was happening in our neck of the woods until one of our B-17s on a reconnaissance flight spotted the Japanese building an airstrip on Guadalcanal. Our sunny vacation was about to come to an end. In early August of 1942 the marines bloodied the beaches of Guadalcanal (code-named Cactus) and secured their main objective: the airfield. By late August, US Navy Wildcats and SBD Dauntlesses began arriving at the newly named airfield. It was called Henderson Field, named after a marine dive-bomber pilot that had been killed at Midway, Maj. Lofton Henderson. One of our sister squadrons, the 67th FS stationed in New Caledonia, was called up to Henderson to assist the marines in defending the airfield from the large contingent of Japanese soldiers still on Guadalcanal. Five P-400s (the British variant of the P-39) were flown the 1,000 miles to "Cactus," where they quickly employed the strengths of the Airacobra.

The P-400 had some minor differences compared to the P-39. I referred to it as "the cheap version" of a P-39. For instance, the P-400 had a 20mm cannon instead of the 37mm, and it also had a low-level oxygen system; they were originally designed as desert tank busters, so there was no need for a high-altitude oxygen system. But in the jungles of the Pacific they were used quite effectively as a close air support killing machine.

A few weeks before I arrived at Henderson, the P-400s of the 67th FS proved their worth at a place not far from the airfield called "Bloody Ridge." Wave after wave of Japanese troops slugged it out with the out-numbered marines on the ground in an all-out attempt to retake the air-field. Only three P-400s were airworthy during the heat of the battle

The P-39 Airacobra was part of the "Cactus Air Force" at Henderson Field, Guadalcanal. COURTESY OF JAMES BUSHA

in mid-September, and what they did that day was nothing short of heroic. With the main Japanese force gathering only yards away from the besieged marines, the P-400s came roaring in at treetop height with their cannon and machine guns blazing, pouring a deadly spear tip of lead into the center of the Japanese troops.

When the firing had stopped and the smoke had cleared, only one P-400 remained airworthy. But the death and destruction those P-400s caused left the Japanese forces in a state of ruin.

By the time I arrived at Henderson Field in early October of 1942 as part of a handpicked group of 70th FS pilots sent to reinforce the 67th FS, the wretched smell of death wafted across the airfield. The most mysterious sight for me was the cooking fires of the Japanese that seemed to be only a stone's throw away from the end of the runway.

There were two things I quickly learned you could count on while stationed at Henderson Field: the daily twelve o'clock noon visit by Zeros and Betty bombers and the twelve o'clock midnight visit by "Washing Machine Charlie," a twin-engine bomber flying with unsynchronized engines. Every twelve hours we were bombed, and if that wasn't enough, the Japanese ships that circled the island shelled us almost daily.

On my very first mission I took off, sucked my gear up, and then started strafing the jungle below. The jungle canopy was so thick I never knew if I hit anything or not. On my second mission my engine quit shortly after takeoff at 400 feet, and I committed the cardinal sin of flying: I turned back to the runway with a dead engine. I nursed every bit of energy out of the P-400 and used up all of my nine lives, just making it back to the airfield.

Although the Zeros and Bettys came over to harass us almost daily, we could not get high enough to tangle with them. As fighter pilots we were frustrated by that, but understood that our main mission was to eradicate the Japanese troops hidden in the jungles around Henderson.

Some of our ingenious ground crew guys on the island filled some 50-pound practice bombs that the navy had laying around with gasoline and we began to drop them on the jungle targets below. That really opened things up and caused a fiery napalm show below in the jungle. Because the marines and the Japanese on the ground were so close to one another, the marines laid out a series of colored panels indicating where their front line was. As long as we strafed the ridges in front of the panels, we were okay.

The flying was pure hell, and so were the living conditions. We slept inside tents in a flooded coconut grove, and our closest friends were the thousands of mosquitoes that feasted on us nightly.

We had no clean water to wash with because we weren't allowed to start a fire to boil it for fear the Japanese would shoot at our smoke from the cooking fire. Our mess kits became infected, and pretty soon, so did our bodies. You name it, we got it: dengue fever, malaria, and dysentery. We became more or less like walking dead.

Sick or not, we continued to fly our P-400s in support of the marines on the ground. Day after day we did what we could with our Airacobras as we held out hope that the tide would turn. Hope came late in 1942, in the form of the P-38 Lightning.

After being sent back to New Caledonia for ten days of treatment, I got checked out in the Lightning and returned to Henderson with a vengeance. Making up for lost time, we flew at altitudes the P-39 could only dream about.

But for all the Airacobra lacked in the aerial combat arena, I have to tip my hat to the P-39s / P-400s. As fighter pilots we made do with what we had, and the Airacobra helped hold the line during the darkest days of the war.

PAPER TIGER
Lt. Peter A. McDermott, USAAC
71st Tactical Reconnaissance Group, New Guinea
P-39: *Brooklyn Bum 2nd*

I guess you could say I really paid for my sins at an early age—all because of my "big Irish mouth." I was kicked out of a Liaison Squadron in 1943 and sent to a newly established home for troublemakers and wayward pilots—the Tactical Reconnaissance Group (TAC/RECON). There I was introduced to the most god-awful airplane, the Bell P-39 Airacobra. To be brutally honest, the Cobra had its fangs removed and was more or less a "paper tiger" in the sky. The P-39 was outclassed by just about every airplane the enemy had. Having no class myself, though, I felt right at home in the little fighter, and exploited its limited strengths in combat.

On paper the P-39 seemed like a first-rate fighter. With a huge 37mm cannon sticking out of the nose along with two .30 caliber machine guns and an additional pair of .50 caliber machine guns in each wing, the Cobra should have had a deadly bite. Unfortunately, it turned out to be more of a dog with an intermittent bark and very little bite. First off, the cannon was a complete joke; it seemed that it worked one out of ten times in combat. With a thirty-round capacity we were lucky to get a few rounds to fire before it jammed on us. Combat was a serious matter, but it was comical to be flying in trail behind other P-39s on a strafing run as the pilots flew all over the sky trying to stay on target and charge the cannon at the same time.

I watched as guys around me pounded their fists bloody on the charging handles trying to get that damn cannon to fire—hell, I've got scars of my own! Thinking back on it, I wish I would have spent more time with

Lt. Peter A. McDermott, USAAC, and his P-39, *Brooklyn Bum 2nd* COURTESY OF
PETER MCDERMOTT

the armament people to learn more about what made this popgun tick.
Thankfully for us, though, we never encountered any Japanese fighters
over New Guinea where we were based. With our limited fuel range and
lack of altitude capabilities, we couldn't fly far or high enough to engage
them even if we had wanted to. Most of our missions were down low anyway, strafing Japanese ground and barge targets. The P-39 was definitely
in its element at these treetop levels; even if the cannon didn't work, those
machine guns could tear the enemy apart.

On a few occasions we even went so far as to turn the P-39 into a
dive-bomber. We would strap a 250-pound bomb to our belly and stagger
up to 14,000 feet where both airplane and pilot were out of breath. Level-
ing off, we simply pushed the nose over and rode the Cobra back down,
releasing the bomb over the target. We got pretty good at it and hit some
of our targets most of the time.

The flip side of flying this low, however, came at a very high price. We lost most of our guys in combat from the accurate flak and ground fire we encountered on these missions. Make no mistake: The P-39 could take some hits—it just couldn't take a lot of them. I must admit that although I was a harsh critic of the Cobra's fighting abilities and considered it a miserable mutt to fight with, the P-39 was a loyal dog; it always brought me back home in one piece.

RUMBLING AND TUMBLING IN A P-39
Capt. William B. Overstreet Jr., USAAC
357th Fighter Group, 363rd Fighter Squadron

When the war broke out in December of 1941, I knew the only way I could do my part for the war effort was to become a fighter pilot. The only problem was that I had to survive flight training in order to make it safely into combat!

I began flying the PT-17 Stearman in California at an air base run by the world-famous aerobatic champion, Tex Rankin. Tex's attitude on flying must have rubbed off on my instructor, Carl Aarslet, because he challenged me right out of the chute.

I only had a few hours of stick time in the Stearman when Carl grabbed the stick from me while we were on a downwind leg to land. He flipped us on over, shut off the engine, and yelled through the Gosport tube, "Now you land it." Instinctively I quarter-rolled the PT-17 into a left turn, lined it up with the runway, and greased it on the mains—after a few bounces, of course! Carl was testing me to see if I would panic or if I had what it took to become a military pilot. I believe Carl directed me down the right path in becoming a fighter pilot. Everything I learned about unusual attitudes was later put to the test when I climbed into the cockpit of a P-39 Airacobra.

I honestly loved the looks of the P-39. It was really a beautiful airplane, very modern-looking, especially with a tricycle landing gear, a rear-mounted Allison in-line engine, and cockpit doors that looked like they belonged on a car. I rather enjoyed flying the P-39, but for some strange reason it didn't like me very much; the P-39 kept on trying to kill me! It probably didn't help that the CG (center of gravity) was way off. With the

Capt. William B. Overstreet Jr., USAAC, poses with two of his favorites: his white-walled roadster and the P-39. COURTESY OF WILLIAM OVERSTREET

engine situated behind the pilot, a 37mm fully loaded cannon sticking out between your legs, and a propeller driveshaft, it always flew out of balance. Heck, it was so sensitive that it would sometimes fly off on its own whenever it felt like it. Usually we could correct its gyrations, but sometimes it totally ignored the guy behind the windscreen throwing the stick all over the place, trying to keep it from wandering off on its own.

When I joined the 363rd Fighter Squadron in Santa Rosa, California, they had just returned from shooting up and bombing the deserts near Tonopah, Nevada. I heard wild stories from some of the vets of the squadron, including my good friend, Bud Anderson, telling me about the bad vices of the Airacobra—tumbling, to be exact. Some of the guys recited a lyric they used to put to a song that went like this, "It'll tumble and spin and soon auger in!"

Fortunately I was young and foolish and couldn't wait for my check-out. Most of my early flights were led by Lloyd Hubbard, who was not only a real good stick but fearless as well. He would take our flight of four P-39s on some low-level work, and at times it felt like we were only inches away from going underground! And if that wasn't excitement enough, he would lead us up near San Francisco where we played a game of follow the leader, looping the Golden Gate Bridge. Of course we received complaints from the locals, but with a war going on you could practically get away with most anything.

Looping a bridge in a P-39 was really fun, but the fun soon faded away on one particular flight in late June of 1943. I had been out practicing aerobatics—loops, rolls, and tight turns. I must have done something to make the P-39 mad at me, because all of a sudden the Airacobra began to tumble. No matter what direction I threw my stick in—right, left, forward, or rearward—the P-39 ignored my imputes. It was time to bail out. We had been warned, of course, about not pulling the ripcord too soon—so we didn't hit the stabilizer on our way out—but at the moment it was mere trivia, because I was having a hard time getting out. Try as I might I couldn't budge the cockpit doors because of the building pressure against them.

As I squirmed around inside of the cockpit, trying to figure a way out, I was able to shoulder one of the doors while pushing the other one with my knee. That seemed to work, and I was able to pop a door off. I squeezed out of the tumbling P-39, waited a second, and pulled my ripcord as soon as I was clear. I felt a violent tug of the chute as it blossomed above me and a few seconds later my feet hit the ground. The P-39 had beaten me to the ground by mere seconds because when I landed, I was surrounded by cannon shells and my bent propeller—everything else was twisted metal.

The next day I hunted down my parachute packer and thanked him for a job well done.

I would be far from the last guy to bail out of a tumbling P-39 in training. Unfortunately, some guys weren't as lucky and were unable to get out in time. The P-39 was definitely a tricky little fighter with some unique quirks, but it taught me how to become an aggressive fighter pilot, and the tactics I learned from flying the Airacobra kept me alive over the skies of Europe.

5

Blue Eyes of the 8th: Spitfires

Col. Kermit E. Bliss, USAF, and
Lt. Col. John S. Blyth, USAF

EAGLE EYES

The Allied ground and air commanders knew early on that in battle, the person or "team" with the best set of eyes held a decisive advantage over their opponent. Target selection, bomb damage assessment, troop movements, and current, up-to-the-minute information on what the enemy was doing and where it was hiding was placed in the hands of a shadowy group of pilots known as the PRU—the Photographic Reconnaissance Unit. In order to be accurate and successful on these missions, the air corps needed a plane that was fast, stable, and maneuverable, one that could reach high altitudes while penetrating deep into enemy airspace. They also had to fly these missions unarmed and alone. The pilots of the 7th Photo Group, 14th Photo Squadron, stationed at Mount Farm air base in England, blindly put their faith and trust in a Reverse Lend-Lease aircraft the British painted baby blue.

The needs and wants of the air corps came in the form of a battle-tested proven fighter whose lineage was flown by so few for so many during the Battle of Britain. Removed from these aircraft were guns and British roundels, replaced by gas, American Stars and Bars, and cameras.

Hidden under a coat of powder-blue paint was the unmistakable elliptical wing that supported a graceful and streamlined fuselage that housed its "heart and soul": a 1,655hp Rolls-Royce Merlin engine. The

Mk IX and Mk XI Supermarine Spitfires became the Blue Eyes of the 8th.

A Different Kind of Fighter Pilot

Commander Kermit Bliss of the 14th Photo Squadron recalls:

When I was commissioned in early 1942, we had a choice of fighters, medium and heavy bombers, and something called PROTU. Someone in our group asked the lieutenant in charge what that last choice meant. The lieutenant scratched his head for a minute and said out loud, "Protu—protu? I don't know; must be some damn Indian name!"

Kermit E. Bliss with his unarmed, powder-blue Spitfire COURTESY OF KERMIT BLISS

No one signed up for this mysterious, unknown acronym, and that gave the air corps a problem. There were a certain number of bodies that were committed to be sent to PROTU, so a well-proven, scientific solution was devised: Everyone whose last name started with A, B, or C was quickly volunteered.

As part of the 14th Photo Squadron, I was sent to Colorado Springs, Colorado, where I began training in Lockheed P-38s and found that PROTU meant Photographic Reconnaissance Operational Training Unit. Instead of guns and cannons, I shot with cameras. After almost a year of high- and low-altitude photo reconnaissance training over the United States, we were deemed combat-ready and sent to jolly old England.

LONG SHOT

For the next ten months I flew alone, unarmed and unafraid (?!) over flak-infested enemy territory in F4 and F5 Photo Recon Lightnings, taking pre- and post-strike photos for 8th Air Force Bomber Command. I also did a lot of aerial mapping over the Continent in preparation for the invasion. The P-38 was a stable camera platform, but when loaded up with gas and film, we couldn't get to higher, safer altitudes, trying to avoid German fighters and flak.

Bomber Command also wanted intelligence on German factories and other industrial targets located deep inside the fatherland. The P-38 was stretched to its limit on range and altitude capability. We knew we could get to the targets okay, but on some missions, with the throttles to the stops, we didn't think we could make it back to England with both motors turning. P-38s didn't float very well in the English Channel either!

Our British counterparts held the answer to our dilemma. The Brits had been flying Spitfires all over German airspace at such high altitudes and they never really had trouble with the Luftwaffe. At altitude, the Spitfire sipped gasoline compared with the gulping gas consumption of the Lightnings. And yet, as the Spitfire burned off fuel, it flew higher and faster.

Another great advantage the Spitfire had was it had parts made out of fabric. German radar had a hard time detecting it compared to the 19,000-pound all-aluminum-skinned P-38s that seemed to attract every flak gun we overflew. Most of the planes lost in our group fell to German 88s and their accurate flak barrages.

The Spitfire was a delight to fly. Each Spitfire we received from Vickers was a handmade piece of art, and, of course, each one flew differently. The Spit was very agile and required little stick movement to get it to do what you wanted. You just simply thought about it and it moved. With the guns removed and two K-52 cameras installed in the fuselage, I took one up to see how high I could get it.

Filling up both wing tanks and strapping on a belly tank, we were theoretically 2,000 pounds, overloaded for takeoff on those little bitty donut tires. If you blew one on takeoff, you were certain to become a torch burning bright on English soil. Directional control was crisp and coordinated as I lifted off from Mount Farm.

The golden rule in reconnaissance was that you fly if it's clear over the target area. It didn't matter if our base was fogged over, rained on, or snow-packed, as long as the other end was clear, or at least predicted to be. By the time I left our base and was over the Channel, I had hit 30,000 feet and was still indicating 100 feet per minute. I passed through 37,000 feet and with a kick in the tail from the jet stream I was zipping along on my way to Germany.

A MOMENT IN TIME

Eighty percent of the 8th Air Force intelligence for Bomber Command came from photo recon. We went in first and took pictures of target possibilities. With hard evidence inside our cameras, the intelligence people evaluated the photos to see if they were suitable targets. Working factories, marshaling yards, aerodromes, V-1 sites, and anything else of interest were photographed by our unit.

After the target was selected and the bombers sent on their way, we hung in the background to await the devastation and destruction that would soon follow. Orbiting at well above 30,000 feet, my cameras froze a moment in time as smoke and dust cleared over the target area. Sometimes the bomber pilots didn't like us too well.

The bomber boys would come back from a mission and report "We really clobbered it! Scratch one factory!" Unfortunately for them, on some

A short time later I was called over to the intelligence hut and came face-to-face with the pilot of this B-26. He had clenched teeth and a red-colored face that exposed a throbbing vein in his forehead. He also wore bird colonel insignias on his jacket.

He began bellowing at me the minute I entered the room, accusing me of taking pictures of the wrong target and not being there at the right time. He went on and on as his tantrum gained momentum. Apparently this colonel had reported to 8th Air Force Bomber Command that his group got terrific hits on this German aerodrome, but my photos showed differently.

My target folder was tossed in front of the colonel and black-and-white post-strike photos spilled from it as it glided across the table. The intelligence people counted 150 German fighters on the field, with more scattered throughout the surrounding woods. There wasn't a bomb crater on it!

My air operations officer checked my cross-out and cross-in times and found that I was over the airfield when I said I was. The color from the good colonel's face soon changed to pale white when he realized he had hit the wrong air base—south instead of north. The colonel stomped out of the shack and took off the same way he came in—hotheaded!

FRIEND OR FOE?
Squadron commander Kermit Bliss recalls:

The other problem we had flying these blue Spitfires was that we were such a rogue unit that no one really knew anything about us. At times our own aircraft attacked us. On one particular mission, one of our Spits had been out on a long-range flight and was on his way back over Holland as he let down to 20,000 feet over the Zuiderzee. Six P-51s were on a fighter sweep in the area below him when they spotted the descending bogey.

The Spitfire pilot paid little attention to them until the Mustangs turned their guns into him. Shoving his rpm to max, the Spitfire pilot watched the P-51s pick up speed as they began their bounce onto him. When the Mustangs drew close to gun range, the Spitfire pilot hauled his stick back in his lap and shot up 4,000 feet at a 45-degree angle, climbing like a homesick angel!

Well above the dazed and confused P-51s, the Spitfire tipped his nose and dove almost straight down. The 51s were full of gas and climbing and the Spit was almost empty and diving. He walked away from them.

When he got back to base he reported the incident to our intelligence officer and me. We decided to have some fun, so we held the report off the teletype and waited.

Eventually the six P-51s returned from their mission and debriefed, and their statements went out across the teletype to let everyone else in the theater know what had happened: "Six P-51s attacked a new Me 109 type in the vicinity of the Zuiderzee. E/A exhibited a phenomenal rate of climb, must have been using water injection or some experimental fuel."

Then we had the Spitfire pilot send his report: "PR Spit attacked in Zuiderzee area by six 51s, climbed away from them and returned to base."

Those Mustang guys got razzed for weeks! First, for not identifying a Spitfire, and second, because it was painted all blue with Stars and Bars!

Our own aircraft attacking us was not our only concern, however.

GLIDING FOR HOME

The gas gauge on the Spitfire was absolutely 100 percent accurate. When that needle reached zero, your engine quit! I found this out the hard way coming back from a long mission over Germany as I flew into a head-wind. I was 75 miles out from England with less than five gallons of gas in my final tank, and to make my dilemma more fun, I was 30,000 feet above the cold, gray-colored North Sea. Thank God I was in a Spitfire!

The British had very politely provided us with this little computer gadget that calculated max range and glide speed. It took into account wind direction, heading, and wind velocity, and gave us a target airspeed to maintain so we could arrive at our destination safely—that is, as long as we had enough altitude under our wings!

I shut down the Rolls-Royce engine and closed up all my radiator doors as I placed the prop in the lowest rpm setting possible. I was now powerless and became a glider pilot, sailing my way back to England. Things inside the cockpit became quiet and cold as the wind whistled through my canopy. I just hoped this newfangled computer worked.

Fortunately for me, it didn't; I was still 10,000 feet AGL [above ground level] when I soared over English soil.

When I hit 3,000 feet I pushed the prop into high rpm and dove the Spitfire until the engine caught and the blades turned. As I touched down on the big recovery field at Bradwell Bay, I ran out of fuel taxiing in. With a glide ratio of close to 20:1, the Spitfire was like a feather in the wind, and when damaged, it was repaired with ease.

Sometimes in a nontraditional way.

HAMMER TIME

One of our Spitfires had picked up a bit of flak and returned with substantial wing damage. We quickly put a new wing on it, but in flight it always wanted to drop that new wing. We tried everything we could to fix it, but had no luck. Bomber Command needed photos and we needed that Spit to fly. A call was made to Vickers and they sent a test pilot down to hammer out the problem—literally!

The RAF pilot took our sick bird up and came back in and asked if we had a rawhide mallet. This madman then began to beat the hell out of

The Photo Spitfires were mainly painted blue in hopes of blending in with the sky, making it difficult for German fighters to spot them. COURTESY OF JOHN BLYTH

the aileron all along its surface. He took the Spit back up again, wrung it out, and returned. He told us "It's better, but not quite." He then directed some of the mechanics to hold on to the aileron while he twisted and bent it with his hands.

Smiling to himself, he climbed back into the cockpit, fired up the Merlin, and jammed the throttle forward. He rolled that Spit right on takeoff! After he landed, he probably didn't notice that our jaws still hung to the ground. He told us very matter-of-factly, "It's fixed. Flies fine, chaps! Any other kites you want me to look at?"

So much for Yankee ingenuity. There was no way in hell you could do that with a P-38! I was thankful for two things: that my last name started with B, and that I flew the best damn plane in the war. Besides, after a while that baby blue color kind of grows on you!

Foto Joes

From the very start, when the airplane was first thrust into a combat role, military commanders on the ground quickly realized they needed hard-copy evidence of future targets, troop buildups, and battle damage assessment from previous bombing raids. The bottom line in warfare: Whoever possessed the greater knowledge of what the other guy was doing held the distinct advantage of not only knowing where to hit him next, but how hard.

Enter the camera-equipped Allied fighters.

Probably the best known of all the Allied Foto Joes was the F4/F5 P-38 Lightning. With its built-in redundancy of two engines instead of one and a high-altitude capability, the Lightnings were stripped of their machine guns and cannon. The weapons were replaced with a variety of vertical and oblique aerial cameras. Depending on the exact model number, the Lightnings carried a combination of cameras that included the K-17, which produced a 9x9-inch negative; the 24-inch vertical K-18 camera, producing a 9x18-inch negative; and a K-22 oblique camera, with lens options of 6-, 12-, 24-, or 40-inch focal lengths producing a 9x9-inch negative. Over 1,400 Photo Lightnings were produced by Lockheed and served in all corners of the war-torn globe.

Although the unarmed Lightnings may have carried more cameras over the battlefields than the F-6/P-51 Mustangs, the Mustangs held their own advantage, as they could quickly switch roles, moving from cameraman to street fighter. The F-6 retained its six .50 caliber machine guns along with a rear fuselage–mounted K-17 camera alongside the two other K-24 cameras—one in the lower fuselage, and one mounted under the fuselage, pointing straight down. The K-24, weighing in at a mere 10 pounds, was manufactured by the Eastman Kodak Company and produced a 5x5-inch negative. The F-6 Photo Mustangs were renamed RF-51Ds and soldiered on during the Korean War in a photo/recon role.

PART II

HOLDING THE LINE: 1943

6

Banshee Wail: P-40

FLYING SKULLS OVER BURMA
Col. Philip R. Adair
80th Fighter Group, 89th Fighter Squadron, 10th Air Force

Itching to Fight

By the time I graduated from high school in Oklahoma in 1940, at the ripe old age of nineteen, I could see that the United States was going to get dragged into a world war. I had grown up in a farming family during the Great Depression and had felt the terrible hardships it caused us firsthand. The effects of the economic devastation continued to linger throughout our state. Finding a good-paying job—or any job, for that matter—was like trying to find fertile soil in the ravaged Dust Bowl.

I tried to join the army at Fort Sill and asked about becoming a pilot. A lieutenant with a very sharp tongue shot me down right away. "Sonny boy," he said, "you got to get yourself two years of college first and then *maybe* we'll talk to you."

I was as depressed as the red clay soil under my feet but was determined to earn my wings. I moved to Wyoming, found work, and enrolled in the Civilian Pilot Training Program (CPTP), earning a private pilot's license in a 50hp Piper Cub with no brakes and a tail skid.

A week later the Japanese bombed Pearl Harbor, and I got the impression from the army recruiter I visited that if a fellow could see lightning and hear thunder, then they would gladly take him!

Newly Minted Fighter Pilot

By September of 1942 I was a green second lieutenant flying P-47 Thunderbolts with the 80th Fighter Group out of Mitchell Field, New York. In the air the P-47 was stable and solid and an all-around efficient gun

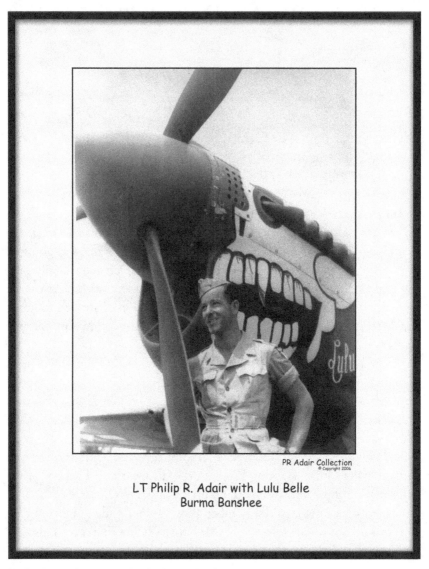

PR Adair Collection
© Copyright 2006

LT Philip R. Adair with Lulu Belle
Burma Banshee

Philip R. Adair and his Flying Skulls P-40, *LuLu Belle* COURTESY OF PHILIP ADAIR platform. But once you pulled the power back, the Jug was more like a homesick brick and came down fast.

In February of 1943, I had flown my P-47 for the last time in stateside training as I watched the Jug I was to fly in combat being loaded aboard a ship that would cross the Atlantic, bound for England. I looked forward to flying and slugging it out with the Luftwaffe as the rest of the 80th Fighter Group prepared to join the fight in Europe. Unfortunately, the military brass had other plans for our group, and I would not see my beloved Jug for a very long time.

General Hap Arnold gathered our group together in the middle of the night and informed us we would be embarking on a very important mission, one that was vital to the war effort. At that time he couldn't disclose our final destination. He did tell us that we could forget everything we knew about the P-47 Thunderbolt and instead look forward to our new mount—the Curtiss P-40 Warhawk. There wasn't a guy in the room who didn't have a shocked look on his face!

The P-40 Warhawk was definitely lighter and slower, and carried a lot less firepower than what we had been used to in the Thunderbolt. I found the P-40 to be a good, honest, and reliable fighter in the air, but it was short on range and was a slow turner.

In less than a week's time we hurriedly trained a total of 25 hours in the air on our new fighters before we abandoned our cold-weather gear and left for parts unknown.

Burma Banshee

After fifty-three days at sea on three different boats, the 80th FG finally landed in India. By the time we arrived in late 1943, the Japanese had been fighting, conquering, and expanding their empire southward since 1937. They had set their sights on Northern India and were already in control of the Burma Railroad by the time we arrived.

It was tough going for the US, British, and Chinese composite forces on the ground as they tried to halt the advancing Japanese. Most if not all of their supplies—including ammo, fuel, and food—were sent up north by air over the "Hump" (Himalayan Mountains) in C-46s and C-47s. Our main job was to protect the Hump route from Japanese fighters that prowled over the thick green Burma jungles, looking for an overloaded, unarmed transport to shoot down.

I was assigned to "D" Flight as its commander, with three other P-40s assigned to me. To signify our 89th Fighter Squadron, we painted our spinners blood red and had a large, white-colored skull painted on both sides of the nose. We knew the Japanese were superstitious and somewhat afraid of anything that resembled death, so we added an extra surprise for them. Because we flew a lot of dive-bombing missions in support of the ground troops, we installed an 18-inch air-raid siren on our bellies and turned it on when we went into our dive-bombing attacks. We called this the "Banshee Wail," and it scared the hell out of the Japanese!

I personalized my P-40 with the name *LuLu Belle* after a girl I had known back in the States. I was also an old car nut and loved the cars from the early 1930s. As a tribute to my passion, I had brought along a can of whitewall paint and painted my main gear and tail wheel tires. I now had something no other fighter pilot had: a customized P-40 Warhawk!

Superstitious or not, the Japanese Zeros were still a constant threat. On many Hump escort missions, they would zoom up, give us the once-over, and hightail it out of there. It wasn't because they were intimidated by us; it was because they had strict orders to leave the fighters alone and attack the transports. They couldn't afford to take a chance of losing one of their fighters because they also had a long supply line to protect.

If a Zero did decide to tangle with us, however, we had been given specific instructions never to try to turn with him. Our instructors said we had two good chances: One was a good chance of being shot down, and the other, with so much dense jungle and rugged terrain, a good chance of never being seen again.

Down and Dirty

Although we were given the title of fighter pilot, I dropped more bombs than engaged in dogfights with other airplanes. We went after the Burma Railroad, a vital Japanese supply line. We attacked road convoys, airfields, and troop camps. But my favorite targets were bridges. We worked with A-36 Apaches and B-25 Mitchell bombers as we went bridge-busting. It must have been a helluva scare for the Japanese on the ground when we

Airborne Burma Banshee

A Burma Banshee P-40 launches for another mission. COURTESY OF PHILIP ADAIR

pushed our noses over and that god-awful sound of our air sirens strapped to our bellies began to wail! Once the bombs were gone, we dropped down and did some strafing as well.

We had a few things in common with the Japanese—mainly, that our living conditions were nothing to write home about! We lived in tents that housed an assortment of mosquitoes and other bugs. Our rations were meager at best. Hell, the Chinese were fed better than we were. When it didn't rain, it was damn hot. And to make matters worse, we had to endure the constant assault from jackals in our tents at night. Somehow we managed to get along and survive.

But I almost didn't on a mission I will never forget.

Uneven Odds

On December 13, 1943, I had just completed my forty-third combat mission—a three-and-a-half-hour patrol over the Hump route, with no

Japanese aircraft encountered. Our four-plane flight had just landed at Nagaghuli Airfield, and the place looked desolate, with all other serviceable P-40s off on other missions.

As soon as I shut down *LuLu Belle*, my crew chief, Carol Peake, began servicing "his" airplane. I walked to the alert tent 100 feet away and waited for the rest of my flight to come back in. I had just laid my head back on the couch and started to relax when all of a sudden the alert sounded.

I took off running for the flight line. Sergeant Peake had hit the electric start and the Allison engine was already running by the time I climbed up on the wing. I hit the throttle, not even bothering to buckle up, and was airborne in less than a minute as I hauled the P-40 skyward.

Our SOP (standard operating procedure) was to climb to 20,000 feet, rendezvous over the field, and stay off the radio, keeping our mouths shut. By the time I had reached 12,000 feet, I had buckled myself in and was searching for the other P-40s in my flight. I began to circle the field, spiraling upward, and saw that none of the others in my flight had taken off yet.

As I was circling, I saw a flight of four aircraft off to the east, just above the haze. By the time I made my next circle, I was completely shocked at what I saw. This was no longer a flight of four aircraft; this was now four flights of twin-engine Japanese bombers! They were in their typical finger-three flight, with three in front and three in back. I counted twenty-four of them heading north and stopped counting when I saw their escort fighters suddenly appear out of the haze.

No Free Pass

I had staggered up to 20,000 feet all alone and had a front-row seat for what was below me. I must have counted more than forty single-engine Japanese fighters flying around in loose formations, with some of the Japanese pilots performing aerobatics for the bomber crews. The Japanese planes were all over the sky, with the bombers staying down low, at 12,500 feet. The fighters, however, seemed to be all over the place, ranging from right above the bomber formation upward, to 20,000 feet. Because of the thick brown haze that hung in the air, the Japanese had not detected me as I neared the pack.

PR Adair Collection
© Copyright 2006

The Burma Banshees
All of the 89th Lined Up
for a long range mission into Burma

Burma Banshee P-40s of the 89th Fighter Squadron line up as they prepare to launch for a long-range mission into Burma. COURTESY OF PHILIP ADAIR

I contacted Control and reported the Japanese formation to them. They responded back and said that what I was seeing was 40 miles to the east, not the 15 miles I was reporting. I tried to tell them they were wrong—that I felt the formation was going to make a 180-degree turn and overfly the 10th Air Force headquarters and bomb it. Control assured me that wasn't going to happen because they had reliable reports from ground stations that the unknowns were farther east.

That's when the Japanese formation began a coordinated turn.

When they rolled out of their turn and took up a new course, it was clear to me that I had guessed right about their intentions. I called Control and gave them the bad news and the ETA of the bomber formation over the Air Depot Group HQ. Then I called Control one last time and said, "I'm not going to let them get by for free!"

I positioned myself above the fighters and the bomber formation so I could hit the bombers just before they reached their bomb release point. I flew out in front of the bombers, off to their left, as I dove down into them. I started to fire at a long range out because I knew that the sight of my tracers would shake things up a bit. I hit the first flight and then swung around into the second flight with my finger on the trigger as I took some shots at them, too. Before I knew it, I was behind the fourth flight of bombers, looking for a target.

As soon as the shooting started, the bombers began to bounce around, moving up and down out of formation. I tacked onto the tail-end Charlie bomber in the last flight and zeroed in on his left engine. I could see flashes on the fuselage and engine area as my bullets tore into him but I couldn't stick around to watch anymore, so I dove underneath him.

I started to break and saw several Zeros heading for me. I had figured this was going to happen, so I pushed the stick full forward into the left-hand corner, pulling negative Gs as I dove away, doing outside rolls. I stayed in my dive with the throttle at war emergency power until I figured I'd shaken the Zeros.

When I looked back, I saw empty skies with nobody chasing me, so I climbed back up for another go at the bombers as they began to reform.

Swiss Cheese
I don't know if the Japanese still couldn't see me in the haze, because no one made a move to cut me off. I started to make another pass on the bombers, but before I could get near them, it looked like every Zero in the

sky was turning into me and wanted a piece of my P-40. I knew I couldn't get close to the bombers—it would have been like reaching into a hornet's nest—so I settled for picking off a fighter or two.

I climbed back up on top and figured I would stay out of range of the bombers, which had already dropped their bombs. I picked out one of the Zeros and tried to get a shot off at him, but he was quick and knew I was gunning for him. He made a sharp turn and disappeared as I picked out another one. This guy was a little more stupid, as he waited too long to turn. I started to fire and he turned right into my bullets. His landing gear began to drop and his engine was on fire as he went into a spiral and crashed in the jungle near Naga Hills.

I climbed back up toward the formation as they neared their lines and went for broke. I thought, "What the hell—might as well take another whack at those bombers!" Stupid jerk! I managed to get into position for another attack, but before I could get in range, I had Zeros on my right, Zeros on my left, and Zeros above me. I was outnumbered almost forty to one.

I didn't think the odds were in my favor, so I went into my escape maneuver once again. I rolled the P-40 over and all I could see was a Zero, mad as hell, coming straight up at me with his cannons and guns blazing away.

I couldn't get out of his way fast enough, but still, it sounded like a shovel full of gravel hitting my fuselage. I heard a *wham, wham, wham* followed by an explosion with a ball of fire coming out from behind the armor plate in back of my headrest. I grabbed the trim tab and turned it all the way forward to assist my escaping dive. As I pushed the P-40's nose downhill, I kept taking hits as other tracers went whizzing by just over my head. The fire in the rear area went out as the ground raced up toward me.

I tried to pull back on the stick and it wouldn't budge. I remembered the elevator trim crank and I started cranking the nose up. The trim wheel was freewheeling and the trim cables shot out as I yanked off the power and reefed the stick back with both hands. I was finally able to get my nose out of the jungle and up into the sky where it belonged, but my troubles were far from over, as I was 125 miles from my base.

It was very hard to hold the nose above the horizon even with both hands as I turned back toward friendly lines. I tried to latch my seat belt around the stick but it wasn't long enough. I kept losing altitude, and my luck turned from bad to worse as another aircraft appeared in front of me, headed in my direction. I was able to get a quarter-mile away from him and saw that it was a Zero, smoking like the devil, losing altitude faster than I was. I figured he was one of the ones I had hit earlier, and we watched one another go by in opposite directions.

I hauled the P-40 around and came screaming up his rear end with a bead on his tail. At 100 yards out with the sight dead center on his engine, I squeezed the trigger, which only brought a *kerthunk, kerthunk, kerthunk* sound of the pneumatic system recharging my empty guns! With so much forward speed, I of course went screaming by him, as I became the hunted. The Zero simply pulled over and started shooting at me. I moved out of the way as his tracers zipped over my left wing. Luckily I wasn't hit as I turned for home once and for all!

I was about 90 miles away from home and my arms were so tired from holding the stick back that I could barely keep the nose above the horizon. As my adrenaline wore off, reality set in and I knew I would never make it back to base, so I decided to bail out. I called Control and gave them the grid map location. As I looked down at the dense jungle below, I said to myself, "Man, if I can just fly another 100 yards, it will save me two days of walking."

Then it hit me—I came up with the best idea I'd had all day. I flipped *LuLu Belle* over on her back, although the jungle was still in plain view below. The P-40 ran pretty good inverted for a couple of minutes before the engine loaded up and wanted to quit. I rolled the P-40 back over, waited for the engine to clear, lost a little altitude, and flipped *LuLu Belle* back over again. I continued doing P-40 flips the rest of the way home until I reached Nagaghuli.

At about a half-mile out from the airfield and at 1,000 feet, I pointed the P-40 toward the south end of the field. I was still inverted as I pulled back on the power and flipped the gear handle down. I squeezed the pump switch, looked down, locked on the gear indicator, and rolled *LuLu Belle* back over as I hit the flap switch and cut the throttle. It wasn't my usual three-pointer, but I could have cared less; we were down in one piece.

When I finally rolled to a stop, I was so tired that I had to be pulled out of my cockpit by some of the ground crew members. On the briefing I found out that the Japanese bomb pattern had fallen short of the HQ area with little damage done to the base. I had sixteen bullet holes in *LuLu Belle*, including one that shattered my trim cable. But the P-40 was a tough old bird, and three days later we had it flying again.

(Philip Adair flew a total of 113 combat missions in P-40s before converting to his beloved P-47 Thunderbolts. Lieutenant Adair was credited with one Zero destroyed and one Zero and one bomber probably destroyed. For his actions and bravery on that December 13 mission, Lieutenant Adair was awarded the Silver Star.)

7

Against All Odds: F4F Wildcat

MEDAL OF HONOR RECIPIENT COL. JAMES E. "ZEKE" SWETT, USMC
VMF-221, USN

Killer Cat

In November of 1942 I had been assigned to VMF-221, not as an original member of the squadron, but as a replacement pilot for all the men who had gone through holy hell at Midway. The group had lost a tremendous amount of pilots and planes on the tiny Pacific island as they had stood and fought the Japanese onslaught.

After my advanced fighter training in Hawaii, I was sent to a place in the South Pacific called Guadalcanal, and became a member of the "Cactus Air Force"—the code name for Guadalcanal. Our living conditions were very basic as we lived in tents next to slit trenches. When the Zeros strafed us on a daily basis, we simply rolled out of our tents into the trench and waited for them to leave. Sometimes our parked airplanes took the brunt of the damage from the strafers.

Our group was assigned the barrel-chested, stubby little fighter called the F4F Wildcat. I liked the Wildcat because it was a good old airplane. It wasn't very maneuverable, but it was an excellent, hard-hitting, almost fortress-like fighter plane. The Wildcat could absorb a tremendous amount of punishment and at the same time return the favor with its six .50 caliber Browning machine guns. The F4F was very sluggish in a turn compared to the Japanese Zeros we went up against. The Zeros were

An F4F Wildcat is flanked by his wingman. COURTESY OF JAMES BUSHA

much lighter than we were and could fly rings around our Wildcats. But if we got behind them and gave them a burst, they lit up and burned easily.

When I joined the squadron, everyone was given a nickname. I was given the name "Zeke" from the Al Capp cartoons and was forever stuck with it. Zeke was also another name for the Zero, so it took some getting used to!

Baptism of Combat

My first combat mission was on April Fools' Day, 1943, as I protected the air over Henderson Field. I certainly felt like a fool as a big air battle raged off in the distance while I droned around, boring a big circle in the sky with my Wildcat. Although I hadn't fired my guns in anger yet, I would more than make up for it on my next mission.

On April 7, 1943, it was still pitch dark when I took off to lead an early-morning flight of seven other Wildcats from our strip, known as

Fighter-2. The runway was totally blacked out and our only reference was a couple of beams of light at the other end. As long as you flew toward the lights and took off before you hit them, you would be just fine.

As we made our way toward the Russell Islands, we made contact with the fighter director, code-named "Knucklehead." We flew around the Russells for a while, never spotting a Japanese airplane. As our fuel gauges began to creep toward empty, Knucklehead told us that there were some Japanese planes stirring around near Bougainville, possibly headed our way. I didn't give that piece of news much thought, because if they were on their way to Guadalcanal they were still hours away.

Our flight returned to Fighter-2 and refueled. After we were topped off we went back up and circled around near Guadalcanal for a few hours. I thought it had the makings of my earlier uneventful mission, just boring holes in the sky.

I took my flight back to Fighter-2 and landed a third time, not knowing that soon I would find myself busier than a one-armed paper hanger! We began to get reports from the coast-watchers up north that the Japanese were on their way down in force. Unbeknownst to me, there was a big storm brewing just beyond the horizon, and it contained almost two hundred Japanese fighters and dive-bombers, all of them heading our way.

Our ground crews topped off our gas tanks once again, and just for good measure, my ordnance man shoehorned an additional fifteen rounds of ammo into each gun bay. I would soon find out that every little bit helped!

We took off again and were still climbing when I was told to take my flight to the Florida Islands near Tulagi, circle, and wait for further instructions. Tulagi was only 40 miles away, with a group of Allied ships anchored offshore that included some tankers, minesweepers, corvettes, and destroyers. Our job was to protect the fleet from the Japanese dive-bombers.

I was still climbing and leading my flight through 15,000 feet when all of a sudden we ran right into the middle of a large formation of Japanese Aichi D3A "Val" dive-bombers and their Zero escorts. My God, there were airplanes all over the sky, and most of them had red meatballs on their wings! I estimated over one hundred fighters and seventy-five dive-bombers. There were just eight of us, and all I could think was, "Holy smoke! We're in deep doo-doo!"

I brought my flight around, turned toward them at full throttle, and dove headlong into the middle of the hornets' nest. Brother, it hit the fan, like, right now!

So Many Choices

Because I was the lead F4F, I was way out in front of the rest of my flight and didn't realize that they were getting mauled by the Zeros. I concentrated on the Vals that were filling my windscreen. The Vals were painted in a dirty olive-drab and were strung out in multiple V-formations. They never looked back as they made their dive toward the ships in the harbor. I guess they thought that the Zeros would take care of all the Wildcats behind them.

They thought wrong.

I nailed one Val right away, just before he went into his dive and flamed it before he knew what hit him. I stayed with the rest of the pack

Japanese dive-bombers, like the ones Jim Swett encountered with his Wildcat, search for their next targets. COURTESY OF JIM SWETT

and had to throttle back because they were so slow; I was traveling a lot faster than they were.

I burned my second Val halfway down into his dive, and I'm sure that bomb slung below his belly didn't help his speed any. My tactic was to get in close to the Vals, hit them hard, and then duck away quickly as I looked for the next one.

My plan seemed to be working pretty well as I tacked on to another Val just as he was pulling out at the bottom of his dive-bomb run. I gave him a couple of short squirts as he began to burn like the other two, splashing him in an instant. Although the Vals had rear gunners, I didn't give them much thought as they shot at me because I was concentrating my aim on the wing root near the pilot. I had been taught early on to squeeze the trigger in short, two- to three-round bursts; that way my barrels would stay cool and not burn out.

The Vals were getting some hits on the ships below as a tanker began to burn and a destroyer took a hit in the stern. Every gun on those ships turned toward my direction, because I was right in the middle of those Vals as the sky filled with antiaircraft fire. The flak from the Allied ships was coming up so hot and so fast that there was no way to avoid getting hit as I pulled out of my dive at around 500 feet.

I was trying hard to get the hell out of there when all of a sudden I took a tremendous hit in my right wing, dead center into my outboard gun. That scared the living bejeezus out of me!

I looked over and saw my gun barrel sticking straight up through a fresh, foot-and-a-half-wide jagged hole in my wing. My right flap was damaged too, but at least my other five guns were still working.

I scanned my instruments and everything else seemed to be working fine on the Wildcat. It was a good time to leave the flak, so I pointed my Wildcat toward the opposite side of the Florida Islands.

I guess the Japanese were trying to do the same, because as I was skirting some low clouds in the area, I ran into another batch of Vals scattered across the sky, trying to form back up for the long flight home.

I was still down low, below 800 feet, as I crept up behind the Vals. I picked the first one out as he made a left turn, and was only 100 feet behind him when I gave him a burst of my machine guns. He burned quickly, and that was number four. I slid over to the next Val and he saw me coming but there was nothing he could do because he was too low. He quickly joined his friends in the sea below.

It was like shooting fish in a barrel, as the slow-moving Vals seemed helpless against my Wildcat. I picked out number six, and as I moved in right behind his tail and raked him with my .50's, right along the side of his fuselage, he began to burn like the rest.

My flight suit was wringing wet with sweat as I closed in on the next Val. The rear gunner, try as he might, could not keep me in his sights as I went for the pilot and walked my short bursts into the Val until he began to burn.

As I turned into the number-eight Val I became overconfident and cocky. I got way too close to him as my propeller swirled behind his tail, just 25 feet away. The rear gunner let me have it right between the eyes as his rounds tore into my windscreen, my engine, and everything else hanging out in the open. I gave him everything I had and killed the rear gunner quickly. I was able to get the Val smoking before every gun on the Wildcat stopped firing at once as I ran out of ammunition.

I knew I had to get the hell out of there before every Zero in the sky swarmed over me, especially after seeing that long trail of smoke from the damaged Val.

Feet Wet

I was only 600 feet above the island as I turned for Guadalcanal. I began to wonder where my buddies were. The entire aerial combat against the Vals had lasted no more than fifteen minutes.

I was noticing my oil pressure gauge racing for the zero mark when all of a sudden my propeller stopped dead. One of the blades was sticking straight up, just like the middle finger of my right hand! I tried to put my flaps down to slow my descent, but with the right one damaged, the left one began to throw me off, so I yanked it back up.

I was probably doing over 100 mph when I hit the water in one large splash. I bounced once and that coincided with my face bouncing off the gunsight, breaking my nose. I continued my dive in the Wildcat, this time below the surface as we sank almost 30 feet together. The F4F had the tendency to float like a lead brick as the water became darker.

I was tangled up in my raft, Mae West, and right shoulder harness as I fought to free myself. I was finally able to get out of my parachute and scrambled to the surface with a belly full of salt water. I'd only been in the water for about ten minutes when I spotted a picket boat heading my way. I fired a couple of rounds into the air from my water-soaked .45 caliber pistol and that got their attention.

As the boat came alongside me, someone up above shouted, "Are you an American?" I yelled back in a not-so-pleasant voice, "Damn well right I am!"

I was picked up and brought ashore on Tulagi. I later found out that everybody in my flight was shot up and shot down that day, but thankfully we all survived to fight another day.

I was full of salt water and morphine when I was met by a marine colonel. He asked me what had happened, and I said, "I got seven airplanes!" The colonel was ecstatic and poured me some scotch, a drink I despise, but I didn't want to seem like an ungrateful guest. I threw it down and promptly threw it back up in front of the colonel!

The next day I was transferred to a naval hospital where I recovered from my injuries. As I rested, all my victories were confirmed, and this fact brought about a lot of attention from Admiral Mitscher. He recommended me for the Medal of Honor for my actions on April 7.

I was only a twenty-two-year-old first lieutenant and Marine Corps aviator when I was presented the Medal of Honor by Maj. Gen. Ralph Mitchell on October 10, 1943. At the time I received it, I couldn't comprehend what the medal meant, but I knew it was absolutely awesome, and it forever changed my life. I had been asked if I wanted to go back home to the United States and meet President Roosevelt. I was grateful, but asked if we could do that a little later. I'd only been out of flight training a little over a year, and besides, there was a war on. I wanted to stay and finish the job of winning it with my squadron.

Medal of Honor recipient Jim Swett stands at attention during his medal ceremony. COURTESY OF JIM SWETT

Medal of Honor Citation

For conspicuous gallantry and intrepidity at the risk of his own life above and beyond the call of duty, as a Division Leader in Marine Fighter Squadron 221 in action against enemy Japanese aerial forces in the Solomon Islands area, April 7, 1943.

In a daring flight to intercept a wave of 150 Japanese planes, First Lieutenant Swett unhesitatingly hurled his four-plane division into action against a formation of fifteen enemy bombers and during his dive personally exploded three hostile planes in midair with accurate and deadly fire. Although separated from his division while clearing the heavy concentration of antiaircraft fire, he boldly attacked six enemy bombers, engaged the first four in turn, and unaided, shot them down in flames. Exhausting his ammunition as he closed the fifth Japanese bomber, he relentlessly drove his attack against terrific opposition which partially disabled his engine, shattered the windscreen, and slashed his face.

In spite of this, he brought his battered plane down with skillful precision in the water off Tulagi without further injury. The superb airmanship and tenacious fighting spirit which enabled First Lieutenant Swett to destroy seven enemy bombers in a single flight were in keeping with the highest traditions of the United States Naval Service.

(James Swett continued to fly combat missions in F4F Wildcats with his squadron VMF-221. In May of 1943 he along with the rest of squadron switched over to the F4U Corsair. James Swett more than doubled his earlier score and ended the war with 15.5 victories, all in the Pacific Theater.)

8

Running with the Devil: P-38

BECOMING AN ACE WITH SATAN'S ANGELS
Col. Perry J. "PJ" Dahl
475th Fighter Group, 432nd Fighter Squadron, 5th Air Force

As a kid growing up on the bow of my father's tugboat, hauling oil from Seattle to Alaska, I had a lot of time on my hands. I use to read the pulp magazines about the aces of World War I, like the Red Baron. That's probably how I became interested in flying. But when I became a fighter pilot, I didn't care about flying straight and level; I was more interested in the fighter aspects of pursuing and attacking your enemy. It was the aggressive instinct of being a fighter pilot in combat—hunting and attacking other airplanes as opposed to being the hunted—that intrigued me the most.

Earning My Wings

My initial exposure to the military was in 1939. At the ripe old age of seventeen, I joined the 41st Infantry Division of the National Guard in Seattle, Washington, because my parents thought that serving a year in the army would do me some good. I guess it was because trouble always followed me wherever I went; thankfully it was always two steps behind!

As a foot soldier my mind was always in the clouds, so when the opportunity presented itself for me to go into aviation training, I was at the front of the line, signing up. After completing preflight I was sent to Cal-Aero in Chino, California, where I almost washed out.

I had been out over the desert on a solo flight in my PT-17 Stearman and began to do some unauthorized aerobatics. As I looped and rolled my biplane around the sunny California skies, I didn't notice the other PT-17 nearby with an instructor seated inside. By the time I got back to base, my punishment was waiting for me: twenty-five tours of walking guard duty. Back to being a foot soldier again!

The only reason I wasn't washed out of flying was because I was the only cadet in my class that hadn't ground-looped the Stearman. I attribute that feat to an excellent instructor I had who took his time with me and showed me how to handle a Stearman, including aerobatics. It was instilled in me early on to be aggressive and utilize the strengths of the airplane in combat situations. By the time I earned my wings I was sent to multi-engine training—not as a bomber pilot, but as a fighter pilot.

Lightning Lessons

I thought the Lockheed P-38 Lightning was massive! As fighters go, it was a big airplane. With twin Allison engines, twin tails, and a deadly weapons package in the nose, the P-38 was all business. I felt the Lightning was much easier to fly than a single-engine fighter; there were no worries with ground loops because of the counter-rotating propellers. The visibility was excellent, sitting up high on three wheels instead of two with your tail dragging. There weren't any dual-controlled P-38s, so you hung on every word the instructor told you about how to fly it and get back down in one piece. The checkout was simple: The instructor kicked you in the ass, slapped you inside, and said go!

In early 1943 I was assigned to the 55th Fighter Group that was stationed in the northwest section of Washington State. Most of the guys I flew with had combat time in the Aleutians, and a couple of them had even tangled with the Japanese. Needless to say they became our informal instructors and showed us what to do and what not to do in combat. The one golden rule that was drilled into us was to never, ever, under any circumstances, get sucked into a low, slow-turning battle with a Zero. Although the Lightning was faster and had more armament and better weapons, the only way to survive against a turning Zero was to keep your speed up—otherwise you were toast!

As fighters go, the P-38 was the hottest ship in the air; at least that was my father's opinion during World War II. He had come to visit me in Washington and I was out showing him around the base when two P-38s came roaring across the field, practically "cutting grass" as they crossed in front of us. My father's jaw dropped as his eyes tracked the low-level duo leaving as quickly as they had come in. He turned to me, and with the biggest smile I had ever observed on his face, proclaimed, "Twenty-three skidoo!" That was an old slang term from the 1920s that meant getting out and leaving quickly. I decided that if I ever got my own P-38 I would paint that saying on my Lightning's nose.

With the war heating up in the Pacific we received word that a recently formed, brand-new, all P-38 group—the 475th FG—was desperately looking for replacement pilots. Because they couldn't afford to send all of us overseas, the instructors decided to have a fly-off to see who was the most aggressive and capable. When the dust had settled, two of us—Joe Forester and me—were selected to join the group in New Guinea in October of 1943.

One of Satan's Angels

After the C-47 dropped Joe and me off in Dobodura, New Guinea, we reported to the commanding officer (CO) for our squadron assignment. Although Joe was only two years older than me, his hair was pure white in color. I, however, looked like a sixteen-year-old kid and stood only 5 feet, 5 inches tall. When we reported to the CO he gave Joe and I the once-over and threw his hands up in disgust. He turned to his executive officer and said, "Oh my God, they're sending me old men and boys!"

I became one of "Satan's Angels" with the 475th FG, 5th Air Force. Joe

Perry J. "PJ" Dahl getting strapped into his P-38 Lightning COURTESY OF PERRY DAHL

and I were assigned to the 432nd Fighter Squadron known as "Clover." The 431st was code-named "Hades" and the 433rd was called "Possum."

My introduction to combat came at an accelerated pace.

Baptism of Fire

There were no milk runs for a new fighter pilot to fly in the Pacific in 1943. My very first mission was to Rabaul—the Japanese fortress of the Pacific. The enemy order of battle was to put up between 100 and 150 Japanese fighters against 18 of our P-38s. Our job was to protect the formation of B-25 Mitchell bombers that were sent in for low-level bombing and strafing. I have to be honest with you: I was all over the sky that day and never fired a shot. It wasn't because of a lack of Zeros; there were plenty of them all around. The problem I had was that I couldn't get any of them to stay in one place long enough for me to get a shot off! I almost obliged them, though, because I came home with a handful of bullet holes in my Lightning.

But I would soon return the favor.

A few days later, on November 9, 1943, I was flying the tail-end Charlie position in Blue Flight near Alexishafen when all of a sudden my element leader broke off and went after a Helen bomber. I stayed with him covering his six o'clock and was dumbfounded to see a Zeke zooming in, trying to get on my leader's tail. This guy must have had only one good eye or was so locked in on my leader that he never noticed me right behind him. The Zeke slid right in front of me in the twelve o'clock position; I think I could have knocked him down with my pistol!

The P-38 carries an awful lot of firepower in its nose: four .50 caliber machine guns and one 20mm cannon. The rounds were a mixture of armor-piercing, incendiaries, and cannon shells, and when they converged at 300 yards they formed a 6-inch circle of death. Heck, you could sink a destroyer with that lethal combination. I barely squeezed the trigger and *BOOM!* The Zeke blew up right in front of me; there was nothing left of him. The guy never knew what hit him.

Unfortunately for me, four missions later the roles would be reversed.

Switching to Glide

With a handful of combat missions under my belt, I was assigned to the tail-end Charlie position in our flight. We had eighteen P-38s up that day on combat patrol as we made our way to Lae, New Guinea.

Somewhere up ahead someone called out "Bogeys!"

For whatever reason, our leader decided to trade airspeed for altitude and ordered us to climb—a bad decision, especially when Zeros are around.

As the tail-end Charlie I was just above stalling speed when the order came to "Drop tanks!" Due to my inexperience, I failed to select internal tanks before jettisoning my belly tanks, and my world went silent in a split second. Both of my engines quit in unison and began sucking air.

It took me less than a second to realize the error of my ways as I pushed the Lightning over and screamed for the deck to keep my speed up. As I switched to internal tanks, both engines roared back to life as I pulled the nose up and began searching for my flight. I called my leader and of course lied to him, telling him that I'd had some engine trouble and had lost sight of the group. He told me to turn for "home plate," as they were busy engaging enemy fighters.

Reluctantly I turned for home, mad at myself for missing out on a good scrap.

That's when I saw the Betty bombers about to make a run on Lae.

I was young and foolish, so I convinced myself that I would just wander over to the Bettys and shoot a couple of them down. The trouble was, I was so fixated on the Bettys that I never saw the Zero diving down at my three o'clock until it was almost too late. This guy was so close he was almost in my cockpit!

As he hammered away at me I threw my right wing up, trying to block the incoming rounds. They found their mark and tore my right engine and vertical stabilizer to shreds. I could feel each of his rounds impacting my Lightning; this guy was really pouring the lead into me. As I looked into my rearview mirror all I saw were the flashes of the Zero's guns and a long white vapor trail streaming from my engine. Trouble was right behind me, and it was time to lose this guy!

I shoved the throttles forward and pushed the P-38's nose downward as I dove for the deck a second time. With both engines turning I was able to lose the Zero, and as soon as I was out of harm's way I shut down the bad engine before it blew up on me.

On the way home a fellow Lightning pulled up alongside and rode shotgun on my wing. When I arrived over my field I made a long approach, threw down my gear, and greased my wounded Lightning onto the pierced steel planking (PSP) runway.

It didn't take me long to realize that had I been flying a single-engine fighter, all of those slugs would have gone into my cockpit instead of my engine. It was a nice feeling to know that while flying the P-38, although you had two engines, you could always make it home on one.

The Old Man and the Kid Make Ace with the Ace of Aces

Right before Christmas of 1943 I claimed a Zeke near Wewak, and a month later I bagged my third one. By April of 1944 we were really on the offensive as we slugged it out with the Japanese day after day. On April 3 our Fighter Group along with the 80th Fighter Group—"The Head-hunters"—were tasked with providing bomber escort to Hollandia. The 80th stayed up high with the B-24 Liberators, as our group was assigned to deck with low-flying A-20 Havocs and B-25 Mitchell bombers.

Lt. Col. "Mac" MacDonald led our squadron in as we protected the withdrawing A-20s. There were so many Japanese fighters around that everyone in our group got in on the action—even one guy from 5th Fighter Command who showed up unannounced.

I tacked onto a Zeke and an Oscar and raked both of them with machine-gun and cannon rounds over Lake Sentani as they both hit the ground burning. My buddy Joe Forester was the tail-end Charlie in one of the flights and had a pair of victories to his credit before this mission. Joe was able to bag three more that day as we both evened our scores to five apiece.

But Joe was about to pass me up when he spotted a fleeing Oscar and went tearing after him. Unfortunately, another Lightning, flown by Maj. Richard Bong of 5th Fighter Command, appeared on Joe's wing and shot the Oscar down before Joe even had a chance. It was hard to be upset with a guy like Bong, as that was his twenty-fifth victory of the war; besides, he still had fifteen more to go before the war ended.

All in all that day our two groups shot down twenty-five Japanese fighters to the loss of one P-38. Not a bad day for Angels and Headhunters.

Trouble Catches Up

By November of 1944, I had been promoted to the rank of captain and was the assistant operations officer. Our army and navy were marching and sailing northward and invading parts of the Philippines.

On November 10 our group was part of a large air armada sent over Ormoc Bay off Leyte. The mission called for our B-25s to go in low and skip-bomb the Japanese troop- and warships that were trying to supply and reinforce the Japanese troops on the ground. Colonel MacDonald was leading our group, and he spotted a lone Zero stooging around up ahead. As MacDonald dove on him, I think the Zero pilot bailed out before a shot was fired. He must have seen the daisy chain of P-38s right behind him!

After Colonel MacDonald shot down the Zero, he called me and told me to take over the group, as he was returning to base for more fuel. Just as he bugged out, I looked to the other side and saw a flight of eighteen Tony fighters in a big V flying just underneath the cloud deck. I circled our flight around and got on top of the clouds as I waited to pounce.

We came zooming out of the clouds right into the unsuspecting Tonys and I knocked off the lead plane with a short burst. The Tonys that remained turned into us as we got into a big swirling dogfight at 20,000 feet.

I was indicating over 400 miles per hour, rolling and turning with the Tonys, when all of a sudden I felt a huge jolt. I looked in my rearview mirror and saw that both of my tail booms were gone. I never saw the guy I collided with. It was surreal as time seemed to slow way down. I could see our base off in the distance and realized I would not be home for dinner. I watched as my right wing fell away while gas poured out of the ruptured tank. As I blew my canopy off, I thought out loud, "Boy, this ain't my day!"

I was having trouble getting out of the airplane and had just unbuckled when *KABOOM!* The P-38 exploded and shot me out, leaving me with a bunch of nasty flash burns. My element leader later told me that there wasn't a piece of my airplane bigger than a quarter left; it had simply disintegrated.

I chose to free-fall for a while because I wanted to get away from the fight. At around 10,000 feet I popped my chute and looked down and saw the whole Japanese navy right underneath me. Then I looked up and saw a Japanese pilot right above me, hanging in his parachute. I was surrounded!

Because he had a smaller chute the Japanese pilot beat me down and hit the water first. He never came back up.

I was floating down through a hailstorm of bullets from the Japanese gunners on the ships below when they suddenly turned their attention to the incoming low-level B-25s as they made their skip-bombing runs on the ships. With the Japanese ships turning tail and making a run for it, I just missed snagging the rigging of one of their cruisers as I splashed into the water nearby. They couldn't have cared less about me as the gun-nosed B-25s continued to assault them.

In the next month I would float in the ocean for a couple of days; be strafed at by a Zero and shot at by a destroyer; and be rescued by Filipino guerrillas, adopt a pet monkey I named Ormak, and live in the jungle. I would eat worms and bugs and lose 30 pounds, and be rescued by American "Alamo Scouts," and sent to Australia for R&R, where I'd lose another 10 pounds "fighting off" the Australian women! I eventually returned to my squadron at Clark Field and ended up bagging a Sally and a Hamp in March of 1945, to end the war with nine victories.

Looking back on it, being a successful fighter pilot meant you had to have that killer instinct. Sure, there were times when you got victories because you were there "at the right time and the right place," but for the most part, if you weren't aggressive in combat, you were either a target or a future statistic on a government chart.

We policed ourselves in the squadron; if you were afraid to mix it up, you were sent packing to fly C-47s for the rest of your tour. That may sound harsh to some, but war was life and death, and in order to survive you had to count on the guy next to you to watch your back. There weren't many second chances in air-to-air combat.

9

Hell's Belles: P-40

LOW-LEVEL COMBAT IN A **P-40** WARHAWK
Capt. William Dave Gatling, USAAF

Off I Go into the Wild Blue Yonder!
The oldest of six kids growing up in Tarboro, North Carolina, I was a wide-eyed eighteen-year-old when I enlisted in the US Army Air Corps (USAAC) in late October of 1940. I was assigned to the 3rd Reconnaissance Squadron in Orlando, Florida, as an aerial photographer, and learned quickly that the air corps was far from ready for war. We lacked pilots, mechanics, and airplanes as we sat back and watched other countries in Europe building up their military air arm. But the air corps knew this too and instituted a program whereby if you were already enlisted in the service, you could "volunteer" to learn how to fly and bypass the college degree requirements. If you earned your wings, you would be classified as a staff sergeant pilot—so that's what I did.

After flying PT-17 Stearmans, BT-13s, and AT-6s, I earned my staff sergeant wings in October of 1942 and was immediately assigned to the 324th Fighter Group, 315th "Crusaders" Fighter Squadron in Manchester, New Hampshire, where I was checked out in a P-40 Warhawk. It was more than double the horsepower of the AT-6, and after my blindfold checkout I learned quickly about getting your head out of the cockpit with 1,300hp roaring out in front of you.

My instructor told me to take the Warhawk up to 10,000 feet, get to know the airplane by doing some gentle turns, and then to do some stalls with the landing gear and flaps down to get the feel of it. I got the feel of it right away—and it was all bad!

As I climbed through 9,000 feet I must have been going too slowly and the P-40 snapped on me, throwing me into an inverted spin. I hadn't planned on stalling the airplane yet and really didn't know what I was doing at that point. We were trained in spin recovery early on and so I did what I was taught and popped the stick forward and stomped down on the opposite rudder. When I did this the P-40 stalled and threw me back into a spin. I watched the snow-covered fields below rapidly spinning around me, and must have repeated this process four separate times before I finally woke up and realized that I was in an inverted spin.

Because I was upside down, every time it happened I popped the stick forward. All I was doing was pushing my nose up and stalling the darn thing. I finally managed to get out of it, but in the process I had lost 7,000 feet. I pulled out at less than 2,000 feet of altitude. I was wringing wet with sweat and had to go back up and do my assigned maneuvers, but I learned more about flying the P-40 on that checkout than at any other point in my training.

When I came back into land, I shot three of the most perfect landings ever performed in a P-40!

Have Guns, Will Travel

On March 8, 1943, after 60 hours of flying time in the P-40, having never fired a single shot from its six .50 caliber machine guns, I was sent overseas to Nigeria. Our crated P-40s were waiting for us to assist in assembling them. Once that was done, we had to flight-test and slow-time our engines ourselves as we cruised over the dense jungles and hot deserts of Africa on our way to Cairo, Egypt, over 2,600 miles away, without even a set of railroad tracks to guide us. The British had established refueling fields every 500 miles for us to land at. Once we hit the Nile River, we turned north to Cairo, with only 1,000 miles of desert ahead of us. Once we arrived in the northern deserts and mountains of Tunisia, we were assigned to the British 8th Army, to assist in pushing Rommel's Afrika Korps out to the sea.

Curtiss P-40 Warhawk wartime ad COURTESY OF EAA

We were all as green as green could be when it came to combat, so in early April of 1943, we had to fly "shadow gunnery missions" to test our shooting skills. We set out in pairs and one P-40 would fly at 500 feet over the hot sunny desert as he cast his shadow on the ground, and the other P-40 would make gunnery runs on the shadow. You could tell right away if you scored hits on the shadow because the sand and dust would kick up in the shadow fuselage. Immediately after that training we were deemed combat-ready and sent to slug it out with the Axis.

Our primary mission was to support the British 8th Army by strafing and bombing the Axis troops on the ground, but on my fourth mission we were sent out to sea to attack a different kind of target.

Lucky Strike

On April 30, 1943, we got a call at our 324th FG HQ that there was an enemy Italian destroyer out at sea and our British counterparts asked if we would give a Yankee try at dive-bombing it. Because the 315th FS had arrived later in-theater, we were assigned to fly with some of the more experienced pilots of the 316th "Hell's Belles" FS. I was chosen as one of the lucky ones to go along. Our ground crews loaded a single 500-pound bomb on the center line of our P-40s, where our belly tanks would normally sit. Needless to say, removing the belly tank cut down on our combat range.

As a new pilot I was positioned as the No. 10 pilot in this string of dive-bombers. We left our base flying in a four-ship box formation with a total of twelve P-40s and climbed to 7,500 feet. Our top cover escort was British Spitfires to shepherd us and protect us from the even-higher-flying Me 109s that were sure to show up—and as if on cue, they did.

When we got to the warship, the Spitfires were tangling with the 109s. Our flight leader called for echelon right and everyone pulled off to the right. It turned into a deadly game of follow the leader. The distance between each P-40 was between 250 and 300 yards. We had been warned that when you squeeze that gun trigger, make darn sure there wasn't another P-40 sitting in front of you!

As soon as we got close to the Italian destroyer and peeled off to dive, the ship started zigzagging and throwing up a huge screen of ack-ack. I remembered my earlier training back in the States to deal with the torque of the Allison engine when I pushed the nose over in a dive. The P-40 was manufactured with the vertical stabilizer offset, to cause the airplane to fly straight when flying at the designed cruising airspeed—around 230 mph, as I recall. As long as I flew straight, the offset stabilizer and the engine torque balanced each other out. The problem was, the faster you went over 230 mph, the more it caused the P-40 to want to turn to the right. And as you can imagine, in a dive-bombing run, the airspeed picks up quickly. Zooming through 230 mph really made that sucker want to turn right. But that was a minor problem compared to the bigger one that filled the sky. All I saw around me was tracer fire, streaking my way.

My eyes locked in on the destroyer down below, using my iron cross-hair gunsight for aiming. When I saw 900 feet on the altimeter I thought, "Holy smokes, I got to get out of here!"

I took my eyes off the gunsight because I got distracted by the antiaircraft fire for a second. When I looked back my nose was pointed way off the target, so I stomped down on the left pedal as I kicked hard left rudder, all the while pulling back on the stick. My hand came off the throttle as I grabbed the wooden "T" handle located on the floorboard just under the throttle and trim tab controls, and pulled it to release the bomb.

I tried to toss the bomb to the left. Bingo! It hit dead center on the deck. The delayed action on the fuse caused to bomb to penetrate the deck before it exploded. When I looked back from my pullout, I saw an enormous array of black, blue, and white smoke pouring from the center of the ship. I didn't see it actually sink, but it was reported that it did.

Too Hot to Handle

On June 5, 1944, I was leading a flight of four P-40s on a recce mission in support of the American 5th Army when one of them developed engine problems. I sent a buddy to go back with the rough-running Warhawk as the two of us, Lt. Jerry Lennon and I, continued on.

We were cruising along at 800 feet, looking for German motor transportation in Italy as part of Operation Strangle, northwest of Rome. It appeared the Germans were pulling out rapidly and there was a lot of traffic up ahead on one of the roadways. There was already a bunch of

P-47s strafing that convoy and they looked like they had matters well in hand, so we went looking for our own targets as we turned north toward the Bolsena area.

We had only flown another 50 miles when I spotted this semi-tractor-trailer with camouflage netting all over it parked under a group of trees next to a roadway. I dropped down to 80 feet and turned toward the truck and tried to give it a squirt, but I couldn't get my guns on it because I was too close—my right wing almost clipped the treetops as I flew overhead.

I decided to go out 500 yards and circle back for another try. The machine guns on the P-40 had been bore-sighted for 300 yards, and as I made my run I kept talking to myself: "Not now, not now—now!" My finger depressed the trigger and my rounds impacted the target. I only saw one tracer round from my guns so I knew I'd only fired about thirty rounds at the truck.

I remember the first explosion, but it was the second one that really rocked me—literally. I had seen gas tanks explode on other vehicles in the past, so I didn't expect anything big to happen on this gun run. Boy, was I ever wrong! The first clue I had that this one was different was the big boiling cloud of black smoke billowing right in front of me. I began to ease left as I pulled back on the stick, and as if I had been moving in slow motion, I saw a 55-gallon drum hovering in front of me in that cloud of smoke, just missing my right wing tip.

Immediately I saw a flash of something that I thought was just a dust or sand cloud. It went on and off quickly before there was a catastrophic explosion followed by a mass of red-colored flames. A mass of gray- and tan-colored residue engulfed me and I lost sight of the trees, the road below, and the sky above. I estimated it to be over 100 yards wide, and I froze on the stick to keep it centered.

Next I saw a white thin cloud moving my way, which turned out to be a shock wave. It felt like a sledgehammer when it hit the P-40. My shoulder straps tightened hard around me. At first it was a push, then a hard pull, almost like a vacuum as I got pulled forward. I thought I was still straight when I entered the fireball and I felt something strike the airplane. For a moment I was confused because I saw a hole in the fireball, but beyond that I saw the ground rushing up at me—I was going in left wing low!

I pulled the stick back to raise the nose and get the left wing up and missed the ground by about 6 feet. I was fighting it the whole time because when I moved the stick back to neutral, still in a climb, the left wing would drop again. I saw some trees up ahead so I tried to turn right but when I did I thought the Warhawk was going to snap-roll on me. I didn't try that again. I cleared those olive trees by the skin of my teeth.

For some reason I looked down and saw this man—must have been a German soldier, because I saw the swastika on his helmet and his eyes were as big as pancakes and his mouth was wide open—I was only 75 feet away from him. Funny thing was, my expression mirrored his as I zoomed past him.

A minute later I was out over no man's land with my wingman about 100 yards away on my right side. That's when the shooting started. There must have been twelve to fifteen different streams of automatic tracer fire arching all over the sky, as the German soldiers on the ground were shooting widely in all directions. Because we were below the treetops they could only hear the roar of our Allison engines and couldn't catch a glimpse of us.

We flew straight ahead until the firing stopped before I even thought about climbing. When I did, I had to do everything very gingerly because any sudden movement would cause my left wing to drop. We were heading north so I had to wait until my compass read 270 degrees so I could aim for the Mediterranean. That's when my wingman called me, when we were only five minutes away from the Mediterranean Sea. I could tell he had some excitement in his voice when he asked me if we were still over enemy territory. He was on his 13th mission and I was on my 175th. He never told me he was hit.

When we hit the coast, I knew he was as relieved as I was as we limped back to base. I was fighting the P-40 all the way and thought I might have to bail out or crash-land, for sure.

I looked in my rearview mirror and saw my wingman and asked him to pull up on my left wing to give me a look to see what he could find. I saw him move below me and that was the last time I saw him that day.

A P-40 with a 500-pound bomb strapped to its belly, and smaller underwing bombs, prepares to hunt for its next target. COURTESY OF TOM ANDERSON

When he didn't show up, I looked back again in the mirror and saw an empty sky. I was still 125 miles from base and couldn't get my crippled P-40 to turn around to look for Lieutenant Lennon. At 25 miles out I called for emergency landing instructions and asked that somebody put that runway dead center on my nose. There would have been no way for me to circle and land.

I came in with a little bit of speed and no flaps as I made a wheel landing. I had to use more right rudder as I was headed left off the runway. I cut the engine and got the tail down as I slowed to a stop. The engine was steaming like a freight train as I began to count bullet holes in the airplane. The heat from that explosion had melted the dope-covered fabric on my ailerons, and they resembled baggy pants on a hobo.

I walked in front of the right wing and there was a large 12-inch-diameter hole in the leading edge, just outside the wheel well. I am sure the airflow over that airfoil was quite disturbed; along with no aileron control, it's no wonder I couldn't keep it level. The oil cooler was smashed in by flying debris, and it was a complete miracle that the propeller wasn't hit.

While the P-40 had brought me back home, I wondered what had happened to Lieutenant Lennon.

The next day Lennon's P-40 was spotted on a beach, its red-colored nose resting above collapsed gear with countless bullet holes smothering the wings and fuselage. I feared the worst and had to wait almost two weeks to hear his story, when he finally walked back to our base.

Lieutenant Lennon told me he had picked up a lot of damage on the way home during our low-level journey. He had tried to call me but his radio must have been shot out. After he bellied in, he was picked up by the Italian Underground and returned to American lines, almost two weeks later. He said the funniest thing was when he tried to bury his parachute in the sand; as his hands were busy digging and throwing sand all over the place and he was sweating like a butcher, he looked back and thought, "How in the heck am I ever going to bury the P-40?" I often wonder what ever happened to that Warhawk.

(William Gatling flew 195 combat missions in the P-40 and 5 in the P-47 before returning back home. He still thinks about all his buddies who didn't make it back.)

10

True Blue Jug Jockey: P-47

With the war in Europe and the Pacific already in full motion, Republic Aviation's contribution to the war effort was greatly augmented with its newly designed fighter, the P-47 Thunderbolt. Affectionately called "the Jug" by its ground crew and pilots, the P-47 proved its usefulness and effectiveness against Axis aircraft, earning the respect and admiration of those who flew her. Republic knew it had a winner on its hands; now all that was needed were fighter pilots to prove it!

SILVER WINGS
Lt. Col. Donald S. Bryan
352nd Fighter Group, 328th Fighter Squadron, 8th Air Force

That damn 65-horse Aeronca Defender saved my butt!

When I entered the service in January of 1942, I had already obtained my private pilot's license. I had a whopping 39 hours in the Aeronca, so when I went to Primary, instructors didn't have to tell me about chandelles, loops, and spins, because I had that training already. My instructors had a little fun with me, teaching me things I was supposed to learn in Basic.

I went on to Basic and the same thing happened: I was taught tactics and air work I was supposed to learn in Advanced. When I got to Advanced, I was labeled a "hot pilot."

After graduation I was sent to fighters. To this day, I still consider those 39 hours in the Aeronca as the most important time I ever had in the air.

My first assignment was at Myrtle Beach, South Carolina, where I was checked out in the Curtiss P-40 and soloed in it two days before I was legally allowed to buy a drink! I soon found myself instructing in P-40s and P-39s down in Florida.

I thought the P-40 was a bastard when it came to flying it. It was one of the hardest airplanes to land that I flew. Every time you landed in the P-40, there would be problems. It didn't seem to make any difference what or how you did things. The only good thing about it was you knew right away which way the wind was blowing from because your nose always started in that direction! If the wind was to the left, you'd stomp down on the right brake and the gear would start to rattle and squeak, and as soon as that happened it would start ground-looping to the left, so you locked the left wheel and it would start back to the right, so you locked the right again, and finally the tail wheel would connect with the ground and you'd roll. I never three-pointed the P-40. You were so close to a stall, you were just asking for trouble. Besides, you had too much to concern yourself with on the recovery from the ground loops that you knew were coming!

I thought even less of the P-39s. I had about 35 hours in P-39s when I was on a training flight near Atlanta. The bearing on the prop shaft went out on me, and I was barely able to make it safely into the field. I got out of the cockpit and said, "Never again. I won't fly that SOB anymore." It had the Allison "time bomb" as an engine, with that shaft running between your legs out to the prop. You never wondered *if* it would fail or break, just when! I knew the Russians loved them and used them in combat quite effectively. I wish we could have given all of 'em to them!

Fighter Lead

Around March of 1943 I was transferred to a newly formed fighter group: the 352nd. I reported in to receive my orders and met with a brigadier general. This general was looking over my file and asked me how many hours in fighters I had. I nervously answered that I "only" had 200 some-odd hours. I thought that being posted to a fighter group, the existing pilots in the group would all be high-timed, high-experienced fighter pilots. The general stared at me for a long time, then looked down at my file, then looked back at me, smiled, and said, "Only?! You just made flight leader, mister!"

I was assigned to the 328th Fighter Squadron at Mitchell Field in Long Island, New York, and that's where I came face-to-face (face-to-prop) with the behemoth monstrosity called the P-47 Thunderbolt. I had seen the Jug's predecessor, the P-43 Lancer, when I was in Tampa, and I wasn't too impressed with them. But the P-47 was quite a different airplane, with its full cantilever wing, employing two main spars and spanning 41 feet. The enhancement of four .50 caliber machine guns in each wing established the Jug as a "true gun fighter."

The "front office" of the Jug contained a huge Pratt & Whitney R-2800 air-cooled radial twin-row engine rated at 2,000hp. The engine alone weighed more than a ton, and as I would find out later in combat, it could take an enormous amount of damage and still bring its pilot home to safety. It also appeared to me that the Jug was built around the engine and supercharging system that was directed and ducted beneath the fuselage. With its 12-foot-diameter four-bladed Curtiss Electric prop hanging on the nose and supported by hydraulically controlled main landing gear, the P-47 weighed in at almost 7 tons, making it the heaviest produced fighter of its time. I didn't care about any of that at the time; I just wanted to fly it!

I was sent to the Republic Factory at Farmingdale where the Jugs were being built and was given a complete and thorough checkout by the Republic test pilots—all in three hours! The P-47 was a hot airplane!

The cockpit was absolutely huge, almost too damned big for my 5-foot-6-inch frame. I had to have cushions all around me. The start-up was easy and straightforward. With that big, dependable R-2800 out ahead of me, I felt very comfortable in the cockpit with the favorable placement of switches, throttle, and gauges. The interior was laid out quite nicely. Like most fighters at that time, you couldn't see a damn thing out in front of you. S-turns were mandatory, unless you had your crew chief or instructor lying on the wing beside you.

With the adjustments of trim, the P-47 handled like a lady. Take-off was effortless and impressive with that big four-blade prop pulling you skyward. Although you could feel the 7 tons you were dealing with strapped to your shoulders, it was a very docile and easy-to-fly airplane with sufficient power. In training, only two to four guns were loaded with fifty rounds in each gun. With the war going on, every bullet and every pull of the trigger had to be justified due to the early shortages of ammunition. Even so, the Jug was an excellent gun platform, which would be proven time and again in aerial combat.

About the only mischievous behavior the P-47 had was compressibility during high-speed dives. Unfortunately for some, this behavior turned deadly when the nose was pointed downward and control loads became excessive. We had been instructed early on to avoid certain angles and speeds during dives.

With my checkout complete, I rejoined my squadron mates in preparation for deployment to England.

Shaking Apart

In early July of 1943, I along with 20,000 other young men set sail aboard the *Queen Elizabeth*, bound for war-torn England. After five quick days of zigzagging across the Atlantic, avoiding stealthy German U-boats, we arrived at our new home.

The 352nd Fighter Group was assigned to a place called Bodney, a base previously used by the Royal Air Force. The airfield was a huge grass field with no runways. Crosswind landings were a thing of the past, as we could now take off and land into the wind every time. Our P-47s began to trickle in and arrive at Bodney, and soon all aircraft were present and accounted for. It felt good to get back into the Jug, putting it through its paces over England in preparation for combat missions that were soon to follow. Acclimating ourselves in formation, gunnery, navigation, and instrument flying was the order of the day. But most important was learning where your airfield was located in the event of an emergency or foul weather, both of which were encountered all too often.

By early September 1943, the 352nd had become operational. On September 9, 1943, the group received its first combat briefing. This is what I, along with the rest, had trained so long and very hard for. Enthusiasm and apprehension filled our heads as we waited for our orders: a patrol mission over the coast of England to fly protective cover for returning P-47s of the 56th and 353rd fighter groups. Maybe, just maybe, a "lone" German aircraft would try to sneak in and would in turn be clobbered by over forty P-47s lying in wait. At the time, it was just wishful thinking by a young, foolish pilot—me!

As the roar of more than forty R-2800s came to life, a feeling of uncertainty and intrigue took control of my body, strapped into this huge monster of an airplane, designed for the sole purpose of destruction and annihilation of the enemy. Seeing and hearing all of these olive-drab P-47s moving and taxiing in one harmonious column to ready themselves for takeoff was awe-inspiring. All three groups would participate in today's mission, with the 486th and the 487th taking off first, followed by the 328th bringing up the rear.

And that was exactly where my flight of four P-47s was located—the back row! I positioned myself to the left with my No. 1, 2, and 3 to the right after lining up and swinging to the left a bit, just enough to see over my engine to the flight in front of me. As the flights progressed on ahead of us, I checked and rechecked instruments, settings, and switches, just to be sure nothing would go wrong on this very first and important mission.

As the flight in front of me began to move, I swung back to takeoff position, nodded my head to the guy next to me, and "poured the coal" to the big Pratt & Whitney. As speed and lift increased, I raised my tail up off the well-worn grass below and began to feel and hear the damnedest noise you ever heard in the cockpit of a P-47. As I rocketed down the grass strip at Bodney, the vibration and noise coming from somewhere in the bowels of my cockpit became louder and more thunderous. I couldn't figure out what in the devil was going on. All I thought was, "Oh, shoot, I'm gonna have to abort. Dammit, the first mission of the group, and I'm not even off the ground yet!"

I was just about to chop the throttle when I looked down and found the "problem." My knees were shaking so much that it was rattling the brake pedals attached to the rudder pedals with such force that they were clattering. Here I was, a fighter pilot with over 500 hours in high-performance aircraft, on my very first combat mission, and my knees were acting like it was their very first flight! When I realized what the hell was going on, they finally settled down.

Our very first combat mission was so simple it was funny. I don't think we even saw the enemy coast, but it was a mission nonetheless.

Unfortunately, the rest of the missions would not be so simple or funny.

Hot Rod Jug

Our primary mission in the P-47 was bomber escort, either on the way to the targets, or providing withdrawal support for returning bombers. Usually the number of returning bombers was less than had gone out due to the lack of fighter protection over the target area. The early P-47s had a limited range in which it flew missions. Later, with the addition of drop tanks, our range of area and coverage increased. We could now bring the fight to the enemy. And early on, the enemy was always itching to fight.

I never thought of myself as a good pilot. My wingmen and others in my flight were hotter pilots than I was. The attributes I had going for me were threefold: One, I had better eyesight than most of the pilots in my squadron. Two, I was a flight leader and was afforded more opportunities. And three, my crew chief on the P-47D had the ability and talent to turn a "soup can" into a rocket!

I had shared a "kill" in late January of 1943 of an Fw 190 near Frankfurt. We came at each other head-on, and I ducked down behind that steel out in front of me and opened fire on him. I saw some hits and we rattled around for a bit, and finally the guy bailed out. The fight had started up high, above 20,000 feet. This is where the P-47 reigned supreme over the Bf 109s and Fw 190s, but once you went below 18,000 feet, things changed in a hurry, and these were not favorable changes! The 109s and 190s could outperform the P-47s at these lower altitudes. The German air force was still being operated by highly skilled and motivated pilots that knew how to exploit their strengths and our weaknesses.

New replacement P-47s began to arrive at Bodney. These newly improved Jugs had water injection connected to the supercharger, operated by a switch on the throttle. This allowed for a higher emergency rating and protection of the engine from detonation when being operated above military power settings.

Donald S. Bryan, USAAC, poses on the wing of his P-47 Thunderbolt, *Little One*. COURTESY OF DONALD BRYAN

I asked my crew chief, Staff Sgt. Kirk Noyes, when *Little One*, our P-47, was going to get this H20 improvement. Kirk just looked at me and smiled. "The 47D2 ain't never gonna get water injection. It isn't in the book for us. We're too old of an airplane."

I reminded Kirk that I was a flight leader, and I wasn't gonna be flying the slowest airplane in the squadron!

Kirk just looked at me, winked, and said, "I'll think about it."

I was the pilot all right—I flew on the missions, I got shot at—and he's telling me he'll think about it! It only took me a few minutes to realize that this P-47D, named *Little One* after my petite fiancée back home in Florida, was in fact "owned" by my crew chief, Staff Sergeant Noyes. He was responsible for keeping my butt alive time and time again. While I slept peacefully on my cot during those cold, English nights, my crew chief would be repairing, replacing, and rebuilding parts I had either damaged or got shot off, all while making sure that "his" Jug was ready to fly the next day's mission, allowing me to safely head off into combat. Kirk was right. He could take all the time he needed to think about it.

A few days later, Kirk came up to me and asked a very direct question.

Don Bryan's tireless ground crew prepares his P-47 for another mission. COUR-
TESY OF DONALD BRYAN

"What would you rather have happen: Have your engine blow up,
forcing you to bail out, or get shot down?"

Instinctively, I answered, "Have the engine blow." I had a greater
chance of survival jumping from the Jug than I did having cannon shells
tear into me.

Kirk smiled and said, "Okay, what I'm gonna do is pull the stops on
the turbo, and in doing so, it should give you about 90 to 100 inches of
mercury instead of the 52 inches you have available now. The burst of
power will only last thirty seconds, and then the whole engine will deto-
nate and blow."

Hell, I was young and stupid. It sounded good to me!

Kirk added, "Just make sure you don't tie in the throttle and the turbo
supercharger together. Operate them separately and control your manifold pressure."

It would not be long until I realized just what a hot rod of an airplane
I had.

Hot Head

During the week of February 20, 1944, while on bomber escort, I was able to prove that a Jug could outfly a 190 at low altitudes, even on the deck.

Just as our squadron had taken up its position, air battles erupted throughout the skies. I noticed a twin-engine Bf 110 diving for the deck after attempting to penetrate our bomber box. Several other pilots from the 328th got hits on the 110 as it dove downward. I locked on to the already-damaged Bf 110 as we raced earthward, passing 3,000 feet. I was probably about 50 feet off my prey's tail when I finished him off with the heavy-hitting Browning machine guns.

I was way too close, as oil and debris from the now-burning 110 began to envelop my Jug, coating everything with a fine, oily mist. With the Bf 110 now dispatched, I pulled up from my dive just in time to see eight Fw 190s above me. Simultaneously, the loathsome 190s observed me destroy one of their own, and began their headlong dive down toward me.

I pulled into a hard right turn and shoved everything to the firewall. The cloud base that day was between 6,000 and 7,000 feet, with thick, heavy, gray overcast. I knew if I could make it into those clouds, I had a strong chance of surviving this melee. But in order to reach the sanctuary of the clouds, I had to fly through a gauntlet of unrelenting German fighters.

A normal P-47D stood a snowball's chance climbing from the deck through the hail of fire and then trying to outrun superior German fighters at these low altitudes. But this was not your normal P-47! I resolved that as soon as I got some hits on the 190s, I would start my climb.

The Fw 190s began firing first, and each time they fired at me, they appeared to knock themselves backward, slowing themselves down. The other thing I couldn't believe I was seeing were tracers coming at me head-on. Hell, I didn't know you could see tracers from the front!

As we passed each other I realized I was still in one piece and the Jug was operating magnificently. That was until I heard the loud *bang* on the left wing. I snapped my head to the left, expecting to see gaping holes in my wing from exploded cannon shells. I saw nothing; the wing appeared fine.

I then looked right and observed the Fw 190s turning into and firing at me. Once again, the loud *bang* on the left presented itself. This time I saw what was happening. My inboard .50 caliber machine gun was cookin' off. I had gotten my guns so hot from shooting down the 110 that they had started firing off themselves. The problem was that the enemy was behind me, not in front, where the guns could be of some use.

I remembered what my crew chief had said and pushed everything balls to the wall.

As I pulled into my climb, I glanced back and saw one Fw 190 sticking with me, pulling vertical and shooting at me. As soon as he fired at me, he stalled out. I was hanging on my prop and I still wasn't in the clouds yet. I rolled it on its back and split-S'ed down and back out. I figured, "Okay, we'll try it again."

Down I went with the Fw 190s hot on my tail. I pulled up expecting machine-gun and cannon fire to strike me at any second, except this time the 190s held their fire.

I picked up enough forward speed and began to outclimb my now-distant prey. Only one Fw 190 was able to stay somewhat close to me as I entered the clouds. A hard turn in the cloud base and I shook my exhausted prey as I disappeared into the mist.

My artificial horizon was tumbling all over the place as I tried to level off. I decided that no matter what it was indicating, turning right side up or wrong side down, I would hold it there until it stopped. As I backed off on the throttle, my instrument finally settled down and reset to absolutely perfect.

I glanced outside my cockpit, peering into the heavy cloud layer. I did a double take as I observed "softballs" made of ice covering the nozzles of the .50 caliber machine guns. With the rest of the P-47 covered in grease and oil from the 110, ice buildup on the wings was denied. It was at that moment that reality finally set in and I began to shake—and not just my knees this time!

In the span of less than a minute, I had done the impossible: I'd out-maneuvered and outclimbed an Fw 190 from the deck on upward. You just couldn't do that in a P-47 except when you had almost 100 inches of mercury at your fingertips.

Chalk up another "save" for Staff Sergeant Noyes, I thought, as I returned to Bodney.

I flew over fifty combat missions in the P-47. I was credited with 4.33 enemy aircraft destroyed (out of 13.33 total). I flew two combat tours in the European Theater of Operations, with my second being in the P-51, flying with most of the same "blue-nosed bastards" I'd flown with in the Jug.

Quite frankly, without a doubt, the P-47 was the best ground support airplane in the world, and held that title until the A-10 Warthog came along. I often wonder what my crew chief could have done with one of those!

China Blitzer: P-40/P-51

There have been countless tales of US Army Air Force World War II fighter pilots weaving over boxes of bombers pulling contrails, high over Europe, and then slugging it out with the Luftwaffe, taking the fight from the lower reaches of the stratosphere down to the deck. The majority of war correspondents were stationed in Europe during World War II, so it was only natural that many of these documented exploits came from the European Theater.

But this story takes place in a far-off corner of the world, over inhospitable terrain filled with malaria, humidity, and subzero temperatures—not a place many war correspondents dreamed of traveling to. Nevertheless, the fighter pilots that protected the Hump routes always seemed to be outnumbered, outgunned, and short on supplies.

Follow along as one young fighter pilot from Texas cuts his combat teeth in the skies over China.

FIGHTER MISSIONS OVER THE HUMP
Lt. Col. Benjamin H. Ashmore
51st Fighter Group, 26th Fighter Squadron, 14th Air Force

Go Get Those SOBs!
When the war broke out in December of 1941, I was a nineteen-year-old kid from north Texas, and like most guys my age, I wanted to enter the fight. My father had other ideas, though. He had made it as far as earning his wings at Kelly Field in Texas, flying Jennys before World War I ended. I'm sure he knew guys who never made it back and had read many

accounts of the horrors of war. He understood a lot more than I did, what I would face. Finally, in early 1942, with constant nagging on my part, he said, "Go get those sons of bitches!"

I followed in his footsteps and entered flight training, flying PT-19s, BT-13s, and the AT-6 Texan. It was while I was flying the BT-13 that one of my instructors casually pulled me aside and said, "I think I'm going to recommend you for fighters." And in my poor old Texas farmboy accent, I said, "What's that?"

As flying cadets, we didn't have time to think about the future. We ran around knowing there was a 45 to 50 percent washout rate. You didn't blink, unless you were ordered to. If you screwed up, you were out, 'cause we had a whole bunch of guys coming along behind us.

But after I understood what flying fighters was all about, I remained focused on earning my wings. That finally happened in 1943, and as a newly commissioned second lieutenant, I got my chance to prove myself at the controls of a P-47 Thunderbolt.

I was sent to Richmond Army Air Force Base in Virginia along with a cadre of others to be trained in the art of being a high-altitude bomber escort. The Thunderbolt was huge, and once in the cockpit it was like sitting under a big tent. It was the biggest cockpit I ever saw in my life; you could have a dog race inside of that airplane.

The only bad thing about the P-47 was that when you got it above 37,000 feet and pushed the nose below 30 degrees, you entered compressibility. The elevator just froze up and the only way out of it was to roll the trim forward and shove the throttle to full power as you tried to pull that stick back with your trembling hand. At about 18,000 feet it would slowly come out of it. It was an interesting ride down, to say the least.

After flying and surviving our newly learned tactics, we would gather and talk about what we were going to do to the Luftwaffe with our Thunderbolts when we got to England. Unfortunately, we never made it to jolly old England. Right before we finished our training, eighteen of us were pulled out and told to report to Miami for further instructions. We figured that we were going to be put on submarine patrol or some damn thing and finish up our training over the Caribbean.

Benjamin H. Ashmore, with hands on hips in front of Shark Mouth P-51C and microphone, waits for Gen. Claire Chennault, standing to his right, to speak. COURTESY OF BEN ASHMORE

Leaving Miami, we had secret orders and were told not to open them until we were over Cuba. We all scratched our heads when they said we were to report to the commanding general in New Delhi, India. Where in the hell was India? And where's New Delhi? I said, "I know where India is. I always painted it pink on a map when I was in grade-school geography." I got many of the guys to chuckle.

It was the last time many of us laughed for a long time.

Young Tiger
Our final destination turned out to be Lahandi Field in Karachi, India. They had some fighters there, P-40Bs that had come from the AVG (American Volunteer Group–Flying Tigers). They didn't look so good, all bruised and battered. To be honest, I hadn't ever seen an airplane look

quite that bad before. The distinctive shark mouths were still on them, buried under mud, exhaust stains, and oil. Our instructors were a group of battle-hardened pilots that had seen a lot of action with Claire Chennault's AVG and Chinese Air Task Force after the deactivation of the Flying Tigers in July 1942.

It was the first time I had fired a gun since Advanced flying school in AT-6s, and the first bombs I'd ever dropped. These were desperate times, and there wasn't a lot of time to prepare us with the Japanese pushing their way through China and the rest of the Pacific region.

The early P-40s were heavy and sluggish, and grew tired quickly. Top operating ceiling was between 21,000 and 23,000 feet, depending on how much you could nurse it up there. It turned like a Mack truck, but it could take a lot of damage, and that was the main reason we had great trust in it.

With my rapid checkout complete, I was pushed out of the nest and joined the 51st Fighter Group, 26th Fighter Squadron—the China Blitzers—of the 14th Air Force, led by General Chennault. We were operating out of the upper Assam Valley and our strip was cut right out of the rice fields, with PSP laid over it. When the rice grew up with the constant rain we had you couldn't find the damn airstrip. It was perfect camouflage, but you had to know exactly where you were going. Turn by the big dead tree off of this end, and that's how you lined up to land, because all the rice fields looked the same.

Another treat was malaria. It affected the squadron 100 percent, along with dengue fever. As a west Texas boy, you couldn't give me anything to deal with it, so you lived with it. Our main mission was to defend the eastern edge of the Hump route, along with protecting air bases in the Kunming area.

Our early missions were bomber escorts. They put us up at 21,000 to 22,000 feet, because the air force had lost many B-24s trying to fly over French Indochina, and they thought they could fly without escort. They found out that they couldn't. Many of the early missions were over Hanoi and the Haiphong area. General Chennault put us down there, and the tactics were to fly in a string formation, at 500 feet above the bombers, just weaving back and forth. Sometimes we were lucky to put up eight

P-40s, if we could get them all running, but most times we ended up with only four of us going, as others turned back with mechanical issues.

The Zeros sat up above us at between 30,000 and 35,000 feet. The fun began when they would push over and make gunnery passes. But if we held our ranks and stayed in our string formation, we could meet any Zero coming in. When you had to turn, you'd turn, and that's when the guy behind you picked him up.

Our tactic was to try to be above them when they dove on the bombers. Then we would dive on 'em, shoot, and get the hell out of there, because you can't turn with a Zero, and you sure as hell can't climb with it. The only thing you can do is dive. It doesn't take a genius to figure out what tactics you have to follow, especially when you're always outnumbered by them. And the only guy that's going to hit you is the guy that you don't see. If you can locate him, he can't track you. When he starts pulling, and it looks like, uh-oh, he's just about got enough lead now to start shooting, you throw that stick to the side and break. You know where you're going, so you take some time, set up again, and set up another sight picture.

One thing we did have over the Zero was the fact that we had pressurized carburetors. We could fly inverted all day long and the engine would never quit. If the Zero stayed inverted too long, his engine was going to quit, and he was going down.

Eventually I was assigned to my own P-40N, and I christened it *Anvil Chorus*. This was a popular Glenn Miller song from the early 1940s. Back in Texas I did a lot of beating on a goddamn anvil, and those .50 caliber machine guns in the P-40s sounded like somebody was beating on it.

Everybody else named their airplanes *Anne* or *Betty*, or something like that. Problem was, the only girlfriend I had had Dear John'd me already, so I didn't want to put her name on anything. Our P-40s also carried the infamous shark mouth as a tribute to our AVG lineage.

Shiny New Fighter on the Block
A lot of our missions also involved ground support, which consisted of strafing, bombing, and rockets. I became the rocket projects officer for our group when we began switching over to P-51 Mustangs in early 1944.

I was told by our group commander to report to General Chennault's office, and when I arrived he said, "Get yourself a sheet metal mechanic, and go to Burma. Don't know what in the hell's going on, but Cochran's First Air Commando Unit is using them on their P-51s."

So, we went down there and I saw what they were doing, got all the information, and got myself a North American Aviation tech rep. We procured the mounting plates in India and flew 'em back up to China, installing the rockets on the P-40s and P-51s. We managed to get them set up with the P-40s first, and they would hang out of the bomb rack. The weapon of choice was the M10 triple-tube rocket launchers, firing 4.5-inch, M8 type, fin-stabilized rockets. We tried to put them on the Mustangs' bomb racks but realized we couldn't carry drop tanks if we did; no way was that going to work, because we needed the gas. We finally got it worked out and began using them. They were impressive as hell, zooming out under our wings, but it was like throwing rocks—not very accurate.

When the first P-51 began to arrive in February of 1944, we had no pilot checkout manuals. Nobody in the squadron had ever had any time in one.

A P-40 is all muscle. Lots of muscle. By comparison, you can fly a P-51 with the tips of your toes and fingertips. And, of course, the first mission we flew in one was a combat mission.

The one thing we found out right away about the B model is that they installed a fuselage tank right behind the pilot in the fuselage. With 80 gallons of fuel sloshing around back there, we learned you can't turn because you get a stick reversal. Instead of pulling on the stick, you're pushing on it. It'd snap on you. We learned to use that fuel first and burn it out as soon as we could, and then we were in business.

Flying the Mustang in combat became a whole new game. Everything we'd learned before was just different. The Mustang could perform with and many times outperform the Zeros. Although it was not as tight-turning an airplane as the Zero, we found out we didn't need that. You could zoom off, get away, and come back and still fight; you didn't have to give up altitude. Once you give up altitude, you're going home—hopefully.

Now we could stand and fight, at least in the air.

War Stories and Combat Memories

By mid-1944 China was falling fast and the Japanese were pouring men into the area, wanting to push us out. They called it Operation Ichi-Go. They came down from the north, through Changsha, Lingling, Kweilin, Liuchow. We operated from a forward base out of Nanning, a stone's throw from French Indochina.

As they were making their way down the railroad, with 40,000 to 50,000 troops marching, hell, it was an easy target. We carried frag bombs and rockets. It wasn't a long haul to get to them, but the P-51 is the most vulnerable airplane to ground-fire that I think was ever designed, anywhere. It's beautiful, and a heck of a fighter—but all the coolant lines and oil lines come back behind the cockpit. A hit from a .25 caliber round anywhere in there, it'll run exactly ninety seconds.

So, we learned real quick that the only pass you make is from about 8,000 or 9,000 feet, abreast in a fingertip. None of this classic peel-off; we wanted as much surprise as we could get over the target, and then come out the other side of the column. And the Japanese tactic for that was pure discipline: Nobody'd dive to the ground; they all stood there and shot straight up in the air with their rifles. Very effective. It was like flying through rain. The only good news was that the aerial opposition at that time was almost nonexistent. The only time we ran into anything was around the Canton–Hong Kong area. It was still pretty heavy there, with Zeros as the main opposition.

Late in the war I had just returned to Kunming after flying two strike missions down in Indochina. When I landed, I was told to report to Yunannyi with a P-51.

I said, "What in the hell am I gonna do over there?"

I was told I was going to rendezvous and fly on a mission with some P-40s. I understood they had some trouble over on the Salween front, and they were trying to open up Ledo Road. The Japanese were bombing some of the Chinese forces that were trying to hold the line. It had been damn good intelligence, because as we arrived overhead, there were two Betty bombers in the valley.

I was doing S turns to keep up to the three bomb-laden P-40s, and as I looked up higher, to the left, I spotted eighteen Zeros. The P-40s gave up the only thing they had—a little altitude—and they were down in the valley.

I said, "Well, hell, I can get one of those damned bombers, and still get back, 'cause I have an airplane that I can fly and fight with."

I went down, lined up on one of the Bettys, and squeezed the trigger.

I watched as my rounds hit home, smoke and flame shooting out from the left engine. I danced on the rudder and my next rounds hit him right in the cockpit, and the Betty blew right there.

Turning around I laid the hammers of that P-51 right back up through those eighteen Zeros. I found myself on top of them as they were going down. They had trapped the three P-40s in the valley, with big mountains on either side. Up on the north end, there was a cloud deck, where the mountains kind of came together, about a 500- to 600-foot deck. As soon as I passed the Zeros, I turned and was quickly riding right back around on their tails.

We were all coming down like the hammers of hell as the P-40s broke and scattered. They hightailed it straight home to Yunannyi.

Now it was just me, right on the Zeros, and hell, they didn't like the P-51, so they broke and went up under that little cloud deck. And I said, "Well, sooner or later, one of them's got to come out." I got up about 5,000 feet above 'em, and, sure enough, one of 'em came out. I made a pass at him. I went after him, but he turned and went back under the cloud before I could get him.

So, I was smarter. I backed off a little farther and let the next one come out a little bit farther ahead. He paid for that mistake, as I nailed him.

I waited and waited, and I heard someone over the radio say, "What's going on down there?" And along comes a P-38 Lightning. He wouldn't come down in the valley with me, but he was an extra set of eyes as he remained my top, top cover. And I waited until almost sundown, but I refused to drop my drop tanks. Didn't need to, because I had all my gas. And I said, "Well, I can stay here, until maybe I can run 'em out of gas."

They had come out of an airfield at Liuchow so they would be getting low on gas soon. I stooged around a while, hoping to get the whole lot of them. My better sense took over, so I went back and landed at Yunannyi.

About three days later I saw some coolies [term used by the veteran] come into our base carrying a three-bladed prop on a pole. Turned out to be the prop off the bomber that I had shot down. Some of the squadron crew chiefs sought out a piece of it and made me a cigarette lighter out of it. I still have it today.

(Lt. Col. Benjamin Ashmore flew a total of seventy-eight combat missions with the 51st Fighter Group. He was one of eighteen men who joined the 26th Fighter Squadron; only six would return home.)

12

Big Chief / Little Chief: P-47

JOINING THE WOLFPACK

As the air war in Europe became broader and additional fighter units entered the fray, it became quite evident early on that a handful of these fighter groups were destined to become "leaders of the pack."

One such group, the 56th, was bestowed with warriors that aggressively took charge. And with a few well-directed efforts, these leaders soon had everything coordinated and working as a well-disciplined unit. These men were the cream of the crop—men like Zemke, Gabreski, Johnson, and Schilling all knew that the overall success of the unit lay in their hands, and they freely passed on their valuable knowledge and lifesaving tactics.

This was a life-or-death area where one mistake could cause a deadly domino effect on the entire flight. Air combat tactics were drilled extensively until every pilot, no matter how high or low in rank, had successfully mastered all maneuvers. Tactical turns, combat spread, bracket attacks, cross splits, and half splits, along with the Thach weave, were just some of the air tactics successfully used against the Luftwaffe by the pilots of Zemke's "Wolfpack."

By the time a new replacement pilot was deemed combat-ready, he was expected to know every move his flight leader made with precision and accuracy. As a new wingman, he was there to protect and defend the guy next to him. With his head on a swivel, he had to have four sets of eyes and the ability to stay with his flight leader through violent combat maneuvering.

Col. Hub Zemke, CO of the 56th Fighter Group, grabs the barrel of one of his Thunderbolts' .50 caliber machine guns. COURTESY OF FRANK KLIBBE

Before he was allowed to join the rest of his fellow aviators, he had to cut the mustard. Combat looked relatively easy compared to being checked out by the group leader or squadron commander.

And for one young eager pilot, flying tight and following orders were just some of the many hazards to be encountered while flying in the Wolfpack.

BIG SHOES TO FILL
Col. Frank W. Klibbe
56th Fighter Group, 61st Fighter Squadron, 8th Air Force

At 5-foot-4 I felt like a midget when I stood next to my new front office. The P-47 was the biggest airplane I had ever seen. It was just plain awesome! Because of my size, or lack thereof, I had to wear a back cushion just so I could reach the rudder pedals. At 14,000 pounds and 2,000 horsepower, this was an airplane! It was built like a battleship and had more firepower than any other fighter of its time. The only thing I wished it had was a metal plate to cover my rear end, because on my first checkout flight with my squadron commander, I got one hell of an ass chewing!

Arriving in England around August of 1943, I was assigned to the 56th Fighter Group of the 61st Fighter Squadron. After getting squared away, fellow classmate 2nd Lt. Robert "Shorty" Rankin and I reported to our squadron commander, Maj. Francis Gabreski. He had a habit of "checking out" the newcomers.

Gabby said to us, "When we take off, we're gonna fly some formation and I'll introduce you to some battle formations and tactics. Then we're going to do a little rat racing so I can see how well you perform."

We took off as a three-ship flight and I was on Gabby's left, with Rankin on the right. We went through our formation drills and other tactics and then returned to base.

After landing, Rankin and I were walking back to Operations and I said to him, "Well, how do you think we did?" Rankin replied, "By God, I think we did all right!" I shook my head up and down in total agreement. I almost broke my arm patting myself on the back for such an outstanding job of airmanship!

Reality hit me right between the eyes when we met Gabby in the Operations shack. His teeth were clenched and his face was rather unpleasant in appearance.

"Where the hell did you two learn to fly formation?!" barked Gabby.

My first thought was, "Well, hell with it. I'm not gonna say anything. I'm just a lowly flight officer. I'll let Rankin do all the talking. He's making the big bucks as a second lieutenant."

Rankin tried to explain to Gabby what we had learned in the States and then about the 25 hours of training we had received here in England. I don't think Gabby heard a word as he began to go into great detail and criticism of what we had done wrong. I was back too far on takeoff; I was too high on this and too low on that; I was too slow on moving out. Rankin was this and that. Hell, he went on and on! Before he dismissed us he said we were going to do it all again tomorrow.

That night, as Rankin and I lay steaming on our bunks, we devised a plan for our next flight with Gabby. I said to Rankin, "When we fly tomorrow, let's tuck that damn Jug right in there. Put the propeller right smack underneath his wing, right on his elevators. We'll make it so damn miserable for him, he won't even be able to hold his airplane straight! I thought we came over here to fight a war, not fly in some damn circus!" Rankin agreed.

We soon learned, however, that we were the clowns and Gabby was the ringmaster.

As promised, we made Gabby miserable. The prop wash from our P-47s was taking its toll on Gabby's ability to maintain control of his Jug. Our four-blade props were splashing against his elevators as he wobbled through the air. We were both mere inches from chewing his wings apart. Gabby gave the hand signal command to move out. Rankin and I thought as one: You wanted us to fly formation, so dammit, we're going to stay right here!

Gabby must have been pissed. He called us over the radio/transmitter (R/T) and said, "Go to battle formation now!"

We followed his orders and backed off.

As we flew around, I wondered what lay ahead for us when we landed.

Frank W. Klibbe poses in front of his P-47, named *Little Chief*. COURTESY OF
FRANK KLIBBE

Gabby was waiting for us on the ground with fire in his eyes. He lit
into us with a great deal of emphasis in his voice. "Let me tell you two
something: When I give a command by hand or voice, follow it! Is that
understood?!"

I was so scared I saluted with both hands! I thought my flying days
would be over before they began. Rankin and I received a far worse verbal
assault from Gabby than the prop wash assault we had given him.

Gabby delivered one final shocking message: "Both of you are on the
mission tomorrow. Dismissed!"

We staggered out of the shack in total shock and disbelief. We had
passed the first test and quickly realized one important lifesaving fact:
Although Gabby was a disciplinarian, he was trying to teach us the neces-
sity for air discipline as a team.

In a few short weeks, I would learn more valuable lessons in survival.

Learning from the Best

For whatever reason, Rankin and I were chosen quite frequently to fly wing on both Col. Hub Zemke and Col. Dave Schilling when they led the 56th into combat. We were expected to fly in a certain manner, with a certain technique. If a guy screwed up, he was told to get on the ball or get out. As a result, our group became very aggressive and close-knit. We could trust anyone we flew with.

Sometimes, though, in the heat of the battle, lack of communication between lead and wingman could get a guy killed!

During one mission I was on, I flew wing on Colonel Schilling. He was a great leader, a great pilot, and a helluva tactician. He allowed only his friends to call him "Chief." I was very fortunate to be included in this circle. He was like a father to me and took me under his wing. Unfortunately, on this particular mission, my wing got in the way!

We were just coming off a bomber escort when Colonel Schilling spotted a 109 on the deck. We were at 25,000 feet when he called the bounce. He peeled off and dove so fast that in order for me to keep up, I had to crank the Jug over and momentarily blanked him out. I lost sight of him on the way down.

As we dove, I spotted the 109 he was after. At the same time, Schilling was called over the R/T by the rest of the group. They had encountered a whole gaggle of Me 110s and thought Schilling might be interested.

Schilling broke off his bounce and pulled skyward. I continued downward, never seeing him. He claimed later that he called me to break it off and follow, but I never heard it. We became separated as I lowered my wing, searching for him. I should have looked up instead of down. Schilling was in a whole heap of trouble!

I returned to base wondering what the hell had happened to my flight leader. I soon found out. Schilling jacked me up in a corner and proceeded to tear me a new ass! When he had gone to find the 110s, some Fw 190s and Bf 109s bounced him and he nearly got his own ass shot off. Bob Johnson had to rescue Schilling, and Schilling wasn't very happy about that!

From that moment on, even after the war, Schilling would always introduce me to people as "his good friend who left him in combat," claiming that he was almost shot down by the enemy because of it! He was a great boss and a great joker!

Earning My Keep

I eventually had enough seniority in the squadron to receive my own P-47. With that large cowling out front surrounding the R-2800, it was a painter's dream. In honor of my high school back home, I had the motif of a large Indian chief with headdress applied to my bird. *Little Chief* and I soon began to tear up the sky in search of German aircraft.

I already had three Bf 109s to my credit and needed just two more to be included in the same circle of men called "ace."

On my next combat flight, the only circle I found myself in was with an Fw 190!

On February 22, 1944, I was flying wing on Capt. Don Smith and had arrived at our assigned altitude of 30,000 feet as we approached the German border. We were in the tail-end flight and could hear Colonel Schilling over the R/T, calling for full throttles. The Jerries had made their first attack on the bombers.

A rare wartime color shot of *Little Chief* COURTESY OF FRANK KLIBBE

As we raced ahead, Captain Smith spotted an Fw 190, nibbling away at a crippled bomber. Smoke soon turned to flame as Captain Smith continued to pour .50 caliber rounds into the 190. The Fw 190's right wing tore away and fell with the rest of the carnage, back to the fatherland. Captain Smith signaled me to take over lead for my chance at the next prey.

It didn't take long at all. I saw the Bf 109 below climbing through 6,000 feet. He was trying to join the fight high above him. I had altitude, firepower, and speed as I rolled the Jug on over. Quickly notifying Captain Smith over the R/T, I never took my eyes off the 109. Even if Captain Smith didn't hear me, I was sure he was right beside me—or so I thought!

My plan was to pull out of my dive a mile or so behind the 109. With my gun switches hot, I began to center the target in my gunsight. I closed to within 1,000 yards and felt my finger begin to depress the trigger. My "target" soon grew another tail, engine, and a big white star! A P-38 came out of nowhere, slid in front of me, and knocked the 109 down. I had no business at this low altitude as I cranked the Jug into a climbing left turn.

I glanced over my shoulder and saw what I thought was Captain Smith joining me in the climb back up. With a feeling of security, I relaxed for a moment until I was rudely awakened by what I had really seen.

My wingman was an Fw 190, and he was shooting at me!

I laid the P-47 on its side and entered the only thing that would save me: a Lufbery circle. We were at 8,000 feet and climbing through this circle of death.

Everything flashed through my panic-stricken mind. What kind of pilot was I up against? Could the Jug outperform the 190 at this low altitude? Where the hell was my wingman?! Now I knew what Colonel Schilling had gone through!

As I pulled harder on the stick, my turn became tighter and the g-forces higher. My oxygen mask had slipped under my nose, adding further discomfort to my already unpleasant situation. As I "bent" the throttle forward into full supercharge, the reliable Pratt & Whitney never missed a beat.

Each time the 190 fired at me I instinctively ducked my head, expecting a hail of bullets to rip me apart. Much to my surprise, they all missed.

I was wringing wet with sweat and fear and wondered how long I could continue this fight. The fact that the Jug was gulping precious fuel at an alarming rate added to my anxiety.

Climbing through 9,000 feet I notice two P-47s below me at 2,000 feet. I called frantically to the pair to come up and get this bastard off me. They flew on, never seeing me or hearing me. Looking up I saw four more P-47s above me at around 20,000 feet. I screamed over the R/T for their help. They wanted to know what town I was near? I shouted back, "How the hell do I know? I'm the Jug with the 190 on my tail!" To expect help with my vague, unintelligent position reports was asking for a miracle.

I had been in the Lufbery for over six minutes now. Slowly I began to widen the gap between us. I was now at a 180-degree position to him. No longer was I in a defensive mode but rather I began to close the gap on his tail. With my fuel status beginning to approach critical, I had two options: The first was to press on the attack and destroy my foe. The longer I stayed in the Lufbery, the greater the chance of more German aircraft showing up. My second option was to make a flat-out run for it. I had to make a choice in a big hurry or I wouldn't make it home. The Jug's gliding capability was akin to a rock.

The 190 made the decision for me. He rolled over in a dive and headed east for home. This was the most gratifying maneuver I had witnessed during the past twelve minutes. It was finally over. I eased back on the throttle and headed for home. I slipped my oxygen mask off, leaned over, and planted a big ol' wet kiss on the canopy. I thanked the ol' girl for bringing me home.

I did not plant a kiss on Captain Smith, who was waving wildly when I landed.

"Am I glad to see you! Where were you?" Captain Smith asked.

I was a little upset, and responded, "You let me ask the questions! Where the hell were *you*?!"

We discussed the matter. Unbeknownst to me, when I had made my dive on the Bf 109, an Fw 190 had turned into my tail and Captain Smith chased him off. In turn, Captain Smith lost sight of me, still in my dive, and joined with another P-47.

I realized at that moment how effective this single tactic was to my survival. The Lufbery is as basic and essential to the fighter pilot as the skill of flying itself. All of the tactics learned while flying with the 56th, in my mind, are to be attributed to the great leaders we had. No other group could match our aggressiveness or discipline. We just needed a little work on our communication skills!

(Colonel Frank Klibbe finished his tour on May 8, 1944. He went out with the same bang with which he had entered the war. On his last mission, he downed two German fighters, bringing his final tally to seven victories. After the war he joined back up with his old squadron and old boss. Colonel Klibbe was group maintenance officer under the command of "Chief" Dave Schilling, and was involved in the first jet crossing of the North Atlantic.)

13

Satan's Playmate: F6F

CREATION OF AN ACE
Lt. Cdr. James E. Duffy
VF-15, USN

Fighting Fifteen
In late 1943, I was selected and accepted into an elite fraternity of naval aviators. I became an original member of Satan's Playmates when we formed in Atlantic City, New Jersey. At the time, I was just about the lowest form of life in the navy hierarchy—an ensign. Yet, here I was, a freshman attending "Clobber College." My mentor and professor was the legendary David McCampbell, CO of the Fighting Fifteen (VF-15).

Dave McCampbell was a very fair and understanding CO. It was understood that if you screwed up, you had a fair chance of getting an ass chewing! He was also anxious to get the squadron in the best possible shape for combat in the Pacific.

When I reported to Atlantic City, I was asked by the air operations officer if I wanted to take a look at what I would be flying. As I walked out to the ramp, there before me was the most beautiful airplane I had ever seen: an F6F Hellcat. My gosh, it looked big enough to be a bomber! The biggest thing I had ever flown before was an SNJ. My eyes took a walk all over her, staring at that huge engine and those big fat wings containing six Browning machine guns.

As far as I was concerned, the Hellcat was the best-kept secret the navy ever had! The checkout was a little unusual for me: read the book,

Brand-new Grumman F6F Hellcats on a factory test flight COURTESY OF JACK COOK

memorize the instruments, followed by a blindfold check and then crank her up and take off. No instructor in the back to bail you out if you messed up.

I had some apprehension on that first takeoff. I worried about two things: First, would I survive the impending crash? And second, would my remains be unrecognizable? I realized this was no SNJ as I rocketed down the runway. I found I was using little effort to control my direction. Grumman had really built a winner with this plane. She was easy to fly and very forgiving. More than my CO was!

Hellcat Checkout
During the squadron checkout CO McCampbell had all thirty-six planes up to teach us a little formation flying. I was in the very back of the division, tail-end Charlie position. It was like being on the end of a whip—very difficult to maintain proper airspeed and position in the formation. McCampbell would go to full throttle, then back down to almost idle, then back to full. By the time his inputs got back to me, I was practically falling out of the sky.

I pulled out a little wider from my wingman to give myself some breathing room. It also kept me in a reasonable position. Apparently my radio wasn't working, as McCampbell kept calling me to close it up as the squadron continued making big wide turns out and back. I think McCampbell had eyes in the back of his head!

All of a sudden McCampbell did a big wingover and pulled up along-side of me, shaking his fist and pointing at me to get my butt back into position. I never moved so fast as I slid back over. He never said a word to me back on the ground and I never pulled out of position again!

By May of 1944 we had been deemed combat-ready and sent on our way to the Pacific. Our new home for the next seven months would be aboard USS *Essex*. Hellcats, Helldivers, and Grumman TBM Avengers (TBMs) filled her deck as we entered the combat arena.

Being the new kids on the block, we were sent on heckler missions to Marcus and Wake Islands. Strafing and raising hell with the Japanese garrisons helped build our confidence. The Japanese on the ground were confident, too—confident that we would keep coming back!

Built Grumman-Tough

Being quick learners, VF-15 progressed into the aerial combat arena. On one particular mission, I learned just how much damage a Hellcat could take and still keep on ticking. I also learned firsthand what it was like being used as bait!

A majority of the time I flew wing on Lt. John Strane. By war's end, John had over a dozen kills, so I developed considerable skill in dodging pieces of Japanese airplanes! As a wingman, you stayed with your lead no matter what the situation. Sometimes, though, my lead was in back of me!

John and I along with two other Hellcats were on a top cover mission over the Marianas. I looked up and saw two Zeros on our right and two Zeros on our left, making the most beautiful gunnery run I'd ever seen. Unfortunately, we were the targets!

I reached for the mic to call the break but I was too late. I could see that two of the Zeros were going to pass under John and me. I rolled right to get a shot off at them but wasn't fast enough. The Zeros went into a big chandelle and one of them ended up right behind me. He was so close I could have hit him with a rock!

I tried to turn as hard as I could but the Zero kept turning inside of me. He started shooting at me but was over-leading me, as I saw the tracers out in front. I quickly reversed and went the other way. Same thing. If I kept this up maybe the SOB would run out of ammo!

I wondered where the hell John was as I continued to turn and weave, trying to shake this guy. I pulled so hard on my next turn that I stalled out. I was raked with machine-gun fire and it sounded like someone was banging the plane with a sledgehammer.

Turning with the Zero was going to get me killed, so I pushed the Hellcat over into a dive. I didn't realize it at the time, but ol' John was right on this guy's tail as we zoomed for the deck. About a third of the way down, John flamed the Zero. Brand-new "made in Japan" holes covered my tail section, wings, and fuselage.

When we got back to the ship, John congratulated me on our new-found tactic. He told me from now on I would be the bait and he would shoot them down. He called it the "Duffy weave." It took me a while to find humor in that!

Payback

On June 18, 1944, I was able to return the favor to the Japanese by putting some "made in America" holes into one of theirs.

I was flying escort for some SB2C Helldivers as we searched for the Japanese fleet. Nearing the end of our sector, this Helldiver started rocking his wings and pointing down. I saw another airplane below about 60 degrees off our nose. At first I thought it was just one of our scouts, but they normally flew in pairs.

I decided to take a look. I pushed the Hellcat on over and dove for the water at full throttle. I leveled off at 50 feet and, boy, was I moving! As I passed under him, my eyes got as big as the red circles on his wings.

He was at 1,000 feet above me as I used all my energy and traded it for altitude. I went into a chandelle and dropped right in behind him. I gave him a short burst in the wing root and he started to burn immediately.

It was a "Jill"—a Japanese torpedo bomber painted up in an ugly mustard-brown color with a red cowling. The rear gunner was trying to get out as the Jill nosed up, half rolled over, and disappeared into the water below.

I was now on my way to earning that degree from Clobber College.

Setting Sun

On June 19 I was up on the deck at dusk, taking in the last flight of the day. I watched in awe as the landing signal officer worked his magic and took a plane aboard *Essex* every thirty-five seconds. Plane after plane landed in unison as the sun began to set. There was one more guy to trap as he made his approach.

It was a beautiful turn to final, his plane silhouetted against the fading light. As he approached the fantail, the LSO began to jump around, waving his paddles frantically, giving this guy the wave-off. This guy was committed to land with his flaps and wheels hanging out. The LSO was like a scared rabbit as he dropped his paddles and jumped over the side into the net.

At the last minute, this guy sucked up his gear and took the wave-off. The large red circles on his fuselage and wings were unmistakable as he flew by: a Japanese Zero! No one on the deck fired a shot at him as he staggered back into the air. We were barely able to close our wide-open mouths, let alone fire a gun!

This poor guy was either lost and mistook us for one of his carriers, or he'd lost one hell of a drinking bet!

The very next day, I would meet some of his fellow pilots at a good ol'-fashioned turkey shoot. It would be deadly serious and winner-take-all.

Well before our arrival in the Pacific, the Japanese had been shuttling their planes from the mainland to Guam. They were in a constant mode of resupply due to the heavy losses they were encountering. For a while, this place was a real hotbed of Japanese fighters and bombers.

Targets Galore

On June 20 it was like an inferno as the sky was filled with fighters from both sides.

Later war, stateside, F6F Hellcats en route to a live-fire training range COURTESY OF JACK COOK

I was a section leader in a flight of four Hellcats as we made a big, wide circle over Guam in our top cover assignment. The rest of the group went down to strafe the airfield but got caught in a hornet's nest of Japanese Zeros.

I listened over the R/T as a big air battle was taking place below. My flight leader's radio was out as I closed in on him and pointed to the airfield. I received the nod from him as the division was turned over to me. At 15,000 feet the four of us raced over to see what all the hollering was about.

There were planes stacked up from the deck to 10,000 feet, all making big circles, fighting one another. Hot damn! The Japanese were everywhere! Every once in a while, a Zero would pop out of the circle and then fight his way back in. We simply waited for one to pull out.

We didn't have to wait very long. I made a run on one of them as I dove from 4,000 feet above the Zero. I was pretty steep and moving like greased lightning when I opened up with my guns and saw hits on his tail. As hard as I could pull, I couldn't walk the hits forward. I was too steep and too damn fast! I pulled up and out and when I got turned around, I found another Zero. He was painted up in all dark green with a touch of yellow. The big red meatball on his wing was a great target. I closed on the Zero a lot faster than I wanted to as my bullets ripped into his armor plate.

I overtook him, pulled up over the top, and rolled the Hellcat over. I was about 50 feet above him, looking straight down on him. His cockpit was engulfed in flame and smoke. I must have hit the 50-gallon center tank right in front of the cockpit. Hell of a way to build an airplane, I thought, as burning fuel poured all over the pilot. Within twenty seconds there wasn't another plane in the sky. Fighting Fifteen did quite well that day!

Making Ace

I splashed an Oscar over the Central Philippines on September 13, 1944, to bring my total up to three victories. All I needed were two more to get my diploma, and on October 27, 1944, I found a willing participant.

There were three of us up over the Philippines just south of Manila Bay, looking and itching for a fight. It didn't take long to find our prey, but catching him was another story. We jumped a Betty and it dove just above the wave tops; we were off to the races!

For some reason I was able to get out in front of the other two Hellcats. The Betty was in the best defensive position it could be in. No one could get underneath her, and with her deadly rear guns, no one wanted to get close. We took some shots at her but none of us were getting any hits.

Finally, with some luck on my part, I managed to get some rounds into her right engine. The smoke turned to flame as the Betty began to slow and burn. The gunners must have been scared to death as they shot wildly into the air. Tracers were arching straight up, nowhere near my Hellcat. They died a quick death as their Betty cartwheeled and slammed into the sea below.

I was getting close to graduation time.

Before I was fitted for my cap and gown, I was introduced to another fine attribute of the Hellcat—that of rocket launcher! I had been up on the deck and noticed some sailors putting some long pointed tubes on our wings. I tried to get close and ask questions, but was ordered to the ready room.

Rocket Man

Commander Air Group McCampbell gave us the briefing, his opening statement short and to the point: "Gentlemen, today we are going to use rockets." He handed us each a mimeographed sheet on the use and firing of a rocket. He then said, "If you follow exactly what this piece of paper says, then you will hit what you aimed at, guaranteed!"

It really didn't matter to the rest of us, as we had never fired a rocket before, let alone seen one. If CAG said it was going to work, then by God, it would work, or there would be hell to pay!

When we got to our planes, six of those beauties were strapped to our wings, three on each side. One by one we launched and followed CAG out for a successful day's hunt.

The Japanese were very foolish that day, allowing seventeen of their transport ships to become our test targets. It was amazing! I did exactly what the instructions said: 30-degree dive, 50-mile lead, and fire the rocket at 3,000 feet. I picked out one of the freighters and let all six of them go at once. Streams of fire raced for the ship below as the rockets stayed true and penetrated the ship's hull. All six exploded inside as the ship began to glow red-hot. The fire inside the ships must have been hellish as the hull began to burn and melt. The sea was full of burning Japanese ships that day, compliments of VF-15's rockets' red glare!

Live Bait

On November 5, 1944, I found myself flying wing to my good ol' buddy, Lieutenant John R. Strane. Before we launched I told him in no uncertain terms that I would be used as bait. He just smiled and winked at me as we made our way across the deck to our Hellcats.

We were up over Luzon attacking some Japanese airfields with the rest of the squadron. Our flight began to mix it up with a variety of Japanese aircraft, as I stayed glued to John's wing.

I saw them at the same time John did. Out ahead in a loose formation was the oddest pair of Japanese aircraft I'd ever seen. A twin-engine Nick fighter was following a much slower Oscar in defense of the Rising Sun. It would soon turn into a setting sun for both of them!

They never saw our flight as they dove right in front of us; their eyes fixed on another Hellcat. John went after the Oscar, and I lit into the Nick. I let off a few short bursts, saw some hits, and then swung back into position on John's wing. John flamed the Oscar as I dodged pieces of burning aircraft. It was his thirteenth and final victory.

When we got back to *Essex*, John came up to me and said, "Boy, you got one, huh!"

I said, "I did?"

He smiled and said, "You sure did! Way to go, ace!"

It was a real good feeling. Not because I had graduated from Clobber College, or the fact that I was one of twenty-six aces with VF-15 during our seven months in combat. I felt good because he hadn't used me as bait this time.

(During VF-15's seven months in combat under the leadership of CAG David McCampbell, the "Fighting Fifteen" were crowned top guns of the navy. CAG McCampbell also became the navy's top ace, with thirty-four victories. He along with the rest of the squadron became "Satan's favorite playmates"!)

KILLER CATS: VF-15 ACES

The USN Grumman F6F Hellcat reigned supreme over its counterparts, with a total of 5,163 enemy aircraft destroyed by war's end. The next closest contender was the F4U/FG Corsair, with 2,140 victories, followed by the F4F/FM Wildcat, with over 1,500 total victories. Even the torpedo planes and dive-bombers got into the aerial action, with the SBD Dauntlesses racking up 138 aerial kills, followed by the TBF/TBM Avengers, scoring 98 victories, while the SB2C/SBW Helldivers brought up the rear, with an additional 43 enemy aircraft shot down.

The bottom of the barrel, in terms of aerial victories, was claimed by the stubby F2A Buffalo. The Buffalo flew twenty-five sorties and accounted for six bombers and four fighters shot down before they themselves became extinct and were withdrawn from service. VF-15 "Satan's Playmates" claimed 310 total victories during their combat tour from May through November 1944. In that time frame, 27 men from the squadron known as the "Fabled Fifteen" claimed ace status while flying the Grumman Hellcat.

When the war finally ended in September of 1945, a total of 306 pilots were able to call themselves aces while at the controls of the F6F.

14

Confessions of a Headhunter: P-38

"SCREWY LOUIE"
Capt. Louis Schriber II
80th Fighter Squadron, 5th Air Force

Training Wheels
In the middle of 1942, after successfully completing Basic training in Pecos, Texas, at the controls of a BT-13, I had a decision to make: become a fighter pilot or jump into multi-engine airplanes and fly bombers. I thought I would be a little lonesome in the cockpit of a fighter and figured I would have better luck with a crew of men and more engines at my disposal, so I chose the bomber route of training.

I soon learned that while flying in the army, you have to be careful what you wish for, and never, ever volunteer for anything. I got the multi-engines just like I had requested, but the plane I would fly in combat, one that saved my butt countless times, was no damn bomber! In fact, the first time I flew one in training, I was a little concerned when the instructors told us that these airplanes were supposed to have gone to the RAF but were rejected because the Brits thought they were incapable of squaring off against the Luftwaffe in combat.

The airplane I was instructed to conquer before earning my wings at Williams Field, Arizona, was an early variant of the Lockheed P-38, called the P-322. The British didn't want them because they had no turbo-chargers or counter-rotating propellers installed on them, so the P-322s that had already been built were turned over to the training command.

I found myself strapped in one with my knees knocking as my instructor gave me my last rites and some advice on how to bring both of us back in one piece.

I started both engines and taxied halfway to Tucson for takeoff as I closed my eyes for a long second and let the Lightning roll. When I opened my eyes and finally caught up to the airplane, we were already passing through 2,500 feet as I retracted the tricycle landing gear.

After that first flight, everything I learned about being a fighter pilot was most enjoyable, as I quickly educated myself on how to fly, fight, and stay alive in the P-38. Of course, I had a lot of help from some great teachers.

Port Moresby, New Guinea

What a thrill it was to fly over the infamous Coral Sea, the sight of one of the greatest sea battles of World War II, as I approached my new home in May of 1943: a 3-mile airstrip just outside of Port Moresby. I was assigned to the 8th Fighter Group, 80th Fighter Squadron, of the 5th Air Force, and soon became one of the newest members of the "Headhunters."

After I had landed at the airstrip, I was introduced to the squadron CO, Maj. Edward "Porky" Cragg, along with the operations officer, Capt. George "Wheaties" Welch, and fellow pilots, lieutenants Jay T. "Cock" Robbins, Cy Homer, and Cornelius "Corky" Smith. All of them welcomed me like a lost family member, and it didn't take long before I was considered part of the gang. Many of my early missions were flown on the wing of Cragg, Welch, Homer, and Robbins, and I was extremely lucky to have such great pilots as mother hens in the Japanese-filled skies over New Guinea.

George Welch was almost an ace before he joined the squadron and was credited with destroying four Japanese aircraft while flying a P-40 during the attack on Pearl Harbor. By the time I had arrived in New Guinea, he was already closing in on double ace status. Cragg, Robbins, and the rest were also knocking on the ace achievement door when I flew with them during my baptism of aerial combat over Wewak, which at the time was a Japanese stronghold on the northwest coast of New Guinea. I

The "Headhunters" pose for a group shot in front of their score card. COURTESY OF LOUIS SCHRIBER

fired at a few Zeros, depleted my ammo, and burned up my gun barrels in unsuccessful duels; I hit nothing but air.

I must have scared the Japanese pretty bad, though, with my display of aerial "miss-marksmanship," because on a mission on August 20, both Cragg and Welch increased their score, each downing three of them.

In early November of 1943, I finally hit what I was aiming at; I guess it was hard to miss that day, as we were outnumbered ten to one.

Raid on Rabaul

Our squadron had been to Rabaul a couple of times in October, and it wasn't a place you wanted to visit often; in fact, it was a place that made the Devil start to sweat. This was definitely a Japanese stronghold, with some of the best pilots the emperor had at his disposal, most of them well-seasoned.

On November 2, 1943, the mission called for our squadron of twelve P-38s, along with another group, to fly low-level out ahead of almost one hundred B-25 Mitchell bombers that were going after some shipping in Simpson Harbor. The B-25s would be protected by a top cover flight of P-38s riding shotgun above them as they made their bomb run in. Our job was to coax up as many Japanese fighters as we could and take them out before the bombers arrived.

Unfortunately for us when we arrived over Rabaul, our Lightning groups became separated by cloud layers. We in the 80th Fighter Squadron found ourselves in the bottom of the soup. We weren't alone, though, as we bumped into over 150 Japanese fighters that rose up to protect their base. The twelve of us had stirred up a damn hornet's nest!

We tore into one another and slugged it out at low level for over twenty minutes. I looked around and saw my wingman shoot down a Zero, and when I glanced back to make sure he was where he was supposed to be, he was gone. That was the last time I ever saw him. It was every man for himself from that point on.

I latched on to a Zero as he weaved and tried to shake me, but our P-38s were superior in everything except maneuverability. I began to fire at the Zero and saw some hits and light smoke coming from his engine. I was able to stay with him through a quarter of a turn as I fired, but I realized it was time to get the hell out of there—I knew the Zero could turn right around on my tail. I left the fight at a good time, because when I looked back I found that I had one of his little friends on my tail as I climbed away from him.

There were Zeros all over the sky, and it didn't take long to find another as I dove down and came zooming in behind one. I got him smoking too before I was swarmed over by an angry mob of Zeros. I was able to climb away from them as they broke off their chase and headed back to Rabaul.

I spotted some low-flying B-25s heading for home, so I latched on to them for navigation and some dual protection. My rest was short-lived, however, as it was time for me to go back to work when I saw a lone, low-flying Zero up ahead, looking for trouble. I chased after him as he began to maneuver his aircraft quite violently. He turned a little too tight as his lower wing dug into the water, sending him cartwheeling down in a big splash. That was my third Zero for the day; unfortunately for me, they were all listed as probables. At least I knew I was hitting what I was aiming at, but it took me forever to get credit for another one.

Our stay at Port Moresby was actually fun-filled when we weren't being shot at, lost in weather, low on fuel, and were safe on the ground. The Japanese would stage their nightly air raids and you could always hear them coming because their propellers were never in sync. Most of the time their bombs missed their mark and fell helplessly away from our tents.

The Aussie and American ground troops were making some headway in New Guinea as they pushed the Japanese farther west. We were given orders to move to Dobodura along with several other P-38 fighter groups, and it put us in range of shorter flights to Wewak, Hollandia, and New Britain. There would be no more 12,000- to 15,000-foot climbs through cloud cover to get over the Owen Stanley mountain range to go hunting the Japanese.

I looked at Dobodura as the true start of the South Pacific offensive against the Japanese. This was also the place where I met another pilot from my home state of Wisconsin as our squadrons prepared to hit Rabaul together.

I saw him sitting alone on a bench outside his tent, and I introduced myself to him. He said his name was Dick Bong, and we chatted about things back home. Dick was a very quiet man that seemed to keep to himself. He was also one of the leading aces at that time in the war. I flew on a couple of different missions with him, and have always said that Dick Bong may have shot down more airplanes than I did, but I shot at and missed a lot more than he did! He was a superb pilot, the top ace of the war with forty victories, and a really nice guy.

This was also the beginning of some vicious air battles. We were not only outnumbered, but on one occasion, outgunned as well, when we lost our CO. Most of these missions took us back to New Britain time and time again, to familiar and fearful places like Rabaul and Cape Gloucester, as we attempted to eliminate the Japanese.

It was on the day after Christmas, 1943, when Major Cragg was leading a bomber escort flight of twelve P-38s in his personal Lightning, named *Porky II*. Unfortunately, his luck ran out when he ran into seventy-five Japanese fighters and bombers near Cape Gloucester.

Porky Cragg had just shot down his fifteenth aircraft of the war, making him a triple ace, when he took some hits and his Lightning spun in and crashed. It was a huge loss of a great leader and good friend of mine, who was only twenty-four years old when he died. Cock Robbins was promoted to captain and became our new CO.

The New Year brought more and more missions to New Britain as we attempted to annihilate the Japanese at Rabaul. I was also assigned my own P-38 that I dubbed *Screwy Louie*. I would go through seven of them before the war ended. I started out in an H model and really enjoyed the performance of it, and actually fell in love with that early model. When they brought in some new P-38Js to replace our Hs, we damn near had a mutiny in our squadron. It wasn't until we flew the J model that we realized we had a hot fighter in our hands. The Js had incorporated two major design changes; one was the addition of hydraulically boosted ailerons, allowing us to roll the Lightnings all day long, with very little effort. The second major change was the use of electrically actuated dive flaps. These new and improved P-38s really showed their stuff when I shot down my first "confirmed" kills of the war.

Hollandia

I got my first official victory on January 18, 1944, and would add to that in late March of 1944.

On March 30 I was flying wing with Cock Robbins as my leader on a bomber escort to Hollandia. I stayed with Captain Robbins, watching him down a couple of Oscars. I spotted a Tony as he split-S'ed away from me and I tacked on to him, in close pursuit. I gave him a quick squirt of a combination of 20mm cannon and .50 caliber machine-gun fire. Needless to say, he went down in flames.

A day later we were up again over Hollandia as I stayed glued to Captain Robbins's wing as he tangled with another Oscar. I snuck down below as Cock chased that guy around the sky. The Oscar split-S'ed away from Cock and dove right in front of my guns as I raked him from nose to tail. Captain Robbins found another one and shot him down, bringing his total to sixteen. I was close behind Cock, with three confirmed, but would have to wait until the end of the year to get another one.

Louis Schriber II sits in his front office of the P-38. COURTESY OF LOUIS SCHRIBER

Our group continued to move from base to base, inching closer to Japan. We stayed at the "hellhole on Earth," Cape Gloucester, New Britain. It rained constantly and there was a metal airstrip about a mile inland from the water's edge that was forever wet and oozing mud. You always prayed you could skid to a stop before running out of runway; some of us didn't, and we were running short of P-38s.

We moved again, this time to Nadzab, which we shared with some B-25s. Packing our tents and moving once again, we found ourselves on a tiny island called Owi. The airstrip at Owi was made of crushed coral, which was a great surface—except for P-38 tires. There were many blowouts on landings and takeoffs, and some of these turned deadly. Our base was also visited by some celebrities, including Bob Hope, Frances Langford, and Jerry Coloma. They set up shop under the wing of a B-24 and put on quite a show.

We had one more celebrity set up shop, with a different type of "show." Charles Lindbergh was in town to teach us young cocky pilots how to conserve fuel. He bunked with Cock Robbins and flew with us for three days, showing us how to lean our mixtures back and get the best fuel range. What we got instead were longer missions and much sorer asses from sitting on our parachutes for eight hours at a stretch. As long as the "Lone Eagle" flew with us, we practiced what he taught us, but the minute he left we went right back to our old ways. You can always tell a fighter pilot, but you can't tell him much!

Mindoro

In December of 1944, our group moved north a couple of more times with Cy Homer as our new CO, and I was promoted to the rank of captain as we prepared for the invasion of the Philippines. Most of our missions were "home patrol," keeping watch over our base and surrounding area. I shot down my fourth enemy airplane on December 22, 1944, in a shiny, new all-metal-finish P-38. The pickings were becoming thin, as we had to shoo away some of our own just to get a clear shot at the enemy. On December 30, 1944, I shot down my last enemy airplane and finally laid claim to being an official ace.

I was leading the squadron on a mission from our base at Mindoro and was just getting airborne when one of my engines began to develop some problems. I told someone else to take over while I went back and got another Lightning. I changed P-38s and took off hoping to catch the rest of my flight. I climbed to 10,000 feet with my throttles to the wall, knowing the rest of the squadron was up ahead.

I glanced over my right wing and saw four Zeros down below in tight formation, just over the mountaintops. Living up to my nickname [Screwy Louie], I thought "What the hell" as I pushed the Lightning's nose over and came sneaking up behind them. They never knew what hit them.

I picked out the tail-end Charlie and gave him a quick squirt as he flamed immediately and crashed below. I went after the next three and got two of them to smoke as they fled in different directions. I called the squadron to turn around and head back, but by the time they got there the Zeros were nowhere to be found. They had escaped into the cloud cover, the two still smoking. I claimed one for sure and added two more probables to my growing list—not a bad way to end my aerial combat career.

My last mission was flown in March of 1945, after almost two years in combat with the 80th Fighter Squadron. In that time I flew over 790 hours of combat, all of it at the controls of a P-38 Lightning. On five separate occasions I had one of my engines either shot out or stopped because of mechanical problems. Had I been in a single-seat fighter I would have had to bail out each time, and would probably not be here today to tell this story.

The most difficult part of chalking up a victory is getting to the target and returning home afterward. The aerial destruction comes from getting in the correct position at the right time to squeeze the trigger. I have often been asked if I was ever frightened during combat. My stock answer is always no; I was too damn busy being scared to death! You are usually only frightened before and after a mission when you have time to think and reflect. Any World War II combat pilot that says he wasn't frightened is one big liar!

(The "Headhunters" of the 80th Fighter Squadron were the first twin-engine fighter pilot squadron to destroy two hundred enemy aircraft in aerial combat.)

P-38 TOP TEN ACES

Although the Lockheed P-38 Lightning was overshadowed by the long legs and killer instincts of the P-51 Mustang and the hard-hitting abilities of the P-47 Thunderbolt in the European Theater of Operations (ETO), it nevertheless reigned supreme half a world away in the skies over the Pacific. To the men in the jungles, the P-38 was simply known as "the ace maker." Unable to turn with its archenemy, the Japanese Zero, the US Army Air Force pilots utilized the "slash, shoot, and dive" qualities of the big twin-engine fighter to their advantage. They could either choose to stick around and slug it out or dive away and wait for better odds.

In the end, the top two American aces of the entire war claimed their victories at the controls of the P-38 Lightning:

1. Richard Bong: 40 victories, 5th AF
2. Thomas McGuire: 38 victories, 5th AF
3. Charles "Mac" MacDonald: 27 victories, 5th AF
4. Gerald Johnson: 22 victories, 5th AF
5. Jay "Cock" Robbins: 22 victories, 5th AF
6. Thomas Lynch: 17 victories, 5th AF
7. Bill Harris: 16 victories, 13th AF
8. Edward "Porky" Cragg: 15 victories, 5th AF
9. Cyril "Cy" Homer: 15 victories, 5th AF
10. Daniel Roberts: 13 victories, 5th AF

15

Bad Kitty: F6F

BAD KITTY
Lt. Cdr. Elvin "Lin" Lindsay, USNR
VF-19, "Satan's Kittens"

Memories of Hellcat Ace
I had well over 1,000 hours of time in the air before I entered combat. Most of that was as an instrument instructor flying the SNJ. Instrument flying really teaches you the finer points of flying an airplane. It also makes you focus, and for some reason I found that it carried over to gunnery work in the Hellcat as well. Every time I got behind a Japanese airplane, I was very focused as my bullets tore into them!

Joining the Fight
I joined VF-19 "Satan's Kittens" as one of its founding members in August of 1943. We gathered at Los Alamitos, California, where the "Fighting Nineteen" was supplied with a paltry sum of airplanes: an SNJ, a JF2 Duck, a Piper Cub, and a single F6F-3 Hellcat. Most of them were not much to write home about as far as fighters go, except, of course, the F6F.

To me the Hellcat was a thing of beauty. It was Grumman-made and damn near indestructible! As a gun platform it was hard-hitting, with six .50 caliber machine guns in the wings, bulletproof glass up front, and armor protection all the way around the pilot. It was certainly better than anything the Japanese had, especially with self-sealing gas tanks, better radios, better firepower, and better-trained pilots.

147

Our skipper was Lt. Cdr. Theodore Hugh Winters, a combat veteran fighter pilot and a great leader. He worked our group up with great skill, and increased our Hellcat numbers as we learned how to fight and survive against the Japanese fighter tactics. We also learned one of our primary purposes: stick with the dive-bombers and torpedo planes while on escort duty. Our sister torpedo and dive-bomber squadrons depended on us to shepherd them in and out of harm's way. Tempting as it was, breaking away from them to add a small Japanese flag to the side of a Hellcat meant that those slow-moving torpedo planes and dive-bombers were sitting ducks. But once released from escort duty, the Hellcat showed its deadly claws when we finally entered the combat zone.

Baptism of Fire

By early July of 1944 we were combat-ready, and VF-19 had its orders: report to the USS *Lexington*. By late July we were hitting and plastering places like Guam, Palau, Iwo Jima, and Chichi Jima with our 500-pound bombs. When the bombs were gone we dropped down to strafe enemy airfields and gun emplacements. None of it was easy work, as the Japanese still had plenty of antiaircraft gun emplacements all over the place, and they were masters at concealing them.

In early September we began to hit various targets in the Philippines in preparation for the landings that would take place later on. Many of my squadron mates began to rack up their scores by shooting down Japanese fighters, bombers, and torpedo planes. Unfortunately, I had to wait until late October for my turn. I bagged my first one, a Kate, on October 21, as aerial opposition really began to heat up. A few days later our subs in the area began to notice the remnants of the Japanese fleet sailing south toward the central Philippines, and our intelligence people thought they were going to try to make a stand against our landings on Leyte. The battle of Leyte Gulf took place on October 24 and 25 as our Hellcats, dive-bombers, and torpedo planes tore into them.

I was part of a flight of Hellcats that launched off of *Lexington* on October 24 as small Hellcat-led search teams were sent out all over the Philippines area to look for targets of opportunity. It didn't take very long to find them.

Lt. Cdr. Elvin "Lin" Lindsay, USNR, poses with his Hellcat that showcases his victories. COURTESY OF ELVIN LINDSAY

My area of operation was near Clark Field, which had always been a hotbed of Japanese fighters and antiaircraft guns. We weren't disappointed, as the Japanese sent up a welcoming committee of fighters to greet us when we arrived overhead. There were Hellcats zooming, rolling, and diving after all kinds of enemy airplanes as the Japanese made a desperate attempt to stand and fight. I bagged a Tojo, followed by a Val, and then ended up slugging it out and splashing two Zekes before we had to turn for home.

Our little group of search-and-destroy Hellcats claimed ten that day, with the entire VF-19 squadron bagging a total of thirty. Although I was now officially an ace, things would become a lot hotter the very next day.

Shooting Fish in a Barrel

By the morning of October 25, our recon flights had detected at least four Japanese carriers and their escort ships steaming south off the east coast of Luzon. Admiral Marc Mitscher was in command of our carrier task force, which consisted of the *Lexington, Essex, Princeton,* and the *Langley.* The previous night he had ordered the throttles opened as we closed the gap between us and the Japanese fleet. By morning we were a little over 100 miles apart when our bomb-laden Hellcats were launched.

Our eighteen Hellcats, each sporting a 500-pound bomb, launched from *Lexington* and joined in a loose formation on a northerly course. There were over sixty other strike aircraft from the other carriers in the air with us as we made our way to destroy what we could of the Japanese fleet. Our flight was ordered to climb to 18,000 feet, and as we got closer we saw Japanese ships everywhere. What I found amusing, however, was that only three Japanese planes were spotted over their naval armada to guard their battle group below.

What the Japanese lacked in airpower they made up for with deck guns as the sky opened up with heavy flak. We spiraled down over cruisers, battleships, and Japanese carriers, including the *Zuikaku,* which had participated in the bombing of Pearl Harbor.

Commander Winters was more like a traffic cop in his Hellcat as he directed our attacks from his lofty perch, placing us over the selected

An F6F Hellcat catches the wire with its tailhook after landing on the carrier deck. COURTESY OF ELVIN LINDSAY

targets below. I saw bombs falling, columns of water rising with near misses and direct hits as ship after ship began to absorb our wrath. When it was my turn to dive I pushed the Hellcat's nose over and filled my sight with the *Zuikaku*. I released my bomb but never stuck around to see where it hit as I leveled off just above the enemy fleet.

Instead of turning for home and the safety of the *Lexington*, our squadron went after the deck guns as we made strafing passes on the ships in hopes of clearing the way for the much-slower-moving dive-bombers and torpedo planes that arrived overhead. With six .50 caliber machine guns in each Hellcat, the firepower was devastating as we clawed away at the deck guns. Many of them fell silent.

By the time the sun had set that day, Satan's Kittens had been a huge participant in helping to sink three Japanese carriers, along with an assortment of cruisers and battleships. For our diligent work that day, many of us received awards and recognition—but the fighting was far from over.

Navy Cross Citation
Lieutenant Commander Lindsay

For extraordinary heroism in operations against the enemy while serving as Pilot of a carrier-based Navy Fighter Plane and Flight Leader in Fighting Squadron NINETEEN (VF-19) embarked from the U.S.S. LEXINGTON (CV-16), while assigned to strike major Japanese Fleet Units on 25 October 1944, during the Battle of Leyte Gulf, in the Philippine Islands. Skillfully directing his escort group on a strike against major enemy surface units, Lieutenant Commander Lindsay boldly dived through the intense barrage of hostile antiaircraft fire and expertly maneuvered his plane to deliver a bombing and strafing attack upon a Japanese aircraft carrier, leaving her burning and in a sinking condition. During the ensuing action, he valiantly led his fighters through antiaircraft fire to deliver a strafing raid upon a light cruiser.

By his brilliant airmanship, indomitable courage and inspiring leadership, Lieutenant Commander Lindsay contributed materially to the infliction of overwhelming damage upon the Japanese Fleet during this Battle. Commander Lindsay's outstanding courage, daring airmanship and devotion to duty were in keeping with the highest traditions of the United States Naval Service.

Lunacy over Luzon

On November 5, VF-19's new skipper, Lt. "Smiley" Boles, was killed while on a sweep near Manila. I became the new skipper of VF-19, and on November 6 was given attack orders that called for me to lead a twelve-plane Hellcat fighter sweep in the Manila area. Our primary target was Nielson Field, with a secondary target of Clark Field.

We took off and joined up on the inbound course, but within half an hour our flight was just about reduced in half, with Hellcats aborting due to mechanical reasons. For each Hellcat that turned back, his wingman had to peel off as well and shepherd him back to the carrier. It occurred to me that my "broom" was losing much of its sweep! But I was confident that we could go in with only two Hellcats—they were that deadly.

As we neared the huge Cavite Naval Base, the antiaircraft fire erupted below. We turned our Hellcats from side to side and never flew straight and level. The huge black flak bursts were so close I wondered out loud if we would make it through. We began to fly a northerly course, losing altitude to stay under the 6,000-foot overcast that was developing in the area as our heads swiveled from side to side, always looking. It didn't take us long to find what we had been looking for.

Suddenly the sky opened up and off to our right were fifteen Japanese fighters circling to the right, a few miles south of Clark Field. Our Hellcats were at the same altitude as we pushed our throttles forward and went into a slight left turn. We could hit them on their blind side.

As I made the turn it hit me: We were outnumbered, more than two to one. Maybe we should break off and climb for altitude. These fighters had 20mm cannons with explosive shells, and they were so close to their heavily defended base. But my fighter pilot training took over as I wobbled my wings, signaling an attack to the rest of my flight. The words of my skipper, Hugh Winters, echoed in my mind: "A good offense is the best defense."

Our Hellcats were in an "open out" formation, with each Hellcat far enough apart from the other and able to turn and help another plane should it come under attack. As we closed in on the Japanese planes, I knew we had to hold our fire until we were within 300 yards, giving us the most lethal convergence of our .50 caliber machine guns.

A big red meatball appeared, huge in the pip of my gunsight. I moved it forward to his engine from slightly left of his plane. With only a very short burst, maybe ten rounds per gun—*poof!* A wild explosion, followed by thick smoke, fire, and pieces falling all over the sky.

I quickly shifted my attention to another Tojo army fighter—another quick burst, with the same explosive outcome. I glanced over at my wingman, Ensign Tatman, just as he exploded a Zeke. I looked to the other side and saw Lt. (j.g.) McLaughlin set fire to a Tony, which crashed seconds later. By the time the Tony hit the deck, Ensign Sassman had exploded an Oscar.

We had just splashed five of them on the first pass, and the odds were becoming more even. The surviving Japanese planes churned up the sky and scattered.

I latched on to an Oscar that decided to pull into a loop with hopes of shaking me; it was an easy kill as my rounds tore into him. I looked around and counted noses. I still had my original flight of six Hellcats as we began to hunt for the stragglers. I found myself relaxing a little bit as I bent my neck back and casually looked up through the top of my canopy.

My heart stopped. I saw the red meatballs first and tried to identify the enemy airplane. I recognized it as a George—a brand-new Japanese fighter—and he was making a damn good overhead run on me!

As he closed on me, his tracers looked as if they were close enough that I could reach out and touch them. I stomped my boot down hard on the right rudder, all that my Hellcat could take, hoping she wouldn't snap-roll on me at 180 knots. The skid seemed to do the trick and saved my life, as the George's bullets passed behind and to the side of me.

The George dove straight through our Hellcat flight as we all rolled over in unison and split-S'ed after the guy. The George kept on pouring the coal to his throttle and finally leveled off about 20 feet above a large sugarcane field.

Lieutenant Seckel lobbed a few rounds into his smoking engine as his canopy came off. It was an unbelievable sight as the Japanese pilot tried to bail out at such a ridiculously low altitude. He never had a chance. His body slammed into a lone tree that was standing in the field. The George cut a large swath into the cane field before it blew up.

As we climbed for altitude Ensign Farnsworth became our kami-kaze—our "divine wind"—when an Oscar tried to ram him head-on. Farnsworth's Hellcat bore the brunt and brought back part of the Oscar's wing that had snapped off and lodged in his Hellcat's wing—a heck of a way to score a victory and save ammunition!

As we turned for home, low on gas and almost out of ammo, we climbed to an approximate homeward heading, expecting to pick up our usual YE homing signal. The navigation signal was dead; no one was picking it up. None of us knew that a kamikaze had hit *Lexington* while we were gone. With no homing device, I resorted to my training and slid the Mk VIII plotting board from under the instrument panel and held my stick between my knees. I began some very rough navigation and plotted that in forty-six minutes, we should see our carrier. I think I aged twenty years (I was only twenty-five at the time) in three-quarters of an hour. We finally spotted ships ahead of us and found our Number 16 *Lexington* sitting on a mirror-smooth sea.

Some of the Hellcats were very low on fuel and fell out first to land. With all of us safely on board, we scrambled down from our Hellcats and headed for the ready room to debrief.

It was a very somber sight when we were told that a Japanese kamikaze had crashed his bomb-laden plane into the island structure and wiped out fifty men, eleven of them from our group. The enemy airplane had also torn away most of the antennas and communication gear—the reason we couldn't pick up the ship's signal.

When we told Commander Air Group Hugh Winters of our great hunting success in almost downing all the Japanese planes we had encountered, except one or two, the only response the CAG gave was, "Why the hell did you let the others get away!" I just smiled and said, "I'll have a scotch and water, please."

That was my last mission of the war, as *Lexington* pulled out for repairs and VF-19 was sent home. I was reassigned to a Corsair squadron and was on my way back to the war, but I never made it, because the atomic bombs were dropped on Japan.

PART III

TURNING THE TABLES— PUSH TO VICTORY: 1944–1945

16

Quick Draw McGraw: FM-2

WILDER WILDCAT
Capt. Joe D. McGraw, USN

In mid-1943, the Grumman aircraft corporation began delivering its latest and greatest fighter to the US Navy: the F6F Hellcat. This new fighter was fast, maneuverable, and heavily armed and armored. It was built "Grumman tough" and soon earned the nickname "ace maker." As a replacement for its little brother, the F4F, the Hellcat was everything the Wildcat wasn't.

During this same time period, the US Navy began utilizing a one-two punch to knock out the Japanese. First, it used the larger fleet and light carriers to attack Japanese warships and vessels, land-based airstrips, and troop concentrations. With a combination of TBM/TBF torpedo planes and Curtiss Helldiver bombers destroying targets of opportunity, the Hellcats were unleashed upon the aircraft of the Rising Sun.

The second death blow to the Japanese came in the form of small Jeep carriers that quickly moved in and established air superiority and close air support for ground troops as the larger fast carriers moved on ahead, pushing the Japanese farther north. These smaller escort carriers (CVEs) would be supplemented by an already-proven fighter, the F4F Wildcat.

With the success of the Hellcat in the Pacific, Grumman was committed to increased production demands for more F6Fs; therefore Grumman Wildcat and Avenger production was transferred to General Motors and its Eastern aircraft division. While in the hands of General Motors, the

F4F Wildcat was given a new name and a new set of claws. The FM-2 "Wilder Wildcat" carried a larger engine and less gross weight, turning the stubby-winged cat into a real tiger. And in the hands of one pilot during the Battle of Leyte Gulf, this plane tore into the Japanese with a vengeance!

In July of 1943, when the navy was replacing the F4Fs with the new Hellcats, I was in operational flight training down in Florida. As a new fighter pilot, I got to fly the exact opposite of a high-performance fighter: the F2A Brewster Buffalo. It was kind of fun flying the old Buffalo, but it was a real lousy airplane for gunnery. It had a fat, round fuselage and a small vertical tail and rudder. When I threw it into a hard turn to make a gunnery run on the target sleeve, pulling just a few g's, the tail got blanked out and the Buffalo went into a skid, causing you to lose your point of aim. The only way to get a hit in an F2A was to fly right up to the target sleeve and "shoot and duck." This method actually turned out pretty good for me later in the war. Thank God it wasn't in the Buffalo!

When my orders came in to report to my fighter squadron, I was really hoping it would be on a big carrier, flying Hellcats. My orders were to report to VC-10, which was a composite squadron of F4F Wildcats and TBM Avengers. So much for my dream of Hellcats. If I didn't have bad luck, I would have had no luck at all!

We began flying war-weary F4Fs in Oregon, and then relocated to Southern California, near the Salton Sea, where we learned how to run strikes against ships made out of wood. These were silhouettes of Japanese ships anchored in the Salton Sea, and I learned how to coordinate attacks with the torpedo/bombers. Our job as fighter pilots was to protect the bombers on the way in, strafe ahead of them, and then pick them up on the other side of the target. That is, of course, if we made it through the wall of antiaircraft fire!

Flying these older Wildcats was like flying a brick. They weren't very fast climbers, but they could dive like a rock! They were stout airplanes, and it was the first real fighter I had flown. They made a helluva lot of noise, but I didn't think much of it as a performer. They were all we had at the time to get the job done.

The Wildcat used the "Armstrong" method of landing gear operation. It took a full twenty-eight cranks—twenty-seven and a half turns to get

Joe D. McGraw, USN, poses in his FM-2 Wildcat with one kill flag. COURTESY OF
JOE MCGRAW

the gear up or down, and one-half of a turn to lock it. You had to be real careful when you put the gear down because if you were over 100 knots setting up for a landing, the wind drag on the wheels would rip the handle out of your hand and smack it across your wrist. You could always tell a Wildcat pilot from the rest: just look for the plaster cast on the wrist and a mighty strong right arm!

In the spring of 1944, our group was getting ready for combat as we reported to San Diego. All of us wanted to fly the bigger birds like the Hellcats and Corsairs that were coming on line. We felt that the Wildcat was underpowered and overweight. Not an ideal plane to go up against Japanese fighters. Thankfully, right before we were ready to shove off, we got brand-new Wildcats. The navy called them FM-2s. I called them awesome!

This new and improved Wildcat had a lighter-weight 1,350hp engine with semi-paddle-shaped propellers. General Motors took out two of the guns, leaving us with four total. They took out some of the armor and lightened it up by almost 700 pounds. The acceleration was so strong from that Wright radial engine that they lengthened the vertical stabilizer and rudder to handle the additional torque. This was a damn hot airplane, next to the old F4F-4.

You could really maneuver with the FM-2. If you didn't let the Japanese Zero sucker you below 180 knots, you could stay right with him. I tried to stay closer to 200 knots, especially in a tight turn, trying to keep those meatballs in my sights! About the only thing you couldn't do with a Zero was a loop. The FM-2 just couldn't make it around fast enough.

Killer Cat

In April of 1944, we boarded our "Kaiser Coffin" Jeep carrier, the USS *Gambier Bay* (CVE-73), and set sail for the Pacific Theater. Our flight deck was 480 feet long, inset with 4x4 timbers mounted on a 512-foot-long round-bottom freighter hull, with absolutely no armor anywhere! The ship didn't ride very well and it rolled a lot in all kinds of seas. Primitive as it was, this would be my home for the next seven months.

We arrived in combat just in time for a good old-fashioned turkey shoot at a place called the Marianas. The new and improved FM-2

QUICK DRAW McGRAW: FM-2

Wildcat I was flying quickly showed its teeth in combat as I splashed a photo Betty bomber. Using my well-proven technique, I got up close to him, shot, and ducked! If I had held the trigger down any longer, I would have run right into him!

A few days later, I was the one who got "splashed."

I had been on a strafing mission and picked up some light flak. My wingman Leo Zeola and I were returning to USS *Gambier Bay* with our wing tanks still attached when we were vectored by the fighter director to intercept some "snoopers" (Japanese torpedo planes) coming in on the deck. We were at 12,000 feet when we went to "Buster."

We pushed our Wildcats over and by the time we were around 8,000 feet we were closing in on 400 knots and moving real good. That was until I felt the bump. Leo yelled over the R/T, "Hey, your drop tank just took most of your tail off and almost hit me!" I already knew something was wrong and there was no way I could pull out of my dive.

I got the canopy back, but I couldn't get it off the rails as I took a look at the altimeter and saw I was screaming through 6,000 feet. I tried to dive over the side but I kept getting slammed back into my seat. Finally, I lowered my seat, hooked my feet on the edge, and threw myself over the side.

At 380 knots, the wind pulled me out and slammed me into the side of the fuselage. I cut my leg on the jagged remains of my tail as I went zooming by it. I looked down at the rising water below but I had no reference to how fast I was falling. When I finally pulled the cord, I was hit with a tremendous jolt and jerked upward. I swung twice in my harness and hit the water hard.

After drinking half the ocean, I was pulled right back up. Half my parachute stayed inflated in the 20-knot surface wind! My wingman, the faithful guy he was, came low over the water, flaps down, canopy open, and "bombed" me with a can of dye marker, covering me with green and blue shark repellent. That damn can missed my by a few feet, almost killing me! I'm sure it was payback for my runaway drop tank that almost hit him!

After "parasailing" for the next five hours at about 3 knots, I was picked up by a destroyer and returned to *Gambier Bay*, less one FM-2 Wildcat!

Things got really busy in the next few months as we pounded places like Saipan, Tinian, and Guam. The real push came when we formed up in October for Leyte Gulf and the invasion of the Philippines.

Fistfight

Our task force was enlarged to six Jeep carriers instead of the normal four. Our job was to provide protection for the cruisers, battleships, and troop transports on their way into the Philippine Islands. Two additional task forces identical to ours also joined us. The sea was covered with ships, and they called us Taffy 1, 2, and 3.

The USS *Gambier Bay* was part of Taffy 3, and on a good day all eighteen Taffy carriers could put up over five hundred airplanes. On October 23, 1944, after the big carriers went in and hit Luzon and the surrounding airstrips with Hellcats and dive-bombers, we moved in as a show of force to maintain air superiority and provide cover for MacArthur's landings.

There wasn't a whole lot of action for us on the first day, but on October 24, 1944, the Japanese put their "sho plan" into action. Using Japanese army aircraft from Southeast Asia and the CBI (China-Burma-India), they hoped to catch us off guard. They just didn't count on a bunch of Wildcats and TBMs ruining their show!

I was one of eight FM-2s on a fighter combat air patrol (CAP) that morning. There was a storm brewing off in the distance, and it contained twenty-two Japanese Lily bombers and twelve escort fighters. By the time our radar people found them, we were out of position. The Lilys were at 18,000 feet and the Zero escorts were 2,000 feet higher and behind. We were at 15,000 feet and had to climb to fight.

Pushing our throttles forward, we made short work of our climb upstairs and got even with the Lilys. On our first pass we made a flat-side run into them and flamed three of them.

Then the Zeros came down on us.

I called out the Zeros and turned into them. I spiraled up through the hornet's nest and slugged it out with them. They got two of our Wildcats right away. They couldn't get a shot at me and I couldn't get a good shot at them. When I rolled over at the top of my climb, I saw the Zeros hitting the deck and kept right on going. They had left the Lilys defenseless!

FM-2 Wildcats prepare to launch as a sister carrier comes under attack in the background. COURTESY OF JOE MCGRAW

I jumped right onto them, coming in fast and close. I squeezed the trigger and ducked. I flamed two of them and heavily damaged a third when eight more Wildcats joined us. Soon there were only two Lilys left as they approached MacArthur's beachhead. One was smoking heavily on the way down and never made it. The last one ran into a wall of flak and disintegrated over the beach.

This was only the beginning of things to come.

All Hands

The next day, October 25, 1944, I stood down for the morning hop because of all the flying I had done the day before. I was getting some coffee when general quarters sounded. As I dashed to the ready room, shells began raining down on us and exploded all around the ship. The Japanese fleet had zeroed in on us; they were 20 miles out, and closing fast.

I raced up to the flight deck with just my helmet, as I couldn't wait around to gather my survival gear. Most of the FM-2s were turning over, and I saw two of them way in the back row on the aft end of the ship, not manned yet. My wingman Leo Zeola and I raced to the FM-2s and as we drew near, Leo's FM-2 began to crank up. I reached mine and scrambled aboard.

As it turned out, this was my Wildcat that I had named *Mah Baby*, with the letter and number code Baker 6 (B6). Leo helped me strap in as a big salvo went off 25 yards from the ship. Leo looked at me and said, "This is getting serious. No more airplanes left." I felt really bad for Leo and shook his hand. I didn't see him again for three months.

The shell splashes were all around the ship and I got some quality prayer time in as I waited to launch. I was the last guy in line to go as a salvo came in and hit the bow of the ship. Timbers flew as 4x4 pieces of lumber were thrown skyward. I poured the coals to the FM-2 and waved the launch officer out of the way as I dodged the holes in the deck on the port bow.

When I got off the deck, just starting to crank my gear up, another salvo went off in front of me. Three telephone poles of water stood in my way! I was so close to stalling speed, still cranking my gear, that there weren't any fancy maneuvers I could do. I missed them by feet as I put the Wildcat into a skid.

That's when I looked up and saw a swarm of aircraft coming right at my nose.

I pushed the Wildcat back down, narrowly missing my squadron of TBMs and FM-2s that were forming up in front of me at 500 feet. I made a hard turn back into them and joined up as we headed out for the Japanese fleet.

It didn't take long to find them, as there were four battleships, six cruisers, and fourteen destroyers. The skipper took us to the base of the cloud deck, at about 2,000 feet, and said, "Fighters into strafe!" Boy, did he love to say that!

I pushed the Wildcat over and poured the coal to her. As I was heading downhill into the vast Japanese battle line, all I could think was, "Man, here I am in a little bitty old Wildcat, looking through my gunsight at the world's biggest battleship, *Yamato*. Boy, this is going to be hairy!" White balls of fire streaked my way as the Japanese gunners tried to bracket me and our strafing fighters.

The TBMs were right behind us as they dropped their bombs on the Japanese fleet. They didn't hurt them much because they were not armed with armor-piercing bombs, but we let them know we were there! Those of us that made it through went back into position as the skipper said, "Anybody got any bombs left?" Two of our TBMs were in the water. "Yeah" came the reply as we did it all over again.

We continued to strafe and harass the Japanese until we ran out of ammo. Aircraft from the other Taffy groups relieved us. Low on gas, we re-formed on the skipper and went back looking for USS *Gambier Bay*. When I saw her, she was dead in the water, keeled over and on fire. I thought of Leo as we turned for Tacloban Airstrip on Leyte. Flying over the emergency strip, I saw fighters nosing up in the mud; it was a real mess.

Not wanting to become landlocked, I used my last 30 gallons of fuel and went looking for Taffy 2. I found them and I got into line and landed aboard USS *Manila Bay*. My plane was "up" and so was I as they refueled me and the skipper said I could fly with them on the very next strike.

I went back up and out to tangle with the Japanese fleet. Another FM-2 and I made a headlong dive into a cruiser and my new wingman took a 5-incher in the nose and tumbled downward. I didn't have time to see if he got out okay. I made ten more runs into the Japanese fleet until my ammo went dry.

After landing back aboard USS *Manila Bay* a second time, they asked me if I was up for more. Refueled and rearmed, I was sent on a CAP flight with eight other FM-2s as the Japanese fleet retreated. Orbiting at 12,000 feet, four of us got vectored to a small group of bogeys coming in at 10,000 feet, passing through a cloud front. I counted fifteen Val dive-bombers and twelve Zeros coming out of the clouds. If this was a "small raid," then we were in big trouble!

We were on a perfect intercept at their eleven o'clock and 800 feet higher than they were. Turning hard left, they didn't see us as we made our run into them. We took out the four lead Vals on the first pass as each of us got one. Looking up, I saw the Zeros push over and come zooming down after us. My division leader was hit immediately, his FM-2 raked by cannon shells. I pulled up and did a little corkscrew through the Zeros. I rolled over at the top, pulled through, and was in perfect position above and behind the Zero lead and his wingman. I let loose with a long burst and flamed the wingman, hitting him in his engine and wing root before he exploded. The Zero lead "exploded" in anger and came after me with a vengeance!

He snapped that Zero up on its nose, whipped it around, and came back at me with his thumb down on his cannon button. I thought to myself, "I don't want to be a statistic on some government report!" I pulled the Wildcat into a knife-edge turn, and skidding with the right rudder I was able to turn back on him. All of his cannonballs went right behind my tail.

I needed to make a very tight turn on this guy and I pulled four g's to get it around. The Zero pilot knew he was fighting a Wildcat, but didn't realize it was a "Wilder Wildcat." He underestimated me and my plane and didn't make his world-famous super Zero turn. I got around on him and put a quick burst into his engine before he could unload his cannons on me. I had smoked his engine as we scissored back and forth, tight on one another. He jerked his stick back and I thought he was going to ram me. I pulled back hard on my stick and missed him by mere feet. I still have a crick in my neck from that SOB!

I whipped the FM-2 into another tight turn, trying to put this guy down. He was dangerous, and obviously an old hand. The Zero split-S'ed and dove for the clouds. He was clever, and turned back under me as I dove down onto him. I looked up and back and saw two of his buddies, one on the right and the other on the left, trying to cut me off. I took a long shot at the smoking Zero and split-S'ed out of there. I didn't like the odds!

Suddenly the sky was empty. I'd never felt so alone. One minute there were airplanes everywhere and the next, nothing.

By the time I found my wingman and our leader's wingman and got back to USS *Manila Bay*, it was starting to get dark. After all was said and done, I had flown eleven and a half hours of combat. That's a helluva long day in a Wildcat!

(Joe "Jody" McGraw flew over fifty combat missions in the FM-2. He is one of only a handful to make ace in the FM-2 Wildcat, with five confirmed victories, three probables, and three damaged. He earned the Navy Cross, the Distinguished Flying Cross, and air medals for combat against the enemy.)

17

Butcher Bird: P-47

SCHOOL OF HARD KNOCKS
Col. William B. Bailey
353rd Fighter Group, 352nd Fighter Squadron, 8th Air Force

The same nagging thought returned to my head once more as I crossed the English Channel: "Did I make the right choice?" As CO of the 352nd Fighter Squadron, 353rd Fighter Group, I was flying a top-of-the-line fighter called the P-47 Thunderbolt. Beside me and behind me at 26,000 feet were an additional fifteen olive-drab P-47s containing pilots whose lives I was responsible for.

Three years earlier I had come to a fork in the road and had to choose my life's path. I had been selected to attend Harvard Business College but I had also been offered a "different sort" of education. I'd opted for the second choice, the US Army Air Corps flying school. When I graduated from "Clobber College," I was eventually posted to the 353rd Fighter Group, and, like the rest, sent to England to fly and to fight in the P-47 Thunderbolt.

The P-47, although "huge" in comparison to other Allied fighters, was a delight to fly. I found it amazingly easy to handle having transitioned from the narrow-geared P-40s. The P-47 with its big R-2800 supercharged Pratt & Whitney out front was intimidating at first, but once inside this spacious cockpit, well laid out from a pilot's point of view, the Jug was a real honest airplane, stable and easy to fly at all altitudes. The P-47 was also an excellent gun platform, both in aerial combat and in its desired use as a "high-speed strafer."

Col. William B. Bailey, USAAC COURTESY OF WILLIAM BAILEY

In the air-to-air combat arena, the Jug's major advantage was that it was considerably faster in a dive than the Bf 109 and Fw 190. However, once at low altitude, it had a marginal turning radius, and in such situations pilot experience and skill were the deciding factors between life and death. The Jug also carried its own set of trump cards—the first being the always-reliable Pratt & Whitney engine, which always seemed to get us back home no matter how much had been shot out of it; and the second, the rugged construction of the airframe, which could take an extreme amount of battle damage yet still fly on as if it were just missing a chip of paint.

Meeting the Enemy Head-On

I refocused on the task at hand: leading my flight in a Jug named *Butch*. I picked this name because it was a short but a bit more refined version of Butcher, which I hoped would be the role of the aircraft in combat.

We were getting closer to the rendezvous point. Assigned with escorting the lead force of B-17s to a place called Schweinfurt, my flight picked up our bomber formation mid-Channel and made landfall in the Dutch Walcheren Island area.

Our intention was to stay with the bombers as long as our fuel status allowed. I had hoped to take the B-17s as far as the Rhine River, but the Germans with their ever-changing tactics had something else in mind. The German scenario called for Luftwaffe fighters to attack the Allied fighters as our formation reached the coast. The German goal was to separate all Allied fighter escorts and disallow their protection of the bombers. Once that was established, the Allied bombers would have to proceed unescorted through a gauntlet of terrorizing German fighters that lay ahead in wait.

There they were, unmistakable, as I called out to our flight: "Twenty Bf 109s coming at us from the northeast!" The 109s were above us and began their headlong dive to attack. All attention was turned upward as sixteen P-47s turned into the threat and accelerated to meet the enemy. Airplanes were everywhere as the melee intensified.

At one point I saw a 109 on the tail of a fellow P-47. I called for the distressed Jug to break and dive. As he did, the 109 started to follow and then broke off and began to climb. As I dove down on the unsuspecting 109, letting loose with my guns firing at close range, I observed many strikes, structural disintegration, and an explosion. Oil covered my windshield as the 109 began its death spin.

The initial attack was completely broken up with four enemy aircraft destroyed and no losses to my squadron. Unfortunately for the bombers, they had to continue on without us due to our fuel constraints. What lay ahead for them was pure hell. Over sixty bombers were shot down as they made their way to the target. That nagging thought in my head never returned. I knew at that moment I had made the "right choice," and I was flying a plane that would help turn the tide!

Much thought was given by the high command about the disastrous Schweinfurt mission. Although we were primarily tasked with bomber escorts, the Jug would now be utilized as the best all-around strafer/fighter bomber in the ETO. Fighter command had a newfound aggressive attitude toward German fighters, both in the air and on the ground. Our group employed new tactics with a new and improved P-47, and our results proved deadly for the Luftwaffe.

Encounter Report
14th October, 1943.
Vicinity Eecloo, 26,000 feet.

As Wakeford white leader, I was leading the squadron as top cover for the bombers at 30,000 feet. We had just made landfall in the vicinity of Flushing when I noticed about 20 plus enemy aircraft, both Me 109s and Fw 190s, coming in above us at 11 o'clock at an altitude of 33,000 feet and above. These aircraft dove to attack and a general dogfight ensued. These enemy aircraft definitely engaged our fighters and made no attempt to attack the bombers. In the course of the fight which followed, the enemy aircraft were split up. I noticed a 109 on the tail of one of our aircraft. I called to break and the 109 was shaken off and went into a half-roll. He dove for about 1,000 feet, rolled back, and leveled off, pulling up in a steep climb.

I followed him up in the climb and had no difficulty in closing. I fired two bursts from a range of 200 to 100 yards, observing strikes on the fuselage. There was a large flash, pieces fell off, and the aircraft spun down, obviously out of control. The engagement was broken off as I flew through pieces of the enemy aircraft with oil from this ship in my windshield. The engagement was witnessed by Lieutenant Willits and Lieutenant Gonnam. And on the basis of their statements and what I saw, I claim one Me 109 destroyed.

Jug Jockey

In the spring of 1944, our group began to receive a new, more powerful P-47. This new Jug contained water injection from the heart of the R-2800, boosting the available horsepower. A clear bubble-top canopy replaced the razorback look, allowing for greater all-around visibility. The use of paddle-blade props added to the new refinements. I christened my new Jug *Butch II* and adapted a new paint scheme.

We had been asked more and more as a group to operate at low level, not only on targets of opportunity when returning from escort missions, but also on an increasing number of specific dive-bombing missions. As a result, I thought it a good idea to have my Jug painted in European camouflage so it would be harder to see when operating on the deck. The idea was to use the RAF Spitfire design, but our paint crew used heavy layers of gray, and the total effect was somewhat different, if not unique. The Jug really stood out from the crowd when black-and-white stripes were added to the wings and fuselage—invasion stripes!

June 1944 was a very busy month for the 353rd Fighter Group. Most missions were low-level, armed with bombs designed to isolate the invasion area, suppress airfield activity, destroy bridges, and interdict any ground vehicle movements in our assigned corridor.

On D-Day, each squadron had the task of keeping eight aircraft in the area from dusk to dawn. I flew two missions that day with much success, but six days later I almost swallowed some poisonous German bait.

On June 12, 1944, we had just finished tearing up and bombing the airfield Evreux, just west of Paris. I observed a fast-moving train proceeding eastbound. Not wanting to let this choo-choo go unscathed, I began my dive onto the train. Eight machine guns all in unison barked as tracer rounds flashed across the freight cars.

As I passed over the train at about 100 feet, throttle to the wall, I began my climb out for another go. I didn't notice the flatcar rigged with folding sides and a canvas top hiding twin 20mm antiaircraft guns. As I roared overhead, large tracer rounds began to streak over my canopy less than a foot away. I stomped down hard on the rudder, skidding the aircraft and pushing the nose down forcibly. Luckily I was not hit as I flew fast and furiously away.

Other P-47s in our squadron encountered similar threats. But one Jug pilot brought home some souvenirs after flying through a farmhouse chimney. The Jug was completely covered with oil, the windscreen opaque. When he landed back on English soil, six bricks were found embedded in the cowling and one cylinder head was completely detached, proving once again the fine attributes that made the P-47 ideal for ground support.

I flew eighteen missions during June of 1944 as my time flying the Jug began to run out.

All-Out Effort
On August 4, 1944, the 353rd had just performed a bomber escort mission to Hamburg. On the way home, pilots began looking for targets of opportunity.

Plantlunne aerodrome, located very close to the German–Dutch border, would fit the bill for that day's strafing run. A high concentration of more than fifty twin-engine He 111 and Ju 88 aircraft were sitting on the ground. Normally a "good" target of opportunity, these German bombers had deadly V-1 rockets mounted atop their fuselages. This was a priority target that needed to be destroyed at once! Due to the low fuel and heavy flak, the squadron made one futile pass and then returned to report their important discovery.

A fully loaded P-47 Thunderbolt of the 353rd Fighter Group COURTESY OF WILLIAM BAILEY

A request was made and granted by 8th Air Force Command to launch a designated pinpoint attack on the German airfield. It was felt that this unusual concentration of enemy aircraft and V-1s was to be used for the sole purpose of an air-launched buzz-bomb attack on London. The 353rd Fighter Group was given carte blanche for anything and everything they needed to successfully complete this mission. The 56th Fighter Group led by Col. Hub Zemke and his thirty-four P-47s would assist in the initial dive-bombing of flak installations and to perform the vital role of top cover.

Aerial photos of the aerodrome provided very detailed information. An attack plan was devised assigning squadrons and flights to all identified flak gun positions using fragmentation bombs on a specific schedule. Following the dive-bombing we planned a traffic pattern and strafing sequence using all available aircraft on command.

At approximately six p.m., I led thirty-six heavily armed P-47s from our base at Raydon. The weather en route to the target was absolutely crystal clear, with no Luftwaffe fighters observed anywhere. The dive-bombing of the flak positions was very effective, and once it was reported they had been suppressed to an acceptable degree, I ordered the strafing pattern to begin. I made a series of four passes across the field, claiming one He 111 and one Ju 88 destroyed, along with a flak gun position.

On my last pass I flew directly over a flak tower, which was still operating, and took a 20mm hit in my right wheel well. As I dove for the deck to avoid further hits, I saw a rise in the terrain. Standing on a small hill observing this controlled chaos stood a German officer in full dress uniform with much silver braid on his hat. I was too low and too close to get a shot off at the traumatized aerial observer as I roared overhead.

As the attack progressed, we altered the traffic pattern due to reduced visibility caused by burning enemy aircraft. Ammunition began to run low as our P-47s continued to zip across the airfield. Like a pack of hungry wolves, I called the 56th Fighter Group "downstairs" to take over and finish off what they could. Using their own disciplined traffic pattern, the Wolfpack cleaned their plate in no time.

Departing the area and heading for home, I was reminded of the "little problem" I had acquired. I had a small scratch on my right arm from fragments that came up from my damaged wheel well. The Jug handled like a lady as I set up to land at Raydon. As I began my flare and touchdown, I began to have difficulty keeping the Jug centered. I held hard opposite brake and veered off the runway at low speed, coming to rest on the grass with no further damage to the aircraft or me. *Butch* had sure earned his name today!

Over thirty enemy aircraft had been destroyed by P-47s of the 353rd and 56th Fighter Groups. The 353rd received commendations from General Spaatz, commander of all US army air forces in the theater, and from General Doolittle, Commander of the 8th Air Force.

(After flying 325 hours in 154 operational missions, Colonel Bailey turned his P-47 workhorse in for a new steed: the P-51 Mustang, flying a second combat tour through April 1945, employing well-proven tactics learned from flying the Jug.)

18

Little Friends over the Beach:
Various D-Day Fliers

THE PLANES OVERHEAD WILL BE OURS ...

They must have been a sight for sore eyes to the soldiers on the beach as wave after wave of fighters, bombers, and paratrooper-stuffed transports, some towing gliders, passed overhead, all of them adorned with black-and-white-painted stripes. The invasion was on, and many of the fighter pilots, expecting a Luftwaffe slugfest, were disappointed by the dismal numbers that showed up. But there were still plenty of targets both on the ground and in the air for those lucky enough to be at the right place at the right time.

Follow along with these "Little Friends" on the historic day known as D-Day, the 6th of June, 1944.

TWIN-TAILED TROUBLE
Capt. Stanley P. Richardson Jr.
55th Fighter Group, 338th Fighter Squadron

In early June of 1944 my original P-38J-CL-X had been wrecked by a fellow squadron pilot while I was on leave. I returned to see my pride and joy lying on its belly with an engine shot out from a previous combat encounter. My bunk mate who was at the controls of my Lightning told me he had had an engine shot out while tangling with the Luftwaffe and made it all the way back to base in England when he got cut off by a

P-38s of the 55th Fighter Group tuck in close on an escort mission. COURTESY OF
JACK COOK

landing B-17. With wheels down, flaps out, and only one prop turning, he
ran out of options, raised the gear, and bellied it in. Thankfully with a war
going on there were many P-38s sitting around, waiting to be assigned.

I was issued a new P-38 and my ground crew got it ready to fly.
Unfortunately, the day I was supposed to give it a test hop, everything was
grounded so the base ground crews could paint black-and-white stripes
on our airplanes—invasion stripes, they called them. I would have to perform double duty on my next flight—a combat mission and test hop all
rolled into one.

On June 5 I was slotted to fly a night mission over the English Channel and over the invasion beaches along the French coast. The P-38s were
selected for this because they were extremely recognizable, with twin
engines and twin tails. Nothing else looked like them. Our instructions to
the troops on the ground were simple: "If you see anything flying over the

beaches, shoot it down, no questions asked. Destroy anything that is not a P-38 entering your assigned patrol area."

We departed our base at Wormingford very late in the afternoon. The weather was terrible as we struck out for our patrol area, with low ceilings and heavy rain. From 1,500 feet I saw countless numbers of boats of all shapes and sizes all over the Channel, heading for France—God, what a sight! We orbited the beaches and I saw some sporadic gunfire but nothing that would compare to the next day. We landed well after dark and trudged to our bunks for some rest.

It was short-lived, however, because very early the next day, June 6, we were rolled out of our bunks at 3:00 a.m., and after eating breakfast and receiving our briefing, we were once again over the beaches by 5:30 a.m.

There were P-38s all over the sky with the 20th FG and the 479th FG milling around overhead with us. There was not a German airplane in the sky that we saw, but had one shown up it would have been torn to shreds with the combined firepower of the cannon and machine guns we carried in our noses. I flew three missions on D-Day and am quite proud to say the Allied Air Forces owned the airspace above the invasion beaches. As our troops on the ground moved inland, we followed from above and went after targets of opportunity.

Personally I liked going after trains, but the Germans didn't take too kindly to that. Early on in the war it was a piece of cake to shoot up locomotives and freight cars; that was, until the Germans added "Q" cars to the mix. They looked like any other freight car until the sides dropped and exposed quad 20mm cannons able to fire in all directions. Our loss rate of fighters knocked down shot up dramatically with these "Q" cars. Strafing trains became dangerous work and a lot less fun!

Live Bait!
Capt. Clayton "Kelly" Gross
354th Fighter Group, 355th Fighter Squadron, 9th Air Force

Joining the Pioneer Mustang Group
Because of the war, new fighter groups were forming at a rapid pace. With 65 hours of P-39 time under my belt, I was assigned to the newly formed

354th Fighter Group and became a flight commander with the 355th Fighter Squadron. We continued to train in the P-39 until we received our orders to ship out and head to England, where we would join the fight. Although we flew Airacobras, we were told we would not be flying them in combat; instead, we would be flying a "new fighter" that was just coming on line.

We arrived in England in early November of 1943, and that's where I met the airplane of my dreams: the P-51 Mustang! Actually, the first model I checked out in was the dive-bomber version called the A-36 Apache. This early model used the Allison engine, had only three propeller blades, had machine guns in the nose and wings, and had dive brakes embedded in both the upper and lower surfaces. It looked fast just sitting on the ground!

After spending two days going over a very thorough cockpit checkout and some last-minute emphatic demands by my instructor—"Leave the dive brakes alone!"—I was sent on my way to check out this new thoroughbred. This was no P-39! I guess I had become spoiled with tricycle gear airplanes and had to go back to my early tail-dragger days to taxi the Apache without hitting something.

The A-36 had a long slender nose and you couldn't see out the front end. We had to "S" turn from side to side until ready for takeoff. I felt the power to be somewhat similar, especially with the familiar Allison engine out in front of me instead of behind, like it was in the Airacobra. But once airborne, it was quite different. I could tell right away it was much more responsive and lighter on the ailerons.

After two flights in the A-36 I was deemed ready to check out the rest of the squadron pilots. We continued to train, and this time it was in the P-51As—same as the A-36, but without dive brakes. We only spent a couple of hours on the A model before the more powerful P-51Bs arrived in mid-November of 1943. From then on the 354th FG would always be known as the Pioneer Mustang Group—the first US Army Air Force group to take the Mustang into combat.

The P-51B was an entirely different animal. It was powered by the well-built and reliable Rolls-Royce Merlin engine; instead of getting tired above 12,000 feet, it only became stronger as it literally took us to

Capt. Clayton "Kelly" Gross, USAAC, sitting on the wing of his P-51 Mustang, *Live Bait.* COURTESY OF CLAYTON GROSS

new heights. The B model had four propeller blades instead of three, but only carried four guns instead of six. With less weight we were able to carry more gas, which meant that now we could escort the bombers to and from the target area.

With the entire group checked out and equipped with P-51Bs, we were moved to our first airfield, called Boxted, which was located near Colchester. Before we went on our first combat mission, we were visited and instructed by the commanding officer of the 4th Fighter Group, Col. Don Blakeslee. Colonel Blakeslee was already considered an old hand, as he had been fighting early on as part of the Eagle Squadron during the Battle of Britain. The thing I remember most was that he emphasized to us that during a head-on attack, the guy that broke first would be at a disadvantage. I silently thought it would be more of a disadvantage if we actually rammed into one another!

Baptism of Fire

On December 11, 1943, I flew my first combat mission: a B-17 bomber escort over Germany. Some of the guys in the squadron already had nose art on their Mustangs. At first I was going to put my wife's nickname, "Lil Pigeon," on it; the problem was, it had a history of bringing bad luck. I had given my first P-39 that name and someone had made a wheels-up landing. The second P-39 suffered a worse fate when the pilot cartwheeled it. The third time was not the charm when another pilot crashed that one as well. I agonized over it until a new name came to me on one of my missions.

We had been out on an escort and I became separated from the group. I was able to latch on to another Mustang flown by Bob Stephens as we turned for home. Bob suddenly called me over the R/T and said, "You stay where you're at and I'll climb above you into the sun and then hopefully we can draw some action."

Although I relished the thought of tangling with the Luftwaffe, I wasn't too thrilled with being the lure. I replied to Bob, "What the heck do you think I am—live bait?"

He just said yes, and because he outranked me, that's what we did.

My neck was never the same after turning it from side to side, looking for an attacking German!

When we got back I had my crew chief paint the name *Live Bait* on the side of the Mustang. Our missions increased during that time frame, as things were really getting busy during the spring of 1944.

Work Up to the Big Day!

Our group continued to fly escort missions during the entire month of May 1944. You could tell something was in the works, as more and more ships were seen in and around the harbors of England, with countless supplies chocking their docks. Most of my time was spent over Germany at places like Berlin, Frankfurt, and Magdeburg, as the bombers continued to pound the Axis hard.

The Germans did not simply lie down and take our attacks lightly, however. On May 28 the Luftwaffe thickened the skies over Germany as swarms of fighters, like fireflies on a hot summer night, came roaring into our bomber formations.

I picked out an Fw 190 and almost got him before I had to disengage for fear of ramming another fighter that crossed closely in front of me.

Separated from my flight, I latched on to another Mustang as we set a course for home.

On our way out our flight of two encountered a stricken B-17 that was having engine troubles—probably due to all the cannon and machine-gun rounds it had absorbed from the earlier Luftwaffe attacks.

Suddenly an Me 109 was coming in fast from his six o'clock, hell-bent on finishing him off. I rolled the Mustang over and shoved my throttle forward. I was still over 200 yards away when I noticed the 109 let loose with his cannon and machine guns. I responded with my own machine guns and saw them tear into his wing root and cockpit area. He snapped over and dove straight down before crashing.

I flew two missions on D-Day, and although we didn't encounter any German airplanes, the scene below on the beaches of Normandy was surreal. There were ships of every shape and size out in the Channel with landing craft zigzagging back and forth. Intense ground fire and flak were everywhere, and we did what we could to help the guys on the ground. We continued to fly in support of our advancing troops, sometimes three missions a day as they pushed inland and pushed the Germans back.

On June 14 we were escorting some B-26 Marauder medium bombers over France and the Luftwaffe finally showed back up. We had a heck of a fight.

I tacked onto a 109. Closing fast, I let him have it at less than 100 yards. He turned over slowly as flames shot out from beneath his engine cowling. I saw no parachute as he crashed below. I was one away from becoming an ace.

By the end of June, the Pioneer Mustang Group had already shot down 370 enemy aircraft. And we weren't done yet! With over 200 combat hours under my belt, I was sent home for thirty days of rest and relaxation. There would be plenty of war left when I returned.

(Captain Gross ended the war with six victories during his two tours, and owes his survival to the P-51 Mustang. The Pioneer Mustang Group was officially credited with 701 aerial victories, and they were crowned the top scoring fighter group of the European Theater of Operations.)

19

Twin Terrors: Flying the P-47
and P-51 in Combat

BIG STUD
Lt. Col. Fred C. Gray
78th Fighter Group

Encounter Report: Plan "Stud," 1540 hours, near Alençon

I led the 78th Group flying P-47s to the Alençon area with the mission of destruction of lines of communication. We arrived over the area at 12,000 feet and stooged around a couple of holes in the overcast.

My wingman sighted a train and I sent him down for it, following on his wing since I had not seen it. We broke out at about 3,000 feet and dropped our bombs at the train, with poor results, getting only near misses and a few on the track. We then strafed it and allowed it to blow off steam.

While the rest of the section was working it over, I moved north and located a loco in a small marshaling yard in Le Hutte. I moved in on it and got a considerable number of strikes all over it. It practically blew up. While my wingman Lieutenant Massa was strafing it, I found another in the other end of the yard and got it also. I got dozens of strikes, as did Lieutenant Massa, but it was cold.

I then took my flight up the line to Alençon and out each rail line from the city for perhaps 20 miles without sighting any rail traffic other than two locos in the marshaling yard at Alençon, which I passed up due to the presence of many civilians in the immediate area who were waving at us.

At this time my Red Leader sounded off on a gaggle of Fw 190s on the deck, moving south, near the city. I finally saw them and tagged on, passing him and coming up on tail-end Charlie. I was catching him without water until he threw his souped-up charge in, when I had hit mine. I caught him easily and he started turning. All those boys I taught back at Matagorda (a bombing and gunnery range in Texas) would have gotten a kick out of my sorry deflection shooting.

I finally got him going straight and got four pretty good bursts into him. He jettisoned his canopy as his engine cut and started out. I was about to overshoot him and skidded out to the side, when Lieutenant Massa gave him a burst. He overshot him and eased up alongside and watched him laboriously crawl out, his jacket and helmet on fire. He got out about 600 feet and his chute worked beautifully.

Col. Fred C. Gray of the 78th Fighter Group (middle) poses with ground crew members. COURTESY OF JACK COOK

I then broke for another, but just as I was about to try my deflection shooting again, my second element leader, Lieutenant Caulfield, beat him up. He turned into me and snapped into the ground, making one hell of a beautiful explosion which I caught on my camera—only now they tell me the damn thing jammed!

I claim three loco's damaged as shared and one Fw 190 destroyed that was shared with Lieutenant Massa. I also confirm the destruction of one Fw 190 by Lt. Peter A. Caulfield. I think these Fw 190s were the ones Spicer referred to when he said, "They fly like Basic students."

NO REST FOR THE WEARY
Capt. William Y. Anderson
354th Fighter Group: Pioneer Mustang Group
353rd Fighter Squadron, 9th Air Force

June 6, 1944: D-Day
"Come on, Lieutenant. You got to get up! The colonel says we got a mission."

Capt. William Y. "Swede" Anderson, USAAC COURTESY OF WILLIAM ANDERSON

I sat up and promptly hit my head on something hard and solid. God, I can't see. My damn eyes are glued shut. I pulled off my gauntlets and spit on my finger to rub the goop that the old Sandman had put in my eyelashes. I finally got to see enough to let remembrance flow back into my soggy brain.

I was under the sink on the concrete floor of the mess hall of the emergency field we had been diverted to after last evening's mission, on account of bad weather over the Channel and our own field. We had landed around 2300 last night, and by the time we debriefed, ate a Spam sandwich, and had a cup of coffee, it was almost 0130 hours. The warmest place I could find was under the sink where the hot water had been running. The time now was just after 0300. We were all pretty tired, but the prospects of seeing the land invasion going on served as a stimulant. The mission was the same as last night, except we could expect more gliders and worse weather over the Channel.

We were providing support to escort the gliders with their C-47 tow ships, about 5 miles inside the beachhead, picking them up off the coast of England and then giving the C-47s withdrawal cover back to the English coast. After briefing, we went out to preflight our airplanes. No ground crews to do it for you here. Drain water from fuel tanks, check oil and Prestone, and top off your fuel tanks.

After I finished my chores and warmed up my engine, I had twenty-two minutes left before takeoff. I sat in my cockpit, listening to my warm engine cooling down. I'd shut it down to save fuel. It was just before daybreak, with hazy, cold rain squalls passing by. I couldn't help but shiver. It was a grim morning.

After we had taken off and kept our rendezvous with the gliders, we began flying our lazy-eight pattern over them. About fifteen minutes out from the beachhead, the sun broke through a big hole in the clouds and it looked beautiful down there, along the coast.

The weather closed in again, so we dropped down with the gliders to about 500 feet. I was pretty nervous flying that low and slow along the coast, but it turned out it'd be the first time in over forty missions that I wouldn't run into any flak. Amazing.

By this time the C-47s had begun to spread out and released their hitchhikers. Most of the gliders were cut free and headed straight for what looked like a postage stamp and plopped into it. I did some fancy turns in line. A few did some fancy turns to line themselves up for a cushy landing. Some would overshoot their targeted field and crash into fences and trees. A few even ran into each other. This, of course, was quite catastrophic. One glider overshot its field and hit a clump of trees. It immediately burst into flames and burned like a thermite bomb.

The C-47s, released from their gliders, circled back across the drop zone, tossing out supplies in blue, red, purple, orange, and yellow parachutes. These chutes were scattered for miles, hanging in trees, off telephone wires, laying in fields, and even dangling off of roofs. I could see people in the streets of small towns and in wagons on the roads. There were cows in the fields and livestock in the yards. It did not seem possible that this great Allied invasion was taking place not too far from here. It was just too peaceful-looking.

After dropping their supplies, the C-47s headed back toward the English coast.

Upon crossing out over the beaches, the peaceful scene disappeared. There were what seemed to be thousands of ships and boats, many flying large area balloons from their decks. There were destroyers, battleships and cruisers, and supply ships of all kinds along the coast. Continuing along the route back to England, we saw more gliders on their way to where we had just left. The Channel was dotted with quite a few C-47 gliders. The air-sea rescue boats certainly had their hands full this day.

After three hours and fifteen minutes of this escort duty, we returned to our base, got debriefed, had a bit to eat, and took a snooze.

HIT THE DECK!
Capt. M. Gladych, Polish Air Force
56th Fighter Group, 61st Fighter Squadron

It was 2100 hours near Croisy. I was flying Red 3 (Whippet Red Three) to Captain Rutkowski. We were circling the convoy on the road (in P-47 Thunderbolts) when I saw four aircraft that I thought were Me 109s. I called my flight leader and dove on them. After about two minutes' chase I was close enough to recognize them as P-51s. I started to turn, as I intended to rejoin the squadron, when I saw four to five Me 109s coming from the east at 100 feet. I reversed my turn to meet them.

The nearest one of the enemy aircraft apparently spotted me against the ground and peeled toward me in a shallow dive. The rest of them proceeded to climb in a wide slight turn. I turned with the attacking enemy aircraft and had no difficulties in closing on it. I had switched the water on and after a couple of seconds began to overtake the enemy aircraft. I slid on the outside and then kicked the bottom rudder, getting on the enemy's tail. I fired, didn't see the strikes, but the enemy aircraft reacted by tightening the turn. I pulled some more deflection and gave him another burst. The enemy aircraft spun and hit the ground.

In the meantime, the remaining enemy aircraft were scared by eight P-51s that came from the south. I tried to get another of the Me 109s of the bunch. I pulled up, closed from underneath and astern, and fired a short burst at the last one. The Hun emitted some black smoke but kept flying.

I abandoned the pursuit because my gas was running low. I headed for home flying on the deck.

I claimed one Me 109 destroyed.

REALITY OF WAR
Lt. Col. Huie Lamb Jr.
78th Fighter Group, 82nd Fighter Squadron, 8th Air Force

I was born in Carey, Texas. My dad had a small ranch out at the edge of Abilene there, and we always rode horses. My dream was to ride horses and play polo. I wanted to join the National Guard where they had a polo team, but my mother wouldn't sign the papers. I was sixteen. Thank goodness she didn't sign because I found by best dream ever flying fighters.

In 1942 I was enrolled at Texas A&M and while there I joined the air corps. After completing all my training, I was assigned to fighters and got some time in P-40 Warhawks before moving into P-47 Thunderbolts. The P-47 was a big son of a gun and packed a deadly punch with its eight .50 caliber machine guns. It was big and roomy inside and an all-around good flying airplane. I got my orders to ship out to England and arrived in early July of 1944.

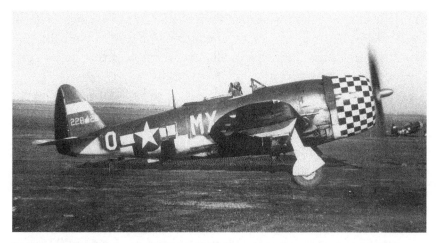

Huie Lamb Jr. at the controls of his P-47 Thunderbolt prepares to launch for another mission. COURTESY OF HUIE LAMB

I was sent to the 78th Fighter Group at Duxford and assigned to the 82nd Fighter Squadron. I was very fortunate to get there, because if you're going to be in a war, it's kind of favorable to have a nice place to stay at night, and we did. But right when I got there the reality of war hit home hard. I remember one particular guy named Captain Roland Wolfe. He said, "You know, I don't want you to take this personally, but I don't like to make close friends with people when they come in the unit." He said he'd lost too many guys. War is hell.

Big Bad Jug

My early missions in the P-47 were mainly strafing locomotives and ground support. There weren't a lot of German airplanes around at first that I saw, mainly because I was busy keeping an eye on my leader. It wasn't until October of 1944 that I finally got my first victories.

On October 12, 1944, I was flying Surtax Yellow 4. In the Hamburg area, we spotted fifteen-plus enemy aircraft, mostly Fw 190s. We dove down to bounce them, and the enemy aircraft broke in all directions, most of them headed into the clouds.

My element leader picked out a straggler in an Me 109 and we circled and came in on his tail. My element leader fired a burst or two at him and then overshot. I came in and fired from dead astern at a range of about 500 yards, getting strikes on both ailerons of the enemy aircraft. The 109 turned gently to the right and I pulled deflection of a ring on him and fired, and the enemy aircraft's engine caught fire.

I pulled up as I overshot and looked back and saw the enemy aircraft falling sideways at about 2,000 feet. I could see the canopy was off and the pilot seemed to be trying to get out. I don't know whether he got out or not, for the 190 rolled over on its back and went straight into the ground and blew up. I saw no chute. I also shot up a loco on my way home in the same area. I claimed one Me 109 destroyed.

On October 15, 1944, Captain John I. Brown and I were returning from the Hanover area after strafing ground targets. Near Osnabrück, I spotted a jet aircraft at about 4,000 feet. We were at about 15,000 feet at this time. I started a steep dive and was indicating about 495 miles per hour airspeed and closing very fast.

When I closed to about 1,000 yards, he must've seen me, and he started to pick up speed and pulled away a little. I gave my plane full power and water injection, which gave me a boost, and started to close on him again, but very slowly. As I got within range and started shooting, he started to turn to the left. I easily turned inside of him and kept shooting during the entire turn, noting many strikes. The enemy aircraft, an Me 262, made about a 180-degree turn and then leveled out.

He started back and led me low over his airfield, but I was so close to him that the flak gunners didn't shoot for fear of hitting him. . . . He made another turn to the left and I kept firing and getting strikes. He turned to the right at about 100 feet off the ground, and the enemy aircraft flipped over on its back and crashed into the ground and exploded. It was then that the German gunners opened up on me big time. My plane was hit pretty hard, and Captain Brown, who was watching my flight, called and said, "Stay low!" Which I did, and was "cutting the grass on the deck." Once clear of the airfield, I climbed back up and headed back to Duxford with Captain John I. Brown. I was glad I was flying my tough old P-47 Thunderbolt that day.

I claimed one Me 262 destroyed.

Cold-Water Ditch

In late November and early December of 1944, we were ordered to turn in our beloved Thunderbolts for P-51 Mustangs. We were not very happy about this, as we thought there was no better fighter than the Jug. I had a P-47D-28. The crew chief and I had waxed it, so it was a little bit faster. It was such a great airplane. But orders were orders, and we transitioned into Mustangs.

My first Mustang mission was on December 29, and it was almost my last.

I was element leader that day, flying my newly christened Mustang that I had named *Etta Jeanne*, after my kid sister back home. My wingman was Lt. John C. Childs. We were over Denmark, heading to our target, when Childs motioned that his radio wasn't working. I was ordered to escort him back to the base.

We were cruising along at 15,000 feet over the North Sea, and my coolant temperature was climbing. I opened the coolant door and it cooled down so I put it back into automatic. I had no way of knowing if it

Huie Lamb Jr. rests his hand on the wing of P-51 Mustang *Etta Jeanne II*. COURTESY OF HUIE LAMB

was open or closed, but I think it froze shut, because then it got hot again. I tried the same procedure and it didn't work.

Up ahead I could see the coast near Orford Ness, just north of Ipswich. I thought I could make it there. I thought wrong, and realized I couldn't make it when my engine began losing power. I made a final Mayday radio call, not knowing if anyone heard me or not.

When the engine started on fire, I tried opening my canopy. I didn't realize at the time that the Mustang had an emergency release, a red handle. I had just read tech orders about it. I don't know why I didn't pay attention to that particular item. But when I finally got the canopy open, I was too low to bail out.

I realized that I wasn't going to make landfall and unbuckled from my seat belt and harness. I got within 4 miles of Orford Ness, so I had to ditch in the North Sea. I came in as slow as I could and stalled out above the whitecaps just as my tail dug into the water. My right wing caught a wave, and I cartwheeled.

It was bittersweet that I had unbuckled. Thankfully I got out of my seat—and the aircraft—as quick as I could before the Mustang sucked me down with it, but as we hit, my face smashed into the panel and gun-sight and I cut it up pretty good, breaking some teeth and cutting my lip. But at least I was alive.

I had always been a pretty good swimmer and thought I could easily swim the 4 miles to shore. Once I was among the waves and got my Mae West opened, I couldn't even see the shore let alone feel my fingers. The water temp was 38 degrees (Fahrenheit), and I didn't know how much longer I could survive.

It was awfully cold and I was sitting on a cushion, so I had a hard time releasing the dinghy. I finally was able to reach down and find one of the fasteners you push in to get loose. I got the dinghy out and got it inflated, but then I couldn't get in it because the Mae West was in front of me and I lost my strength to do so.

Unbeknownst to me, my wingman John Childs had circled where I went down and then flew toward Orford Ness, using the lighthouse there as his guide. He flew over to Martlesham Heath airfield and saw an air-sea rescue RAF Walrus taxiing out. Because he had no working radio,

Childs landed and taxied up to the Walrus, got out, and let his Mustang's engine continue running. He later told me he didn't want to take a chance on having to start it again. Then he raced over to the Walrus and told the crew that they had a man down and he'd lead them to me.

The intrepid rescuers took off, with Childs having to circle over the slower-moving Walrus, and thirty-five minutes after I had ditched, the Walrus landed nearby. Turns out it was the Walrus pilot's first rescue. He did a great job. The radio operator did a heck of a job picking me up with all that water and stuff hanging from me, which only made me heavier. I remember being pulled out of the water and then I passed out.

I was rushed to a hospital as they packed hot-water bottles all around me and loaded blankets on top of me to bring my body temperature back up. Ten days later I was back flying with the squadron again.

I bought the Walrus crew a barrel of beer for pulling me out of the drink. It was the least I could do for saving my life.

Shooting Gallery

On March 19, 1945, I was flying Surtax Yellow 3 when we approached an enemy aerodrome in the Osnabrück area. Some bogeys were called out at nine o'clock low on us, and our flight went down to investigate. The planes were Me 109s. We bounced two of them, and I got strikes on one Me 109, on wings and cockpit.

I pulled up to join Yellow Leader. I'm not sure what happened to that Me 109, but I claimed it as damaged.

I then called out an Ar 234 low, at nine o'clock. He was flying at about 200 feet. Yellow Leader then dove on him, and he got strikes and started his right jet smoking black smoke. Capt. W. H. Brown then overshot him, and I came in and got many strikes on him from astern. I set his left jet on fire, and he jettisoned his canopy, and I kept shooting and got more hits. Then the whole plane started falling apart. I overshot him and looked back and saw him crash into the ground, close to the aerodrome that had been shooting up heavy and light flak at us. The pilot did not get out. I claimed the Ar 234 shared destroyed with Capt. W. H. Brown.

We then joined our flight and I started home. We bounced ten Me 109s and Fw 190s on our way out. I was then bounced by four Fw 190s, and I broke into them. I fired on one, observing strikes, but ran out of ammo before I could finish him off. I claimed one Fw 190 damaged.

Hitchhiker

The very last mission I was on, April 25, 1945, was the only mission during which I ever saw British Lancaster bombers and British Spitfire fighters over France; B-17s also. The mission was to go to Berchtesgaden and bomb Hitler's mountain retreat at Berchtesgaden, Austria.

We had a two-seat Mustang we had converted from a war-weary B model and we named it the *Gruesome Twosome*. The mechanics took the middle fuel tank out and put a seat in the back of the pilot. I took Lt. Col. Ben Prescott, the flight surgeon of the 66th Wing of the 8th Air Force, as he'd always wanted to go on a mission with the fighters, but General Doolittle wouldn't let him. They'd let him go on bomber missions, which to me has much more danger involved than that in a fighter. I had a wingman with me, Lt. Elsey, and the two of us could just kind of go wherever we wanted, just fly around. We didn't see any Germans, but my rider seemed to enjoy his first fighter sweep, sitting back there for six and a half hours. We landed back at Duxford without firing a shot.

When the war in Europe finally ended in early May, I had been promoted to captain, and our focus at Duxford shifted. We began training for combat in Japan. Some of the new pilots in the squadron were upset. I remember getting together with them, and they were all sad instead of being happy about the war being over. They had wanted to go into combat. They'd done all that training and in their minds were ready for action. They didn't realize how dangerous it was. My last parting advice to them was, "Careful what you wish for, fellas."

20

Swede's Steed: P-51

FOOLS' FLIGHT
Capt. William Y. "Swede" Anderson
354th Fighter Group: Pioneer Mustang Group
353rd Fighter Squadron, 9th Air Force

April Fools' Day, 1944. We had been told to stand down the night before, so we'd enjoyed a wee bit of a party at the club. It was therefore quite a jolt when we were awakened at 4:30 a.m. the next morning and told, "Briefing, fifteen minutes."

At the briefing, we found out we were to escort the Big Friends [Big Friends were the bombers, and Little Friends were the escorting fighters] to Ludwigshafen and provide withdrawal support in our P-51s. There were quite a few cumulus clouds along the route, which forced the three squadrons to circumvent the larger buildups. On one such deviation, we found ourselves to be quite a bit south of the rest of the group. Before we could rejoin them, however, someone called out, "Bandits coming in at one o'clock high." I looked over in that direction and saw a gaggle of about twenty to twenty-five Jerries driving down on us.

Just before they reached us, they dropped their fuel tanks, and I'll tell you, there was some wild scrambling to get out of the way of those things and not run into one of your own men trying to do that same.

Of course, we broke up into individual dogfights and I found myself on the tail of an Me 109. We ratted around until we were down to about 15,000 feet, when I got a hit on him. He started to smoke a little and proceeded to split us and head for some lower clouds dead ahead. I followed him, confident that I had a sure victory in my grasp. He dove into the tops of those clouds, but due to his smoke, I could almost follow his flight path through the clouds. Up he popped again, and I, after him. Then down into the clouds he would head again.

We played this game for about five or six minutes, and on one of his pop-ups, he went into a fairly tight turn to the right. I, of course, turned a bit tighter than he, in order to catch him, and he dove into the cloud deck again. I dove with him, confident that his time had come.

Just off my right wing, I saw this great bulge. I hauled back on the stick and passed over two or three gray bulges before I realized that he had suckered me into a bunch of barrage balloons. I got out of there, of course, and checking my altimeter at the time, discovered I was down to 1,500 feet.

I turned north and started climbing for altitude and looking for any signs of the rest of my outfit. I saw some activity off to my left, so I headed in that direction and joined up with two other P-51s. We headed toward the northeast, where the bombers were supposed to be. I saw flak and I knew we had found the big guys.

We eased over the top of them for a while until some of the Me 109s came in on them. We met Jerry head-on and off we were again, giving chase. The Me 109 I met head-on never fired his guns. I pulled over in a sloppy loop, hoping to get on his tail. I went through this fair-sized cloud and came out right behind an Me 210. I don't know where the hell he came from. Anyhow, I gave him a guess lead and fired, saw my armorer piercing incendiary rounds (APIs) light up on his left engine, and it started throwing pieces. I followed him down and I fully expected him to bail out, but he didn't. I gave him another squirt and hit him again all over the fuselage. He dove through the clouds and, by this time, I was a little leery about diving through clouds at low altitude.

I found an open spot and dove through it. Getting under the clouds, I started looking for him and found him still on about the same course he was on when we'd entered the clouds. I took another deflection shot at him and got one strike on him that I could see. I was on his tail and he kept heading down with me behind and it dawned on me that he was

"Swede" Anderson sits on the wing of his P-51 Mustang, *Swede's Steed*. COUR-
TESY OF WILLIAM ANDERSON

heading for a clearing dead ahead. I couldn't believe that he was going to belly in, but he did.

I looked at my airspeed indicator and I was doing over 300 miles an hour at this point, as I pulled up and looked back. All I could see was a long burning streak tumbling across the ground, not much of anything else.

I poured the coal to my Merlin and headed for home. If I couldn't find anyone to fly mutual support with, I'd find the contrail level, if there was one, and drop just below it. It just made it easier for me to see if anyone was trying to sneak up on me from above.

When I got home, I had one jammed gun, two burned-out gun barrels, and two rounds left in my good gun. It was certainly a Fools' Day.

Apple Blossoms and Doodlebugs
On June 17, 1944, our squadron had just completed a dive-bombing mission near Bayeux, France, where we had unloaded our 500-pound bombs into railroad embankments and train tracks. "Kinsley," our controller,

called us over the R/T and said there was a bandit crossing the Channel near our position. I split-S'ed and went after it. I made visual contact with it and saw it was a V-1 buzz bomb flying at between 3,000 and 4,000 feet. I called these flying rockets "doodlebugs" because of the ear-piercing racket they made.

As we crossed the coast inbound near the Isle of Wight, I dove down on the V-1 and began to fire at it with my .50 caliber machine guns. I saw flashes on the doodlebug and knew I was hitting him. You had to look out for two things while chasing and firing at a V-1: One was the friendly fire from the antiaircraft gunners on the ground who put up a wall of lead, trying to knock these little rockets down. And the other thing was you didn't want to get too close to the tail of the V-1 while you were shooting at it, because if that thing blew up in front of you, it was sure to take you down with it.

Fortunately my strikes hit the V-1's rocket tube, blowing it completely off as the powerless doodlebug nosed over and went straight down into a beautiful flowering apple orchard, where it exploded. There was a great shower of pink and white apple blossoms thrown skyward amid the smoke and flame from the explosion.

After I landed I asked my CO how many doodlebugs I would have to shoot down to make ace.

Even though I was credited with over seven additional aerial victories—eight, if you include my V-1 kill—I never paid much attention to victories or damages. I just went up and did my job.

Catching the Next Train

On August 3, 1944, while escorting B-26s who were bombing low-level German airfields in the Caudebec area, I saw a train puffing merrily along. I told my flight to hold their positions; I'd be right back.

I peeled off and peppered that engine till it looked like Old Faithful in Yellowstone. I rejoined my flight and we crisscrossed overhead till they dropped their bombs and headed back. Just off the corner of my eye, coming out of the sun, hell-bent for nasty to our B-26 friends, were four 109s. I pulled up to meet them head-on, with the Merlin screaming at war emergency power and my flight right behind, doing the same. We made them veer just enough so only the leader got a good shot at them. The lead B-26 took a hit in the left engine and it started to smoke.

I fell in behind the leader of the Jerries and proceeded to punish him for his attack on our friends. I became so engrossed in shooting that sucker down that I was overrunning him. He was already smoking and I suddenly realized I was going to ram him.

I hauled back on the stick and at the same time leaned forward in order to keep from blacking out—and ran the damn stick into my mouth. I blacked out for a few seconds, and when I got myself all together again, all the B-26s were still on their way home, one with an engine feathered and four ground fires from four Me 109s. We got every one of them.

When we got back to base our flight surgeon cut out two teeth that I had broken off, hitting that control stick.

The next day we flew the same mission. All I found that day was a train pulling the train that I had shot up the day before. *Zap.* One more choo-choo out of commission.

Upon seen my combat film from August 3, I realized that all the tracers I saw weren't mine. While I was zapping the leader, his wingman was trying to do the same to me, until my wingman, bless his heart, did him in.

Passing the Torch

On August 7, 1944, we had just moved from our base near Omaha Beach to a deserted German airfield near Mauron, out on the Brest Peninsula. We were on a fighter sweep, looking for targets of opportunity, just north-east of Paris. I remember looking down and seeing the trench line still visible from World War I, and it gave me an eerie feeling.

The controller called to let us know that there were some bogeys reported over Chartres, so we headed over that way. We found some Me 109s and Fw 190s, just west of Chartres, and bounced them. I picked out a 109 and dove under him. I don't think he ever knew that I was there. I got him in my gunsights and at about 100 yards put the bull just below him and squeezed the trigger. I pulled my nose up, moving the gunsight bull through him, and walked rudder slightly. He just came apart and went down like a brick. It was the first shot I had with my D model P-51.

It, of course, had six .50 calibers instead of the four .50s that the B model P-51 had.

Later on that day, we were out on patrol again. This time it was a little closer to home. The Germans had thrown in several Panzer divisions in an attempt to cut the Americans off in the Brest Peninsula. There was a fierce tank battle raging just east of the town of Avranches. We were assigned to hit targets of opportunity from Argentan to Vire to Laval.

My wingman called and said he had two bandits at twelve o'clock low. We were only at 2,000 feet at the time, and I couldn't see them. I told him to take the leader and I'd fly his wing. He dove down and I, of course, followed. It was only then that I saw two 109s, right on the deck. We both opened fire at the same time, he, on the leader, and I, on the wingman. The lead 109 blew up, while mine nosed over into the treetops.

My wingman pulled up and was frantically calling for help. He couldn't see. His canopy was covered with oil, but fortunately, it was German oil. I told him to open his canopy a bit so he could see a little better, which he did. It was still a little tricky for him to land in this condition, especially since this was his very first mission.

(Capt. William "Willy" Anderson ended the war with nine and a half air victories and was a member of the Pioneer Mustang Group, 354th Fighter Group, 353rd Fighter Squadron. To honor his Swedish heritage, he christened all of his Mustangs Swede's Steed.*)*

2 1

Requiem for a Fighter Pilot: P-51

CHANGE IN PLANS

Col. Richard G. Candelaria

479th Fighter Group, 435th Fighter Squadron, 8th Air Force

After earning my wings I was sent to fighters, and I graduated from Williams Field, Arizona, at the controls of the most beautiful fighter ever built—the twin-engine P-38 Lightning. Actually, it was called the RP-322, which was the reconnaissance version. It didn't have the supercharger, so you couldn't go as high. But outside of that it was a P-38, without the ammunition and the guns.

I expected to go to combat along with my fellow, now fully qualified, fighter pilots. But my orders said, "Stand by." In the military, that's the only problem: Everything is uncertain. You can't plan for it. Others plan for you.

At any rate, I became a flight instructor at Luke Field [Arizona] in AT-6s, teaching instrument flying from the front seat while a cadet sat in the back, covered with a hood. I was not very happy with my new assignment. It was painful. Very, very painful. Just a terrible disappointment. However, I must say that once I got started and began talking to cadets and knowing that they would be graduating soon, and going into combat, well, that really put my heart and soul into it. So, I said, "Well, if that's what I have to do, that's what I have to do."

But two months later there was a new change in plans. The call came for fighter pilots, single-engine fighter pilots. I signed up with a large number of other guys and, lo and behold, I'm on my way to Harding Field

Lockheed's newest fighter, the twin-engine P-38 Lightning, would eventually fight on all fronts of the war. COURTESY OF EAA

in Louisiana. That's where I got to see the P-47s. They had an operational training unit there, and all I needed to convince myself I made the right choice was to watch them come in and then peel off in a fighter approach, pulling beautiful contrails off the wing tips. I learned gunnery and bombs in P-40s, and by the summer of 1944, I had orders to pack warm winter gear for my next assignment—England.

One of Riddle's Raiders

Arriving in England in July of 1944, I was assigned to the 479th Fighter Group, 435th Fighter Squadron. The group was known as Riddle's Raiders, after Lt. Col. Kyle Riddle, the CO. Things were really looking up when I was reunited with an old flame: The 479th were flying P-38s. I was elated and thought, "Hot dog! I'm back where I really wanted to be. I'm in combat. I'm in P-38s."

And all of a sudden, here come all these single-engine aircraft: Mustangs. Our unit was the first one to transition to P-51s, so we started fighting missions with two squadrons in P-38s, and one of P-51 Mustangs. Others were planning for me again; what was a guy to do?

Although the P-38 was my first love, I must say this: Out of all the aircraft I flew, one of the best aircraft I have ever flown was the P-51 Mustang. All I've ever wanted from the time I was in junior high school was the P-38s. Growing up in Southern California, I would bike over to the airfield and watch them flying out of Burbank. At any rate, now I would get to go to combat in a P-51. And my very first mission in a P-51: Berlin. And I would be flying wing on the squadron commander, Maj. John Glover.

After launching we started out over the North Sea. Out of landfall, the sea was glistening below and the clouds were behind us. I was flying along, very happy, when boom, the engine quit. *Oh no. Not now. Not before we get to Berlin.* Nobody had even shot at me.

I started down and called the squadron commander, telling him, "My engines quit." He told one of the others to go down with me, because you always try to stay in pairs.

I switched the tanks from the wing tanks, and the engine started, so I thought, "Oh, okay." I climbed back in formation and switched over to the wing tanks again. I was flying along for another maybe half a minute, and boom, the engine quit again, so down I went again. I realized the tanks weren't feeding; that was the problem.

So, I kept working the tanks and sure enough, the engine started. By then, everybody was gone. This time, nobody went down with me. A short time earlier, there had been a couple hundred aircraft in the air around us, all heading for the rendezvous point. And the next minute, not a soul in the sky. I thought, "Well, I know where we're going. I know the rendezvous point." So I set course for it.

I caught up with the first box of bombers with their escort. Sure enough, we were headed for Berlin, but guess what? Every time I got close to another group of fighters—they were all Mustangs at this time— they'd turn into me. They didn't know who I was.

Because the Germans had captured some P-51s intact—or almost— and patched them up, they would fly them with the US Air Force or the Allied stripes, with German pilots. They'd get close enough and shoot down a couple of bombers, and dive for home. So, I understood what was happening. I stayed up there out of range of the other fighters and tried to

479th Fighter Group P-51 Mustangs form up. COURTESY OF JAMES BUSHA

get close to somebody. I was like the ugly duckling wanting to come home to Mama. Nobody wanted me.

So, I flew along and we went to Berlin. I watched them bomb Berlin, and there was a lot of flak but no fighter attacks that day. I was pretty independent at that point. I could do almost anything I wanted because I didn't have to fly in formation.

Then I spotted the silver noses and the yellow tails; I had found my squadron. Sure enough, I went up there and joined up with the squadron leader and headed home with them.

I flew many more combat missions, and there were enemy aircraft, but since I was flying wing, my job was to make sure that nobody got on my leader's tail, and therefore I didn't get a chance to shoot until the mission of December 5, 1944.

Aerial Circus
Lieutenant Colonel Riddle was leading the group that day as we made our way to Berlin. We got the word from Ground Control that Germans

were forming up; they were coming down from Norway, and coming up from Austria, so it was going to be a big fight that day. There was no question about that. We also knew the Berlin patrol would have jets.

We had first encountered the jets in August of 1944, and we had seen plenty of them and chased them, but we just couldn't catch them. They would hit and run, and of course that was the smart thing for them to do, because they really could not outfight us. They could not outmaneuver us, so they used their speed judiciously and would fade away into the distance. Although you'd chase them, we would say, "They've got to turn. They've got to turn sooner or later." Well, they disappeared before they turned.

Northwest of Berlin I was flying Yellow Four position. We were heading 130 degrees at 30,000 feet when an enemy gaggle of more than eighty airplanes was sighted about 4,000 feet below us, at eight o'clock, going away from us. At that point, there were ten of us that were left in the 435th. Others had aborted or had been sent off to other responsibilities.

The group leader called a bounce and I followed my leader into a sharp left turn. We closed on these as they started a gentle climbing turn to the right. My leader fired on one and got strikes on him. Two Fw 190s turned toward him and I opened fire on one at about 80 degrees deflection, but saw no strikes. The second one straightened and I closed on him and opened fire. I saw strikes in the cockpit and all over his fuselage. He went into a slow spiral to the right, in flames. I didn't see the pilot bail out, but a few seconds later the plane exploded. I pulled up toward my leader and watched his man bail out of the spinning aircraft.

I followed my leader on another pass, but the enemy aircraft split us and went into the clouds. We pulled up once more and my leader fired once more from very close range. I saw strikes on his fuselage and his canopy flew off. The enemy aircraft then pulled up sharply and fell away to the right. Two Fw 190s made a pass on us and I turned into them and they rolled over and started barrel-rolling straight down. I followed, firing at them every time I got them in my sights. I saw no strikes, but the canopy of the last plane came off and flew past me.

A moment later, I saw the pilot go out and go past my right wing, still in a half-sitting position. The plane went into a flat spin to the left. The other plane leveled off and caught up with four others. When they saw me closing in, all five peeled off to the right and dove to the cloud layer. I followed, but lost them in the clouds. Observations: Enemy pilots were not aggressive. I claimed two Fw 190s destroyed.

I was going to go back up and join up with my squadron. And again, there had been a huge ball of aircraft going in all different directions, and aircraft blowing up and flaming, and so forth. Now, not a soul in the sky. It was just amazing. It was a matter of seconds, and everybody was gone.

And then I spotted another single-engine aircraft, so I started toward it. Friend or foe? If it was a foe, I was going to engage; if it was a friend, I was going to join him. Well, it turned out to be one of the 434th Fighter Squadron guys, with his red tail and silver nose. I came up and joined up on him as we headed for England.

Pride and Joy

I inherited my first Mustang, a K model, from Vern Hooker. I christened it *My Pride and Joy*. It was painted in gold letters in curved script, like the Romans had on their scrolls. This Mustang certainly lived up to its name on the April 7, 1945, mission.

I was finally going to lead one of the sections, and I was going to get to fire first, of course. After the escort I could take them wherever I wanted to.

We were escorting B-24s that day. I went through the briefing and all that, and went down from the aircraft, and, as usual, I was greeted by the ground crews. I climbed in, strapped myself to the Mustang, and signaled for my flight to start engines. The flare went up and we started taxiing out. I was going to be leading. Hot dog.

All of a sudden, I feel *barrump, barrump,* and the aircraft is hard to steer on the ground. The tail wheel had gone flat. Why now? I had to pull off to the side and let the others go by me. They went out and started getting ready for the takeoff. They began departing in twos without me.

Suddenly, the crew chief and a couple of the guys came up and said, "Don't get out. Don't get out. We'll have it fixed in no time at all." I said, "Okay." I sat back down and put the straps back on. The nose came down, the tail came up a little bit, and there was a lot of noise behind me as I watched my squadron take off element by element, joining up and circling the field.

Just then the tail came down and the crew chief came up and said, "Okay, you're ready to go." I saw the last one disappearing into the undercast as they joined up. And they were gone.

I went taxiing down as fast I could to take off. I didn't even wait for the signal of the flag man, just gunned it, went down the runway, got airborne, and then turned. Everybody was gone. Nothing but clouds. I thought, "Well, I know where they're going. I know the course they're taking, so I'll take a couple of degrees off, maybe 3 or 4 degrees, and 1 degree for Mother." I didn't want to run into anyone, so I put the Mustang on a higher climb power than usual. I may have figured that by the time they broke out, I'd be able to overtake them.

I climbed out on instruments all the way. When I broke out of the clouds and hit landfall, I hit Belgium. They usually didn't attack until after we were inside Germany.

Every day, the Luftwaffe would retreat a little farther if they were going to attack. By March and April of 1945, they were back behind the Rhine, so, I really wasn't expecting any trouble. I got there ahead of the squadron by a good three to four minutes—I was smoking!

I went looking for my box of bombers. I picked out the box I was supposed to escort, called over the R/T, and said, "Lakeside 4-0 rendezvous." It was acknowledged, with no more transmission, and I started my little escort dance, going up and down, doing race tracks and S's. I pulled up above the bombers to get myself some good speed. You kept it at higher than normal cruise speeds because your guns were harmonized at 375 miles an hour, so you wanted to get up to that speed as soon as possible. That way if you encountered an enemy aircraft, you would be able to start firing your guns immediately.

Jet Killer

At about 3:45 p.m. I saw two objects coming toward me. Two dots. And they got bigger and bigger. They were Me 262 jets, painted in polka dots, and they were moving fast as they came toward the formation. I thought, "Oh boy—I got them all to myself." I called them out that I was engaging them. I had altitude on them because they were just below the bomber formation, heading for the bombers. I estimated they were at a 45-degree angle. I dove into them and met them head-on. I glanced at my airspeed indicator and saw I was doing between 460 and 475 mph.

I tried to make them break away, and sure enough, they broke away. But not before they were headed right for me. I thought, "Well, I better start firing." They dropped their nose slightly, just enough so that I couldn't bend the airplane down fast enough to get any kind of a lead on them. So I went right over the top of them, and they kept going toward the bombers.

But then they turned and made a big, wide arc. That gave them a chance to pick up full speed. By that time, they were really moving, close to 500 mph.

I began cutting them off as they started back toward the bombers. By that time, I really had a good angle, so I got close enough that I could fire, but he saw I was closing on him. I was almost in range, and he turned away.

I had so much speed by that time that I was able to start to get a little closer. Then, he poured the coals to it and started to pull away from me. I knew what was going to happen. He was going to be gone. So, I fired at him as he was pulling away, and I saw the right engine, big puff of smoke came out of it, then more smoke started to trail out. I kept going after him, figuring, "Well, if he's only got one engine, I may be able to catch him and stay with him to get close enough for another shot."

He turned away from the bombers and went into a wingover, pointing the 262 straight down. He was easy to see because he was trailing lots of smoke.

I started going with him, and I looked in the mirrors. I had two mirrors on each side that the crew chiefs had put on. And here was the second Me 262. He was trying to line up with me, and about that time, I saw his nose light up like a neon sign. I knew he was firing. I dug my boot on the left rudder pedal and he hit me right in the wing. Just barely nicked it, and I saw a little piece fly off.

He took off the running light. I thought, "That's as close as you're going to get." I knew no Me 262 was going to out-turn me, so I started a tight turn, and sure enough, he broke off. I turned back toward him and saw him heading down. And about that time, I saw the Me 262 I had hit, still going straight down. And now, much more smoke was coming out of the engine before he disappeared into the undercast. He must have been doing his maximum of around 600 mph or so. Knowing what I know now about jet aircraft, I'm sure he couldn't have pulled up. There was no chance of catching him as he disappeared, so I started back toward the bombers, and looked for my box again.

About that time, I saw green flares from the tail-end Charlie of the stream of bombers. That meant fighters. I climbed above them and looked and couldn't see anything.

As I scanned the sky my eyes lit up. Coming out of this little cloud bank I saw a huge gaggle of Me 109 fighters.

I've Got the Whole Luftwaffe Cornered!

They were in a good formation for a change, but it was a very peculiar one. They had one leader with four wingmen. There were three leaders with four wingmen. And then there was one that was ahead of them. Wherever he turned, they turned. They obviously were following him. This guy had a bright yellow nose running all the way down the cowling, from the windshield to the spinner. This guy wanted to be seen. So, I figured, he's the leader, and I thought, "Well, the rest of the guys are going to be here any second."

I called them out and the squadron CO said, "We're just about a minute or two away from rendezvous. We should be there pretty close to the right time." Well, it was too late, because the German fighters had hit the bombers over Belgium instead of over Germany.

At any rate, I called them out, but I thought, "Hot dog! Look at all those black crosses. I've been praying for a black cross." Then I thought, "Dear Lord, I only want them in twos and threes. I didn't want the whole bunch all at once."

Anyway, I stopped worrying at that point. I realized that I had to get the leader, because wherever he went, they went. So, I came down with plenty of speed and almost overshot him. I slid out to the right and slid back toward him, and then I went on a wild ride. This guy was good.

Couple of times, I thought he was going to get me. He was so darn good that the others couldn't even get close to us. They seemed to be getting in each other's way. They weren't used to combat or flying a good formation. He and I started going round and round. Up and down. We went way below the bombers. We kept going down and down, spiraling down toward the ground. Several times we were canopy to canopy. And he almost out-turned me a couple of times, but it's harder to out-turn a Mustang to the right. If he'd gone to the left . . . well, I don't think he could've out-turned me anyway. Nobody had ever out-turned me before, so I didn't think this guy would have—but he sure was a good stick.

Oh my God, he did some fancy stuff I'd never heard of. And I had a terrible time. I'd think I had him, but I'd be about to fire, and all of a sudden, the pipper on the gunsight would slide off to the right or to the left or above, and I just couldn't line up on him. And a couple of times we were going down and pulling back sharply, and when I say sharply, I mean we were really pulling some heavy g's. The pipper, which is a gyro precession system, started to slide down, which means you have to pull the nose back up and keep it on him. At times the pipper was down by the rudder pedal, so I knew he was really turning.

I finally got to him. He kept zigzagging back and forth, but we were getting pretty low. He wasn't going to have much more time to maneuver. We were just above the undercast, and I got him. I hit him good, and I saw what first looked like coolant belching out. Then smoke started coming out, and I just gave him a short burst because I figured I would have a lot more of his friends to deal with; better not to waste any ammo.

I gave him another parting short burst to make sure before sliding off of him. Then I saw the canopy fly off, and he bailed out. The aircraft went into the woods and crashed, so that was another kill.

I pulled up to go into a tight turn because anytime you are in a fight, the first thing you do even after you get the guy in front of you is you turn tightly, because there's bound to be somebody on your tail. And boy, this time I had a hornet's nest full. All I could see was black crosses all around me.

I started doing vertical reverses and changing my direction. Then we all went into a Lufbery circle. I thought, "Oh boy, we're going to the right. That's good—I can out-turn anybody to the right," and sure enough, I hit another one. And he went in, and right behind him another 109 was throwing his flaps down. So I slapped my flaps down, brought them up and pulled them down again. I tried everything. I slid around, did a roll-over, then a barrel roll around, until I could get on the next guy.

We were just over where the first one had hit. The second one that I hit wasn't very far away, and I was able to nail another one. I gave him a short burst and then pulled up. I saw him crash near the other two. I didn't even bother to keep looking; I turned around, looking for the next guy. I got on the next 109, who was above me and to my right. To my left were some more 109s, and I could see two more sliding up toward me from behind. So, I thought, "Better make this a quick one, and turn around," and sure enough, just one quick burst and he flipped over.

This guy was as green as they get because as soon as he saw that I had a bead on him, he got rid of the canopy and he bailed out, and the aircraft hit the ground. I pulled around one more time. I'd been calling into the squadron, because I was getting a little nervous now, and I told them, "Well, these guys better hurry up because I don't know how long I can keep them cornered."

Anyway, I latched on to another 109, the last one that I hit, and he cartwheeled. I glanced at my watch and saw that less than three minutes had elapsed since I'd first encountered the jets. That's the thing about combat—time seems to slow way down. Then I saw three P-51s diving down. They wore silver noses, so I knew they were our flight. And sure enough, one was George Williams, the other, "Hot Shot" Charlie King, and the third guy was Charles Heathman.

Earlier on the ground Heathman had said to me, "Well, a lot of the guys don't always want to fly with you because you're always getting into trouble. You're the most aggressive guy in the squadron. We don't always want to seek it out."

I guess he was right. I had a knack for finding trouble.

We all joined up and circled the wreckage. I was going to try to take pictures of it and they said, "Well, there's four of them. They're real close together."

We then climbed back for the others, but they had just disappeared. I think they saw the rest of them coming down, and figured, "Well, there must be a whole bunch behind them. We better get out of here. If we're having trouble with one guy, we'll have much more with the rest of them."

The remaining 109s disappeared into the clouds and the undercast, and we climbed back up. We went to join the rest of the squadron, but I had to leave early because I had dropped my tanks early; I was running low on fuel. So the three that had joined up with me followed me home, while the rest of them kept on escorting the bombers.

When we got to England the others landed. I couldn't resist doing a victory roll. I knew I'd been in the fight of my life, and maybe I had been hit, so it was not a good idea to put the aircraft into violent maneuvers. But I thought, "What the heck." I came across the airfield and did a couple of rolls over the field before I came in and landed.

As I was I taxiing in, everybody was holding their hands up because they could see that the gunports were clear of tape. You broke the tape whenever you fired. The guns were always taped over to keep the air out of the barrels. My crew chiefs got up on the wing and they were patting me

479th Fighter Group Mustangs, looking for trouble COURTESY OF JAMES BUSHA

on the back; they actually lifted me out of the cockpit. I told them what had happened.

"Oh, you got five?" they asked.

And I said, "Well, I know I got four. Maybe five."

When I went to briefing, the others had arrived. I told them what I knew, and they said, "Well, you have to claim the 262, because if you hit him—and the right engine obviously was on fire—it caused the other damage, and he hit the undercast going at full speed. There's no way he could have pulled up."

And I said, "Well, okay. But I didn't see him hit the ground." I don't know if he actually hit the ground or he pulled out. At any rate, I put in for a kill, but the killjoys over at the Victory Credits Board decided it was a probable. Because I didn't see the pilot get out, and didn't see the aircraft hit the ground or explode, I was forced to call it a probable.

Later on, I had other witnesses that I didn't know about at the time—the bomber crews. They claimed that the 262 broke out into flames before he hit the undercast. But that claim came much later—when I ran into them as a prisoner of war.

Unlucky Thirteen

It was April 13, 1945—Friday the Thirteenth. We were northeast of Berlin near East Prussia, very close to the Polish border. On this mission I was assigned to Outlaw Squadron instead of Snow White. Snow White stayed with the bombers no matter what. Outlaw Squadron could go out and look for enemy aircraft or whatever they could find; or if they were on the ground, they could get them on the ground before they could take off.

We spotted a German airfield and I thought, "Well, there's an aircraft on the ground. Let's go get him." So we went down and made the first pass, which is always a diving pass. What you do is you roll over and you do a split-S and come down, so that you pick up as much speed as possible, and you're almost in a vertical position.

I saw two batteries of four guns each, and I said, "I've got the guns spotted. I'll go down and get them, and then you guys can set up a traffic pattern. We'll just knock the bejeezus out of them."

Well, that was a mistake. You never go down a second time. You always make one pass and keep going. I broke the cardinal rule. I went down and I got the first gun and was headed for the second battery of guns. But oh my God, there weren't two guns like I thought. All of a sudden, all the camouflage came off the other guns that were hidden, and they lit me up.

There were red marbles coming up my way, there were white sparklers—that was the light flak: 40 millimeters, 20 millimeters, and an occasional 88, but the 88s were bursting above me. They tore up in front of me and I ran right into it. And sure enough, as I headed across the field I jumped the hedge, staying as low as possible to make as small a target as possible, and zigzagging, but it was too late to zigzag. I have always zagged when I should have zigged.

My airspeed indicator went down to zero; a handful of 20 millimeters had gone through the instrument panel and hit the firewall. A lot of glass and so forth came flying back toward me, but, fortunately, my Mae West was thick enough to stop most of it. A few pieces got into my stomach and I felt something very warm. Blood was pouring out near my left ear. A lot of blood means real damage, but there wasn't any pain. You don't get pain when you've got all that adrenaline. You don't feel it.

My left arm was getting numb and there was blood there, but it was a small wound. I wasn't paying attention to the blood because I was trying to keep the engine running. I opened up the scoop and put it on manual, and opened it up. The others say it didn't come open. Hell, I couldn't see it. And one of them said, "Candy, I think you got a fire." They were right; it was getting very warm in there. And I said, "Yep. It's getting warm. I think I'll get out."

I didn't want to take a chance if there was a fire, because I had a fuselage tank that still had about 40 or 50 gallons in it. I wasn't going to take a chance, so I looked for a place to belly in, but there was nothing but trees that I could see.

Nothing clear there, so I headed for the Allied lines. I headed for Hamburg where I thought I could get to, but my Mustang had other plans. It was time to get out.

I went out over the side, pulled the ripcord, and my parachute blossomed. All of a sudden everything was really quiet, and real nice. I almost enjoyed it. I was swinging there in the air and then I heard aircraft engines. It was my flight coming back. They were going to cover me.

Sure enough, they did. I hit the ground and waved at them. I ran toward a haystack and thought, "No, that's the first place they'll look."

The Hunter Becomes the Hunted

There was a bunch of woods in front of me, so I headed for it. I got in there and saw that I had a lot of blood, and I couldn't figure out where it was coming from. My helmet was gone, and I reached up, and right above my ear, right behind my head, I had deep abrasions on my scalp. And then my left arm had been nicked, evidently by a bullet or something, because the flight suit was torn there. I remember I was upset because it was a brand-new shirt; my uniform was tarnished!

I buried my Mae West, which of course is a bright yellow, and I didn't want that to be seen. I went farther and then buried the parachute. The sun started to go down, I kept walking, and I kept walking, in a southwest direction. I had my little compass with me. I came to a lake and went around it, and by that time, it was dark, so I thought, "Well, if I get in the water, maybe I can swim across, and if they have dogs, they won't be able to trail me."

So, I took off my boots, tied them up, and put them around my neck. I thought, "Gee, I shouldn't have buried that Mae West. It sure would have come in handy."

I still had a little ways to cross, but the water was too darn cold, so I thought, "The heck with this." I headed for the shallow part and waited a while, then went ashore, dried out a little bit, put my boots back on. These were big fur-lined boots, big slumpy things, but, oh boy, they kept your feet warm.

I spent the night hiding out. The next day, I started walking again. I kept walking through the woods, avoiding anything that looked like homes or population of any kind. I walked the next two days until I ran into two soldiers. And then, bad things happened.

I'd been so careful. I had gotten past the edge of a field and all of a sudden, I heard "Halt! Halt!" in German. I thought, "Oh no." I looked around. I hadn't seen these two soldiers. Actually, they were Panzer division guys, because they had the black uniform, and they didn't have helmets, they had caps.

I was wearing a white scarf, not only to keep my neck warm, but to keep my neck from getting chafed, because your head's swinging from left to right constantly. So, I took the white scarf off and I waved it. I was ready to give up. And bang! I heard this report. I hadn't heard anything else, but I saw this quick flash, and a few seconds later, another report, and, whoa, they were shooting at me. The second one fired at me, so I waved it again, and I dropped to the ground and held it above me, waving the white flag.

I could hear their report, but before I heard the bang, I would hear like a rustling through the brush or tall grass, and then a thud as it hit the ground. So, I began rolling. I guess they could still see the waving of the brush because they fired at me again. Now they were walking toward me. I could hear them talking to each other. One of them even laughed. They had no intention of letting me surrender. They were coming toward me, and I kept trying to get lower and crawl backward, but I couldn't get any lower.

Then I realized I had a .45 pistol that I wore in a shoulder harness. I took out the .45 and I could feel my hands trembling. Was I scared? I guess I was. Anyway, they fired again and I saw them coming. They weren't putting the rifles to their shoulders. They were firing at waist level. I thought, "They're not going to hit anything that way." Either they were trying to scare me, or they were trying to get me to sit up or stand up or run. And I thought, "If I run, they're going to hit me in the back."

They were coming toward me, and the one on the left was a bigger guy than the other one. He had this great big belt buckle with a big swastika on it. I was lying as flat as I could, and I was resting the pistol. I held the .45, aiming right at his belt. He got closer and closer, and then he saw me, and he lifted the rifle to put it on his shoulder, and I fired, and I didn't see anything else.

I must have blinked when I fired because all I saw was the soles of his boots as he tumbled over backward. I immediately turned toward the other one who had swung his rifle toward me. Then I hit him and his rifle went flying off. I fired two more times. I fired three shots at him. I don't know which ones hit him, or if two of them hit him. He went down. With the .45, if you get hit in the wingtip, on your fingertip, you're going to go down. They were so close that I just couldn't miss.

I waited a good five minutes. Then, I crawled up to the first one. I had hit him in the head, almost between the eyes, on his forehead. There was a little hole in the front of his head, and the whole back of his head was gone.

I crawled over to the other one, still aiming the gun at him. He was dead too. I thought, "Oh well. I better get their weapons, and at least I'll have a couple of guns." Then I stopped myself, thinking, "If I get captured, and I may, they're going to know I'm the one that killed these two guys—and they're not going to treat me too nicely, so I better just leave them alone."

So, I took off. I put a fresh clip in my .45 and started trotting and zigzagging and got away from there.

For the next day and a half I kept moving. I hadn't had any water, and, boy, I was thirsty. I came to a stream and I could see some animals, some cows and stuff, and they were drinking downstream. So I went down and I took a drink. I filled my little rubber bag, and put some Halazone tablets in it to purify the water.

I noticed a big wagon, and it had what looked like hay in it. All of a sudden, from behind it, I heard this yell, and here were these two guys. They looked like they were farmers. I didn't know. They were in their forties, I guess. They had these pitchforks with two prongs that were razor sharp.

They began running toward me. They weren't that far away, and I looked and remembered hearing stories of pilots getting pitchforked. They'd get pinned to a tree, and the attackers would call the military, but sometimes by the time the military got there, the pilots had died.

I thought, "Oh, they're going to use that pitchfork—not as long as I have that .45."

I waited, knowing that they were not very accurate at long range. I waited, and they kept rushing me. I took the gun out with my back toward them. Then, I turned to the side and pointed the gun at them. They kept coming. I told them to halt. They kept coming, with their pitchforks raised. I fired, and hit the first one. I hit the second one with just two shots, and they both went down. They were obviously dead, sure enough.

I took off and started running again. I headed south, and kept going for another seven or eight days before a squad of German soldiers caught up with me in an abandoned cabin. These guys treated me fair, and a German doctor treated my wounds. I ended up sitting out the last few weeks of the war as a POW.

Checkertail Ace: P-51

JOINING THE CHECKERTAILS

Col. Barrie S. Davis

325th Fighter Group, 317th Fighter Squadron, 15th Air Force

By the time I caught up to the 325th Fighter Group, they had been on the move a lot, chasing the Germans from the deserts of North Africa into Italy. On March 29, 1944, hardly a month before I joined the Checkertail Clan, they had moved to Lesina, where I joined them.

Two days after I joined the 317th, a dapper-looking major with no wings on his chest directed us new arrivals to Maj. Herschel "Herky" Green's tent, where we had our first look at the legendary fighter pilot. Major Green had been with the 325th Squadron when it crossed the Atlantic on an aircraft carrier in January 1943.

The previous day, one of the older pilots had told us a little bit about Major Green, the leading ace of the Mediterranean Theater. He became commander of the 317th in March. We were eager to see him and meet our new boss, but we were a bit disappointed. He was three inches taller than I was, much thinner, had somewhat of

Nineteen-year-old Barrie Davis just after earning his wings COURTESY OF BARRIE DAVIS

a beak nose, and looked older than his twenty-three years. His tent was not fancy, especially considering that he was the squadron commander. The wall tent's only special feature was a small AM radio salvaged from a wrecked fighter, which was tuned to Axis Sally and her American songs.

"Sit down," invited Major Green. He shook hands with each of us. "Welcome," he continued. "I want to tell you that the German Air Force isn't through. Their pilots are good, and they are dangerous. Don't let anyone tell you they are finished." After a few more words, Major Green indicated we could leave.

We knew we were going to have a lot of learning to do after that first day, but we also realized we had a great leader to teach us.

Switcheroo

In May 1944, we traded our rugged P-47 Thunderbolts for P-51 Mustangs. We knew the P-51 was better than the P-47 for long-range escort. A Thunderbolt carried two external wing tanks, and each contained 165 gallons of gasoline. It had 305 gallons of fuel in internal tanks, making a total of 635 gallons (although with only 269 gallons internally, and 150 in the droppable wing tanks).

Although the Mustang had much greater range, some of our pilots were apprehensive. They knew the P-47s were bigger, more rugged, and had proved over and over again that they could bring pilots back after suffering unbelievable damage. The Mustang, with a liquid-cooled in-line engine, had lots of plumbing, carrying coolant and oil from the engine to the radiators in the rear of the fuselage. It seemed far more fragile. "One bullet could take me out of the sky," a pilot complained.

In addition, the Thunderbolt had eight machine guns. The P-51B and C had only four. We felt almost naked with this loss of firepower. Once our P-51s had arrived, the tails were painted with the group's yellow-and-black checkerboard decoration, while our numbers were painted on the sides. My number was 24. Names were painted on the nose. I had the name *Honey Bee*, which was my mother's nickname.

On June 28, 1944, the 325th Fighter Group flying P-51 Mustangs had a mission to sweep the skies in the Budapest area, warding off any enemy fighters that tried to thwart the bombers in their mission. I was flying as element leader in Wayne Lowry's flight when someone spotted formations of thirty to thirty-five Fw 190s and Me 109s below. Drop tanks fell from our wings as we dove to attack the enemy fighters. The Germans were intent on the bombers and only saw us at the last minute. We dove out of the sun at 18,000 feet and the battle soon turned into a melee. So many US and enemy planes were twisting and turning in such a small portion of the sky that it seemed impossible to sight on a Messerschmitt or Focke-Wulf without a Mustang crossing the line of fire.

Finally, I tagged on to an Fw 190, laid my gunsight on its tail, and began shooting from dead astern. The four .50 calibers in the P-51's wings chattered as pieces flew off the Focke-Wulf. Then, running full bore, I nearly climbed up the Fw's tail when the pilot chopped his throttle. I shoved my stick forward and my head slammed against the canopy. My P-51 nosedived just below the Fw 190. The fight ended as quickly as it began as enemy fighters scattered in every direction, trying to evade pursuing Checkertails.

I returned to Lesina knowing I had laid fatal damage on the Focke-Wulf, but I could not report firsthand that I had seen it destroyed. I would claim at least a damaged 190. During debriefing, I told of the fight, and when I finished my story, I asked if we could review the gun camera film when it was developed, to see if it showed more than I could tell.

My flight leader overheard my request and said, "Davis got it. I saw an Fw 190 flame, and then it exploded."

I had chalked up my first kill.

Blackout

I was flight leader on July 3, 1944, and the 325th Group had a mission of protecting bombers and attacking targets in the Giurgiu, Hungary, area. The 317th Squadron provided sixteen planes in four flights. One plane of my flight had problems soon after takeoff and returned home. I continued with my three-plane formation south of Budapest, several thousand feet above the rest of the Checkertails.

Looking around I saw three vapor trails. With my two wingmen following, I made a slight turn toward the sun in the east and began climbing. When we reached 33,000 feet, three Me 109s turned in to us. I fired three short bursts at the first two and then closed on the third, firing two short bursts from about 300 yards and 30 yards' deflection. Coolant streamed from the Messerschmitt, and it split-S'ed in an attempt to escape. I latched on to him and followed as he dove straight down.

At 18,000 feet pieces broke loose from the Me 109 and then the right wing tip and right stabilizer ripped away. Still, we dove faster and faster. My airspeed indicator moved past 510 miles an hour, above the Mustang's red line. At 15,000 feet, the enemy jettisoned his canopy and bailed out. His chute deployed immediately, but it ripped loose from its shroud lines as the helpless pilot passed over my right wing.

I pulled back on the stick, and the centrifugal force generated by the high-speed pullup forced blood from my head, causing me to gray out. And then, as centrifugal force continued, I lost consciousness. My vision returned gradually. I looked outside and found I was in a climbing turn. I looked ahead and was surprised to see shell burst. The altimeter said I was passing through 18,000 feet. How come I was seeing small-caliber antiaircraft burst over 3 miles in the air? Uh-oh, that wasn't flak.

P-51 Mustang ace Barrie Davis with his mount, *Speedy* COURTESY OF BARRIE DAVIS

I hauled back on the stick, threw it to the right, and jammed right rudder. Looking back, I saw an Me 109 lobbing shells at me. Its pilot was a poor shot, or else he would have nailed me with the first round. A quick tight turn put me back behind the Me 109, and I fired three bursts at 300 yards, with no hits. At 250 yards, I began firing from dead astern and continued firing until I was about 50 yards behind him. Flashes appeared all over its fuselage, mostly around the cockpit. I kept shooting, and the Me 109 went into a steep dive. At 13,000 feet, it exploded.

Suddenly, it seemed the lights went out. The world went black as a tar-like substance covered my windshield and canopy. It was oil from the enemy fighter. I couldn't see outside the cockpit and I knew it was time to leave the battle and go home.

I set a compass course for Lesina and began a long climb, hoping no other enemy fighters were in the vicinity. If I could get to 30,000 feet and stay there until over the Adriatic, I might be safe from both German fighters and flak. An hour later, cruising at 31,000 feet, the black oil began to thin on the sides of the canopy.

I approached Lesina and called for landing instructions. As I dived at the runway, I pulled up into a double victory roll and circled to land. With my canopy all the way back, I looked out the sides of the cockpit to make a smooth landing. I taxied to my assigned tie-down and John Mauney, my faithful crew chief, climbed carefully up on the oil-slicked wing. He opened the canopy and asked sadly, "Did your prop spring a leak, sir?"

"That's German oil," I replied, much to John's relief.

Unlucky German

On a beautiful morning in August, we escorted bombers to Bucharest. For the 325th, it was an uneventful mission. We watched for enemy fighters over the target, and when another group took over our escort duties, we set a course for home.

Below us and to our left cumulus clouds were building into towering thunderheads. Showers were forecast for Yugoslavia in the late afternoon. When we approached Yugoslavia, we dropped down to 12,000 feet. The sixteen planes of the 317th Squadron were flying in a long line. I was fifth from the left end. Oxygen masks came off, and those who smoked began to light up.

When a plane approached from the left, at a distance, we believed it was a P-51 from another squadron joining us. Then, with a jolt, we realized it was a Messerschmitt 109.

Immediately eight Mustangs broke left, firewalled throttles, and roared after the plane, whose pilot must have been daydreaming worse than we were. The 109 turned tail and headed straight for the towering cumulus cloud. Four P-51s were behind the 109 and me. There was no way I could get it first, but I conjectured that if I dived under the cloud he was entering, maybe I'd be waiting for him when he came out.

I circled underneath the cloud at 5,000 feet, watching and waiting. Then, I saw a parachute float out of the cloud. Somebody had scored a victory, and the enemy pilot had bailed out.

As the pilot floated downward, I saw his plane coming from the cloud in sweeping turns. It looked as though someone was flying it. Tighter and tighter it turned, losing very little altitude with each circle. Then, it banked toward the hapless pilot, cut through the shroud lines connecting him to his parachute, and spiraled down to crash against the mountain below. The pilot plummeted to earth while his parachute floated slowly after him.

"Who is going to believe this?" I thought. "We get the airplane and the airplane gets its pilot."

Even Fighter Pilots Get Bored

On August 12, 1944, the 325th had a mission to strafe radar stations on the French coast. It was preparation for the invasion of southern France that took place later in August. "Stay on the water," was the command during morning briefing. "Anyone above 50 feet is subject to be shot down." That was sufficient motivation to keep us low.

A 325th P-51 Mustang, *Bee*, sits on the ramp waiting for its next mission. COURTESY OF BARRIE DAVIS

It was fascinating, seeing nearly fifty P-51s skimming across the water, pulling rooster tails with their prop wash. One pilot was overly cautious in his efforts to escape being shot for flying too high. He flew closer and closer to the water until, finally, his prop cut the waves, the Mustang cartwheeled across the water, and then disappeared from sight. Score one for the water.

As we approached the coast, I searched for anything that might be radar. Suddenly I saw what looked like a massive antenna behind buildings. I had a split second to shoot, and I sprayed the antenna and passed low across the building. It probably was not a radar antenna, but I had done the best I could. We gained altitude, re-formed our formations, and returned to Lesina. To me, it was a wasted day.

The next morning we were back over southern France, this time escorting B-24s' bombing gun positions in the Sete area. Again, there was no enemy opposition. Another dull day for fighters.

Outnumbered But Not Outgunned

On August 22, 1944, we completed our mission of providing target cover for bombers attacking an oil refinery at Odertal, Germany. No enemy aircraft were observed. As usual, my flight was easy on gas and, with plenty of fuel, we stayed with our Big Friends.

While the remainder of the group set course for home, a call for help was heard. Looking back, I saw two Me 109s attacking a straggling bomber. I led my four-plane flight in a tight turn and pushed the throttle forward to close on the attackers. One Me 109 attacked the B-17 from the rear. I cheered when I saw the attacking Messerschmitt explode and go down in flames as the guns on the Flying Fortress found their mark. A second Me 109 dove away as we approached.

Fifteen miles west of Lake Balaton, Hungary, six Fw 190s swarmed around a hapless B-17 at 17,000 feet. With an engine flamed and other damage, the big bomber began spinning downward. We counted parachutes—one, two, three, four, five—but there were no more. At least four of the crew went down with their plane.

I shoved my throttle forward and led my flight directly at the enemy fighters, firing short bursts at two before tacking onto a third. I kept firing as the range shortened from 500 yards to 50 yards, noting hits around the cockpit. The enemy aircraft went into a spin at 12,000 feet and I followed it down, breaking off at 1,000 feet when I found another Fw 190 following me. As I climbed, for altitude, I looked back and saw two planes burning on the ground. My wingman, John Conant, confirmed the kill. He said he watched the Fw 190 crash.

The fight was far from over. More struggling bombers were limping home. We gained altitude and turned north where six Me 109s were attacking a B-17 and a B-24. The attackers dispersed as we came near. I followed one Me 109 down to 3,000 feet, then broke the attack to return to the bombers. Another Me 109 came at me from the rear. I broke left, and after four turns, I was on the German's tail. Suddenly, his plane slowed as though it had brakes. It was the same trick enemy pilots had used successfully in the past. Cut the throttle, drop flaps, lower landing gear. Often, an attacking American would zoom past the German before he could cut his speed and he'd find himself being the hunted instead of the hunter.

I chopped throttle, dropped flaps, and flew underneath the Messerschmitt as we both slowed more, and more, and more. I looked directly overhead and counted rivets on the bottom of the Me 109. I saw oil streaks extending from the engine. My indicated airspeed dropped below 100 miles an hour, and I wondered how much slower the Mustang could hang in the air. The enemy pilot rocked his wings, trying to see where I had gone. But I was directly underneath him and he never saw me. Satisfied that he had escaped, he rolled to the right in a shallow dive. I banked directly behind him and began shooting. I fired and fired again. I pulled on the trigger and held it. All six machine guns were chattering, but no hits were showing. I was puzzled.

We strung tracers, fifty rounds from the end of the ammo belts, so we would know when we were nearly out of ammunition. I watched red tracers come from my wing guns and my eyes followed them as they went around the fuselage of the German plane, over its wings, and converged in front of the propeller. I was so close that the guns were shooting around both sides of the Me 109 fuselage. I kicked rudder slightly and saw hits on the fuselage and around the cockpit. Smoke streamed from the engine. At

2,000 feet, the pilot bailed out. I was so close that I saw the nails on the bottom of his boots as he left his plane and sailed past me.

That night, we celebrated with drinks in our tiny squadron's officers' club, listening to Axis Sally. She told of vicious battles fought that day by the gallant Luftwaffe against the 15th Air Force. According to Sally, the victorious Germans had destroyed numerous American bombers and successfully defended themselves from hundreds of US fighters.

"We must've done pretty good," I told the other three members of my flight, "for the Germans to report there were hundreds of us."

(Barrie Davis ended the war with six aerial victories.)

Angel in My Pocket: P-47

LOW-LEVEL P-47 THUNDERBOLT COMBAT
Lt. Col. Robert V. Brulle
366th Fighter Group, 390th Fighter Squadron, 9th Air Force

A BURNING DESIRE TO FLY

I crashed and burned during my very first aerial adventure. As a young boy growing up in Chicago, I made rubber-band balsa-wood airplane models. One day, to impress the neighborhood gang, I sprinkled a little gas on the nose of the airplane, climbed up on our garage roof, set the plane on fire, and launched it. It promptly dove straight into the ground, setting my father's well-kept lawn on fire. My father forbade me from ever doing stunts like that again. Although I promised him I would stop, I was hooked on flying and wanted to be a fighter pilot, like Errol Flynn in the movie *The Dawn Patrol*.

On Thanksgiving Day, 1942, my path to the skies began as I was sworn into the US Army Air Corps and went on active duty in late January of 1943. By the time I earned my wings, I had a total of 208 hours of flying time in Stearman PT-17s, Vultee BT-13s, and North American AT-6s. And just like my hero, Errol Flynn, I became a fighter pilot on February 8, 1944.

Tricks of the Trade

After cutting my teeth in a P-40 Warhawk for ten hours and finding out firsthand what the deadly combination of a long nose and a powerful engine could do on takeoff—if you didn't keep enough right rudder in to counter the effects of torque—I was sent to Bradley Field in Connecticut to meet the airplane of my dreams: the Republic P-47 Thunderbolt. With a gross weight of over 7 tons, the P-47 was a behemoth. Powered by a Pratt & Whitney R-2800 radial engine, the Thunderbolt could zoom to 40,000 feet and cruise along at 400 mph. (Ironically, in combat I never went above 18,000 feet, as a majority of my missions were down on the deck.)

The P-47 was rock-solid in the air, especially in a dive; it dove just like a grand piano. Our stateside instructors warned us about the effects of compressibility in a dive. Loss of control and frozen controls all followed in an uncontrollable dive. We were taught that our only option was to wait until we passed through 15,000 feet, when the shock waves would disappear in warmer air. Low-level navigation also took some getting used to, especially in a fighter that moves quite quickly over the ground. Thankfully all of our practice was back in the States, where we controlled the skies—unless, of course, we were jumped by some hotshot marines in their F4U Corsairs. The Corsair could outclimb and out-turn us, but we could always out-roll them.

As the training hours ticked by, the air corps finally trusted us enough with real bombs and ammunition. Gunnery training was performed over Long Island, as we fired at towed targets. Then we practiced dive-bombing, with 100-pound bombs strapped under our wings. I was a better dive-bomber pilot than I was shooting my guns because I always waited until the last second to drop my bombs. That did have its drawbacks, however, as more than once I came back from combat missions with damage to my P-47 caused by my own bombs.

With over 75 hours of P-47 time in my logbook, I was deemed combat-ready and sent to England in late June of 1944.

When I arrived at Atcham Field, the final training phase before assignment to a combat unit, I met my new instructors. These pilots were all combat veterans with the 8th Air Force who were being rotated home after finishing their tour. There were four of us that drew a captain from the 56th Fighter Group (Zemke's Wolfpack), and he made us forget everything we were taught back home on how to fly a Thunderbolt. We

Robert V. Brulle seems to have been swallowed whole as he sits in the massive cockpit of his P-47 Thunderbolt. COURTESY ROBERT BRULLE

stalled the P-47 going straight up; we did extended spins and negative-g maneuvers; and we performed a split-S at 2,000 feet and survived.

It was during this training phase, which only lasted 25 hours, that I got myself into some very dangerous and unusual situations. But one thing I found was that I really became at home while flying the Thunderbolt.

Down on the Deck

In late July of 1944 I was assigned to the 366th Fighter Group, 390th Fighter Squadron, of the 9th Air Force. Having missed the D-Day invasion of Normandy by almost two months, I joined my new squadron near Omaha Beach at a forward airstrip called A-1. We shared our base with a P-38 Lightning unit, and most of my early missions were in support of the breakout from Normandy, along with some sporadic escort missions of B-26 Marauders. For the most part, however, we stayed on the deck, looking for German targets of opportunity—and there were plenty to find in that arena.

The Germans were for the most part in a full retreat back home. Vehicles of all shapes and sizes seemed to be everywhere, and so were their murderous flak guns that accompanied them. In order to make a claim of a destroyed vehicle, we had to either leave it burning, see it explode, or strafe it twice. Once a German convoy was spotted, our initial attack was to drop our 500-pound bombs and then set up a pattern to strafe them. I was taught early on to focus on one target and not to try to strafe the whole column. The trick was to give it a short burst. With eight .50 caliber machine guns focusing on one place, it was a tremendous amount of firepower that was sure to be unsurvivable.

As the GIs on the ground advanced, so did our P-47 group. From Normandy we were assigned to A-41 near Dreux, France, then on to A-70 at Laon, France, before moving into Y-29 near Asch, Belgium, in November of 1944. The mission briefs seemed to become shorter and shorter: search and destroy German barges, trains, and armor. Trains had their own set of problems because the Germans were camouflaging flak guns on flatcars that were hidden behind canvas sides. When we came roaring in to attack, the sides came down and the flak came up. Although the P-47 could take a tremendous amount of damage, we continued to lose many good men and aircraft to the murderous German antiaircraft fire.

The month of December ushered in fog, rain, and heavy snow—a perfect cover for the German push toward the Ardennes region of Belgium. While the German Panzers on the ground pushed forward, creating a bulge in our front lines, we could only hope and pray the weather would clear so we could assault their advance.

The day before Christmas Eve the weather cleared and the sky was filled with fighters and bombers from both the 9th Air Force and the 8th Air Force as we slugged it out with the Luftwaffe in the sky and the Panzer troops on the ground.

One of the 352nd Fighter Group P-51 Mustangs, *The Hawk-Eye Owan*, that was part of the New Year's Day melee COURTESY OF SAM SOX

Around this same time, P-51 Mustangs of the 352nd Fighter Group of the 8th Air Force, known as the "Blue-Nosed Bastards of Bodney," were temporarily assigned to Y-29. Their job was to provide top cover for us while we performed our dive-bombing and strafing missions around Belgium and Germany. Our tempo only increased as we flew multiple missions each day, forcing the Germans to give up the ground they had gained. The New Year was right around the corner. As we held out hope that the war would be over soon, we also took no day for granted. We knew there were surprises around every corner.

New Year's Surprise

To welcome in the New Year, the Luftwaffe sent over some night raiders to drop sticks of bombs near our base at Y-29 around midnight. The antiaircraft fire from our guns was impressive, but it kept us up half the night. I was one of eight pilots in the squadron that would fly a mission the next morning, and that night I complained to my crew chief, Staff Sgt. Al Czaplicki, that I had yet to see a German aircraft during my tour and figured I would never have the opportunity to shoot one down. Little did I know how wrong I would be just a few hours later.

My bubble-top P-47 was down for maintenance so I was assigned a razorback model that belonged to the group commander, with the nose art of *Flying Carpet*. Around 9:00 a.m. the eight of us taxied our Thunderbolts for takeoff toward the southwest for our short flight to the front lines. While our group lined up for takeoff, there were twelve P-51s from the 352nd Fighter Group, led by Col. John C. Meyer, pointing their Mustang noses toward the northeast, waiting for us to lift off. Once we were airborne, the Mustangs would launch and shepherd us to the front lines so we could bomb and strafe the ground targets while they flew high cover and protected us from any Luftwaffe fighters that may be in the area.

By the time our P-47s had lifted off and made a 180-degree turn we knew something was wrong. One of our Thunderbolt pilots observed antiaircraft fire to our left, and as we turned to investigate I was amazed at what was below me: the largest gaggle of German fighters I had ever seen. Roaring in at 200 feet, it was a mixture of over fifty Fw 190s and Me 109s attacking Y-32, a nearby British airfield.

I jettisoned my bombs and armed my guns as I made wingover to attack. I caught a glimpse of the blue-nosed Mustangs all lined up below and then shifted my focus to an Fw 190 that was out ahead of the gaggle. As I locked on him I began chasing his tail as he dove a few feet above the deck at full throttle.

Because he was so low I couldn't get guns on him, my bullets zipping harmlessly out in front of him. I chased him a bit more before I noticed a white puff of smoke from his engine. He chopped his throttle, thinking I would overshoot him. I instantly jerked my throttle back as I found myself flying canopy to canopy with him.

For a second I became frustrated and thought about pulling my .45 caliber pistol and firing it at him. But he shoved his throttle forward again and I slid back into my familiar spot behind his tail. The German pilot's luck finally ran out when I observed a group of trees looming up ahead in the distance. The Fw 190 pulled up as I pulled the trigger, unleashing eight .50 caliber machine guns. The German fighter exploded and my windscreen was instantly covered in oil.

Simultaneously I spotted another Fw 190, and as I locked onto his tail, cannon shells began to arch over my canopy. I began a roll to the right, then snapped into a hard left turn. I looked behind and saw an Me 109 lobbing cannon shells at me. I pushed the throttle through the gate and went to war emergency power as I tightened my turn, completing a full 360-degree turn.

The 109 broke away as I went looking for another target. It wasn't hard to find one, as there were fighters all over the sky.

I zeroed in on another 190 and gave it a squirt, nicking him before my guns ran dry. I turned to the west at 200 feet and flew directly over Y-29—a big mistake on my part. The trigger-happy antiaircraft gunners protecting our base opened up on me as I wagged my wings, signaling that I was a friend.

I climbed to 3,000 feet, just below the cloud deck, where I had a front-row seat to the action below. I watched both P-47s and P-51s slugging it out and chasing Luftwaffe fighters in all directions. I even dove on an Me 109 that was being chased by two Mustangs; one of them bagged him as the 109 took the bait and turned toward me.

Spotting a break in the action, I decided to return to Y-29 and land. Thankfully I wasn't shot at by my own gunners this time. As I turned off the runway, two Me 109s roared nearby, strafing the field, a P-51 hot on their tails. The gunners on the ground all opened up on the 109s and, unfortunately, didn't lead them enough, as their rounds impacted the poor P-51, piloted by Lt. Dean Huston, who was seconds away from shooting both of the 109s down. With his engine shot out, Lieutenant Houston dead-sticked his Mustang into Y-29.

By the time the German sneak attack, code-named Operation Bodenplatte, was over, we had lost one P-47 and had two others damaged, with eight confirmed German victories and no loss of pilots to our group. The 352nd Mustangs had a field day, with twenty-one victories among the twelve Mustang pilots. Even the antiaircraft gunners claimed four victories, not including any P-51 Mustangs!

For the Germans who had unleashed over eight hundred fighters that day on various Allied airfields throughout Europe, they not only ended up losing countless fighters but experienced pilots as well. Any hope the Luftwaffe had to turn the tide of the war had evaporated, transformed into the smoking wrecks of German fighters scattered across Europe.

Our celebrations were short-lived, however, as we resumed our ground-pounding missions on our march into Germany. By the time the war ended in Europe, I had accumulated over 156 flying hours of combat in seventy missions.

I later flew the P-51 Mustang and P-80 Shooting Star jet, and wouldn't trade my P-47 Thunderbolt for them in combat. The P-47 could not only hold its own against Fw 190s and Me 109s, but it could also withstand the murderous ground fire. Although beat-up and bruised on many missions, the P-47 always brought me back home. I was one of the lucky ones, because in fifteen months of combat, our group lost 95 pilots and 135 aircraft. I truly had an angel in my pocket.

24

Killer Corsair: F4U

An Ace with the Death Rattlers
Capt. Albert P. Wells
VMF-323, US Marine Corps

In 1943 I was a twenty-one-year-old green second lieutenant when I joined VMF-323 at El Toro as a replacement. The original squadron had gathered earlier at Cherry Point, where they began forming a marine fighter squadron called the Death Rattlers. Unfortunately, they didn't have any fighters; the early pilots had to learn fighter tactics in SNJ trainers before F4U Corsairs began to trickle in.

The squadron CO was a twenty-three-year-old "boy" major named George Axtell Jr. Although he was the same age as most of us—and the youngest CO of a fighter squadron in the US Marine Corps—he was a no-nonsense commander who instilled discipline in all of us and made us the best damn marine fighter squadron of the war! Although most of us feared him and had to endure his wrath, he was a damn fine CO—even though he placed me under arrest twice.

The first time was when we were training at Camp Pendleton and I came back with a bunch of wires hanging from the belly of my Corsair. By the time I landed, Major Axtell had received a phone call that one of his Corsairs was "flat-hatting" and had snipped some wires. He asked what I did and I told him I must have flown between two mountaintops and sliced a wire. Of course he didn't believe my bold-faced lie, and I was

US Marine Corps pilot Albert P. Wells waits for the takeoff signal at the controls of his Corsair. COURTESY OF ALBERT WELLS

confined to my bunk for ten days. Behind his back we called him the "Big Ax"—and boy, could he wield it when he was angry!

For the next four to five months, we got down to business. Major Axtell really worked us hard and showed us how to fly and fight in a

Corsair. We did a lot of gunnery—one guy towing a sleeve while the rest of us riddled it with bullets dipped in paint. From there we practiced dive-bombing and close air support, all of which we utilized on an almost daily basis when we got into combat on Okinawa, supporting the mud marines on the ground.

Combat in Okinawa

We landed on that godforsaken island in early April of 1945. The actual ground assault landing occurred on April 1, and we catapulted our Corsairs from a Jeep carrier on April 9. I remembered the day quite vividly, because the next day was my twenty-third birthday. Actually, I shared the same birthday with a very popular guy in the squadron named Louie Brown. We were both born in 1922, and to find out who was "older," we both wrote home to see the actual hour we were born! Since our training days we had saved a bottle of booze that we vowed to open on our birthday once we got into combat.

When we landed on the afternoon of April 9, we were greeted by a marine colonel from the Wing who gave us a big lecture and guaranteed that we were going to be taken care of, and that we wouldn't have to fly in bad weather. The very next day in the early-morning hours, around four a.m., it was raining like hell. It was pitch dark out and I thought, "Well, there ain't no way we are going to fly today." As usual, I was wrong.

We were told to get in our airplanes and wait for the signal to take off. I was soaking wet, as the canopy glass kept fogging over. It was ridiculous at best, as I would open the canopy to get some air flowing and then immediately become soaked again. It seemed like a lifetime of waiting and wondering until Major Axtell came over the radio and said we were going to take off.

The weather was really terrible, and the rain was coming down hard, but he took off first, followed by everyone else. No one joined up because we were immediately on instruments when our wheels left the ground. It was pretty hairy, with Corsairs flying all over the place.

Somehow after droning around we were able to get low enough, below the clouds, and find the airfield and get back in. We lost one pilot that day when we returned to base: Louie Brown, my birthday mate. I ended up drinking the bottle of booze myself that night, in honor of Louie.

First Kill

Because of the weather we stayed on the ground the rest of that day, and it was more of the same on April 11, with heavy rain and overcast, so we were ordered to stand down. But on April 12 the rain began to let up, and once again we were in our Corsairs in the very early morning.

Just as dawn arrived on Okinawa, my plane captain was sitting on my wing and we were talking when all of sudden he jumped off and began running away. Tracer rounds were streaming down the the runway—Japanese airplanes were shooting at us!

The whole squadron began cranking up their Corsairs to take off and shoot down some Japanese airplanes. The problem was, our airplanes had sat there in the rain and were now stuck in the mud. Two or three guys tried so hard to get their Corsairs un-stuck that they ended up having their props pull them right over on their noses. Fortunately I was able to free my Corsair and waddle over to the runway.

On that mission I was supposed to be the seventh guy to take off, leading the second section of the first division, but I found myself first in line on the runway. I sat there for a minute, because I really didn't know what to do—wait for orders to take off, or just go? The decision was made for me when a Tony fighter flew low over the east-to-west runway heading south and dropped a bomb on a tent near the runway, which housed the controllers, killing most of them.

I knew I wasn't going to wait any longer. I slowly shoved the throttle forward, trying to get my tail up to flying speed while I dodged rain-filled bomb craters. The Tony had made a gentle left-hand turn heading back north to Japan, and I was able to keep him in sight the whole time. I was able to get my Corsair airborne and stayed inside of his turn; he never knew I was behind him. Because this was my first combat, I wanted to make sure I did everything by the book. I charged my guns hydraulically, turned on all the switches, and even remembered to turn on the gunsight, but it was too bright in the darkness, so I turned it off just before I took off.

F4U-1D Corsairs of VMF-323 escort an F-5 Photo Lightning. COURTESY OF ALBERT WELLS

I was less than a thousand feet high when I slid behind the Tony and opened up with my six .50 caliber machine guns, at fairly close range. He immediately did a split-S and I began to follow him down. Fortunately I broke away from him before he hit the water below.

I pulled up and got really excited as I congratulated myself. I wanted to go after more Japanese airplanes, but found that my Corsair wasn't performing very well, and I couldn't figure out why. The engine seemed to be running well and the instruments were all reading fine. Finally I looked down and saw the problem: In my excitement I'd forgotten to pull the damn gear handle up!

Needless to say, when I returned to base and received accolades from my fellow squadron mates for achieving the squadron's first kill, I didn't acknowledge the fact that I'd done it with my wheels down.

Ground Support

To me the ground support missions were a heck of a lot more challenging and rewarding than shooting down an enemy airplane on a combat air patrol. On a ground support mission, you always accomplished something. We strafed targets, bombed them, threw napalm at them, or launched rockets on it all in support of the marines on the ground. On CAPs we would go out and circle the ships below and drone around for three hours, waiting to be directed to an incoming bogey.

On one particular ground mission we had been directed to cruise around a certain area where a lot of suspected Japanese artillery was located, wreaking havoc on our ground marines. We dropped down low and began buzzing all these dirt roads. Just as I rounded a bend in a road, I saw a hut with a thatched roof in front of me. Suddenly the whole roof flashed bright yellow, which indicated they were hiding artillery inside. Instinctively I hit the rocket button on the throttle without even thinking. I was only 50 feet off the ground and 100 yards away from it, moving fast.

The rocket got to the hut just as I was passing overhead, as pieces of the hut and whatever lay inside came up in this great big cloud. A palm beam went into my right wing and lodged in my oil cooler. I knew it had penetrated because I was rapidly losing oil pressure and could see the oil pouring out.

I reefed back on the stick and climbed for as much sky as I could get. Thankfully it was a nice clear day and I was only 10 to 15 miles away from the air base at Kadena. I really didn't think I was going to make it, but the Corsair kept on ticking and I was able to make it back in okay. The front lines were only about 10 miles away, and there was never a day we didn't have something to shoot at. We had total air superiority, and the only Japanese aircraft we saw were the kamikazes that went after our ships that were stationed offshore.

Devil in Disguise

A bulletin posted on our ops board before one CAP mission said to be on the lookout for an F4F Wildcat with an inverted "T"-like marking on one of its wings; it had been observed flying over the front lines. Once it passed overhead, Japanese artillery opened up and hit our troops in the front lines.

It was speculated that this F4F had somehow been captured by the Japanese and they were using it for spotting artillery against our people.

Shortly thereafter, one of our flight leaders, a guy named Ed Murray, was leading a division of Corsairs when one of the guys spotted an F4F flying nearby. Ed peeled off and flew under the guy, and, by God, it had an inverted T painted on a wing. Ed announced to the rest of the flight, "That's it, that's it—let's go get him!"

It was a comedy of errors as the next Corsair in line mauled that Wildcat. The third Corsair in line was on deck to attack when he said, "Wait a minute—there are a couple more over here with the same markings." The Wildcat was riddled with bullet holes; it was amazing it had even stayed in the sky, let alone continued to fly. The order was given to "knock it off" as the Wildcat staggered into our base to land, followed by the red-faced Corsair pilots. We all wanted to apologize to the guy for a case of mistaken identity, but we knew he was going to be mad as hell and would probably whip the whole bunch of us! So much for our intelligence.

CAP Encounters

The whole reason for a CAP was to try to locate the incoming kamikazes before they got to the picket ships. On one memorable mission we had three divisions of fighters circling the ships below at staggered heights. The low group was at 2,000 to 3,000 feet, the middle was between 8,000 and 10,000 feet, and the high group was up to intercept anything that came in high.

We drew the short straw and had the low combat patrol. We must have been circling for over three hours. It was getting dark and we knew we couldn't fly at night because there were no lights on at the air base to guide us in to land. We told the ships we were heading back, but they insisted we stay overhead because they had reliable intelligence there were Japanese torpedo planes headed our way. The crews on the picket ships were very concerned, as you can imagine, because they were the targets of the kamikazes. To me that was the real tragedy of Okinawa. In fact, I saw one destroyer take a direct hit from a Japanese airplane, and it sank in less than five minutes.

Just before dark I dropped down real low, which I liked to do because the ocean was black and the sky was gray, so if there was anything coming in, you could silhouette it against the contrast. I was leading the second section of the second division. I was halfway through my turn, heading away from the picket ships, when I suddenly saw an airplane heading for the ships.

I racked the Corsair around into a real tight turn. By staying down low I was able to keep him silhouetted against the sky, and I quickly overtook him. The problem was, I was overtaking him too damn fast. I realized that if I didn't do something right away, I would pass right on by him. The other concern I had was that I didn't want to start shooting at him; with all the other friendly airplanes in the sky, I wasn't positive it was a Japanese airplane.

I knew what had worked for me in the past, so I slammed the gear down along with the flaps and I got slowed up real fast. I was able to get

The aces of VMF-323 pose on the wing of a Corsair. COURTESY OF ALBERT WELLS

behind the guy, real close. It didn't take me long to figure out who was in front of my nose. The guy in the rear looked like he was throwing oranges at me as the tracer fire from his machine guns streaked right toward me.

I opened up at very close range and pumped him full of rounds. He didn't have a chance, and splashed into the water below.

I quickly pulled up to avoid hitting him and then dove to the deck again, and saw another one going 90 degrees to me out ahead. It was going to be a heck of a deflection shot, but I was able to lead him enough that when I fired, he flew right through my tracers and blew up into a big ball of fire before crashing into the water.

Those were easy victories compared to my final one.

Last Kill, Hardest Kill

In early June we had been sent up to cover the invasion of Ie Shema, which was an island that lay on the northern tip of Okinawa. Our job was to thwart any Japanese airplanes that might try to attack our landing troops.

After boring circles in the sky, we were just about to be relieved when one of the radar controllers said they had a large unidentified blip coming down from the north, heading our way. They asked us to investigate, which meant we had to go through an overcast to try to find them.

The four of us struggled to stay together as we climbed up through pea-soup clouds. Finally we broke out on top and were greeted with bright sunshine, white puffy clouds, and almost thirty Japanese Zeros. They flew in a tight, well-disciplined formation and were heading down to attack the invasion force.

We were 90 degrees to one another; they were coming down and we were going up. They saw us immediately, because they dropped their belly tanks and prepared to fight. In the past we had done countless hours on scissoring, and how the wingman always protects the lead. Well, that totally went to hell. It was every man for himself as the four of us began to slug it out with the Zeros.

They seemed to be everywhere—in front of us, behind us, and on our sides. I would try to get on the tail of one but would have to break it off because I'd have a couple on my tail. I kept firing short bursts when a Zero

An F4U Corsair eases by as it gets its photo taken. COURTESY OF ALBERT WELLS

crossed in front of me. I was able to lock onto one for a few seconds with a deflection shot, my rounds hitting him forward of the cockpit. There was a large burst of flame and smoke forward of his cockpit, but, unfortunately, I stalled out before I could do any more damage.

My Corsair fell off on a wing as I went back down in the clouds. When I regained control I was under the clouds, where I saw a lone Zero heading back toward to Japan. I began to chase him, thinking, "Oh, this one is going to be easy; I'll just get behind him and let him have it."

Boy, was I wrong! Before I'd even got into range to fire, he pulled straight up as if to go into a loop. I followed right behind him, but suddenly he flipped over, inverted, and came back down, right at me. He was so close over my head that I could see the brass from the rounds he was shooting at me falling out of his wing. Had my canopy been open, I could have reached out and grabbed his neck—we were that close!

He rolled out on the bottom of his dive and I began to chase him once again. That same scenario happened seven or eight times. I tried different things to get him but had no luck. The only reason we didn't shoot each other down was because we were too damn close and couldn't lead one another.

Finally, when he was coming down and I was going up, I started firing like before and he did the same, but this time I jerked my Corsair's nose down. When he passed me I looked up and saw his cockpit was full of flames. He had flown right through my bullets.

I watched him trailing smoke as his Zero went almost straight down and hit the water with a big splash. That was a bittersweet moment for me, because although I shot down an enemy airplane that day, I wish I could have had a drink with that guy and talk about flying. As far as I was concerned, he was a better pilot than me, but I happened to have the better fighter that day.

(Al Wells ended the war with five confirmed victories.)

25

A Long Day's Knight: F4U

ROMAN CANDLE
Lt. Col. Darrell Smith
VMF-312, US Marine Corps

"You're burning underneath. You have got to get out of that thing!" came the frantic call from my wingman. My F4U Corsair was now a Roman candle streaking across the sky, spitting oil and fuel and causing thick smoke and flames to envelop the entire plane.

At 12,000 feet, the Yellow Sea off the coast of Korea looked calm and undisturbed, with many ships down below, including the one I had been catapulted from only hours earlier. They reminded me of children's toy boats in a very large bathtub. A carrier landing, which had been an option only minutes before—when the engine was only cutting in and out, and then only smoke was visible—was now out of the question. A water landing was my next possibility. Placing the Corsair near one of the many ships that were below me appeared to be somewhat feasible, although I was concerned about survivability.

But that all changed when the smoke turned to flame. I began running through my checklist, paying particular attention to my parachute straps, checking to make sure they were attached to me and that they were tight in all the right places. An eerie calmness came over me. For a few brief seconds my life flashed before my eyes. The first thing I envisioned was of course my family and loved ones, but after that, my thoughts turned to my life as an aviator . . .

Hooked on Flying

As a child I lived in Long Beach, California. When I was in first grade, Charles Lindbergh flew across the Atlantic, and when he returned he toured the United States and stopped near my hometown. I snuck out of school that day and ran to the airport to see this legend of a man and the aircraft that carried him on his historic flight. My short little legs didn't propel me fast enough, and I missed seeing Mr. Lindbergh. But there, sitting in the field, looking larger than life, was the Ryan monoplane that conveyed him for over *33 hours* on his epic flight.

Corsair pilot Darrell Smith
COURTESY OF DARRELL SMITH

A large crowd was still gathered around the plane, and being a lot shorter than the masses that were there, I was able to burrow my way through the crowd, right up to the front. I reached out and grabbed ahold of one of the wheels, one of the very same wheels that had made the longest touch-and-go known to man. I was touching the *Spirit of St. Louis!*

From that point on I knew I wanted to fly. I had just completed two years of college when the war broke out. I enlisted in the navy as a marine pilot. A naval recruiter had told me that the navy had more to offer, such as extensive training in fighters and dive-bombers, and it had carriers. I was hooked!

Wings of Gold

After completing Primary in the N25 "Yellow Pearl" and continuing on through Basic in the BT-13 "Vibrator," I went through Advanced in the SNJ at Pensacola, Florida. I had asked for fighters because I was hearing about all of the air battles in Guadalcanal and that area, and I wanted in on that. I was accepted and sent to Opa-Locka, Florida, for operational training. Because of the shortage of "front-line" fighters, we were given SNJs and F2A Brewster Buffalos for training. The F2As were war-wearies that had come back from Midway because they didn't fare very well in combat.

The F2A had some very bad drawbacks. For example, it had the Curtiss Electric props that had a nasty tendency to go into low pitch and race away, becoming uncontrollable. You could roll the F2A once, but if you tried to stay upside down the oil pressure would drop off and you would run out of oil because it didn't have pressurized oil. These Buffalos were beat up so badly that no two of them had the same instrument panel arrangement. The plane captains who were responsible for each aircraft strapped us in and briefed us on "their" airplane as to where the altimeter, oil pressure gauge, and so on were located on the particular aircraft.

The other severe drawback was the raising and lowering of the gear. I had been briefed quite thoroughly about all the procedures for lowering the gear in an emergency. If the hydraulic system failed, there was a pressure tank located in the cockpit that you could open and blow the gear down. If that didn't work, they had two D-rings that were attached to cables under the instrument panel, and you were to reach under and grab them and pull them back, and this would pull the cocking pan out, along with the gear. Finally, if that didn't work, there was one last recourse: On the side of the cockpit was mounted a pair of wire cutters that you were to use to cut the gear cables. I could see myself trying to fly and at the same time reaching down there and blindly cutting wires and cables and probably cutting rudder and aileron cables and everything else!

I had my first accident in a fighter aircraft while flying the Buffalo. I had the wheels down and locked—or so I thought—and when I touched down, one of the wings started to dip down and I thought it was just the hydraulics, but suddenly the wing kept going down and the other wing kept coming up. The prop came back over the hood and gravel was flying everywhere. I couldn't believe what had just happened. I was sitting in the cockpit with my hand frozen on the stick, just staring straight ahead in shock.

The crash crew arrived right away because as a standard procedure they followed all the F2As right down the side of the runway every time one landed. One of the rescue fellows jumped up onto the wing and then up to the cockpit. He reached in and turned the ignition switch off and said, "I don't think you want that on anymore before the LT gets here, do ya?"

"No," I stammered.

There was an inquiry, and at first I was informed that it was 100 percent pilot error, even before I had a chance to speak. When I informed the LT what had happened and explained about the hydraulic problems, the lieutenant stared at me for quite some time, not saying a word. He put his pencil down, folded his arms across his chest, and I thought I saw a faint smile come across his face. He said to me, "I don't think anybody knows what happened out there," and he changed it to 50 percent pilot error and 50 percent mechanical. This was a moral victory for me.

After finishing up my training—in one piece—I was sent up to Cherry Point, North Carolina. I was there to be interviewed by some of the South Pacific fighter pilots who had just returned from combat, guys like Marion Carl and John Smith. John Smith interviewed me and I must have said something he liked, because I was told to report to Parris Island. They were forming a new squadron named VMF-312, and I was one of the last ones to fill out the squadron.

The squadron was commanded by Major Richard M. Day, and in his honor the squadron was nicknamed "Day's Knights." To make the squadron even more recognizable and distinctive, bands of black-and-white checkerboards were applied to the rudders and cowling area.

We began combat flight training using one F4U Corsair and ten AT-6s with .30 caliber machine guns. Eventually, we became combat-ready and proficient in the Corsairs, learning the Thach weave and other maneuvers designed to keep us hotshots from filling up the sights of a Japanese Zero.

In early July of 1944 we arrived at Turtle Bay Airfield in Espiritu Santo. The strip was cut out of a large coconut grove. We also received brand-new FG-1 Corsairs made by the Goodyear Company. I really enjoyed flying the Goodyear-built Corsairs, as they were extremely well-built and dependable—not like the Brewster-built Corsairs, which seemed to always have problems, not unlike the troublesome F2A Buffalo. We lost quite a few pilots in training accidents as we were preparing for a hot combat zone.

Battle-Ready

In the spring of 1945, we were catapulted off the USS *Hollandia* and flew into Okinawa, seven days into the bloody campaign, to take the island landing at Kadena Air Base. We began to fly CAP sorties immediately, protecting the vast armadas of ships in and around Okinawa from the ever-present kamikazes.

On one particular mission I was up with three other Corsairs on station off Okinawa. It was a very cloudy and drizzly day with low-hanging clouds and minimum visibility. We reported in to one of the many destroyers that formed a protective ring around the island and were given immediate vectors to a "bandit" that was north of us, heading back to Japan. This particular bandit was moving a lot faster than we could go and was believed to be an aircraft that was used by the Japanese to lead kamikazes down from Japan to the destroyers.

Usually flown by experienced pilots, these "fast movers" would lead kamikaze formations to within visual distance of our ships and then turn for home and retrieve another kamikaze formation, starting the cycle all over again.

The bandit we were chasing was definitely heading for Japan. The four of us were in the soup when we received a vector that was at our ten o'clock, 4 miles out. We had the throttles jammed against the stops, trying to catch this guy, when the next vector came in stating that he was now at our one o'clock, 6 miles out. This guy was walking away from us!

After playing tortoise and hare with this bandit, we informed the destroyer that we were not going to catch him and were given vectors back to our field. We were still in the clouds and the little light we had was now fading to dusk. Another concern was our fuel status; because of the large amount of fuel we had expended during our hide-and-seek game with the bandit, all of us throttled back to conserve fuel. We agreed to land at an auxiliary field on an island about 40 miles off of Okinawa, where they had set up a floating dry dock to repair battle-damaged destroyers.

We began our descent through the clouds and rain and broke out at about 1,500 feet, still in our slow flight configuration right over the middle of this island. Unbeknownst to us, just minutes earlier they had been bombed by a couple of Betty bombers that had somehow snuck through. I was now a sitting duck. The whole island lit up in a hail of 40mm, 20mm, and small-arms fire; if they had had slingshots at their disposal, I'm sure they would have used them to shoot coconuts at us!

I began taking hits immediately to my Corsair. One round hit the stabilizer on the right side, causing temporary loss of control. I heard and felt a very big bang, and the radios that were mounted on the side of my cockpit were now in my lap. The right side of the instrument panel had curled up over the oil pressure gauge. The stick began to vibrate uncontrollably in my hand and I thought the engine was going to blow. I also felt a burning sensation in my right lower calf, and when I reached down to feel my leg and brought my hand back up, it was covered in blood. Dammit! I had been hit by friendly fire, and I was bleeding, too. What else could go wrong?

I tried peeling the instrument back so I could see the oil pressure gauge, and of course I couldn't do it. In the process I cut up my hand and fingers and now they were bleeding as well. The entire flight had scattered when the shooting started and I was now all alone. I knew I couldn't land down there in that shooting gallery, and the closest field was on Okinawa, 40 long miles away, all over open water. I figured the engine was going to go at any time because of the constant vibration.

I looked out the corner of my eye and saw the large amount of damage that had been inflicted on my Corsair. There were large pieces of tail section missing, and it finally registered that this was the cause of all the fluttering and troubles. I was faced with a very tough decision: First, I could bail out into the darkening sky over water, with little chance of anyone finding me; second, make a water landing, which may or may not work depending on the sea conditions, which I could not discern because of the darkness; or third, I could press on and hope that I could find the airfield.

I chose to continue flying, as the engine seemed to be operating normally.

I flew on for what seemed hours but was only minutes, when I spotted the ring of battleships around Okinawa. I knew our sailors were gun-happy because of the constant kamikazes, and I was concerned that they would mistake me for one.

I made it past the ships okay, and arrived over the airfield out of position, outside of the lane I was supposed to be in. I began to set up for my controlled crash, and—God, I got a green light! No one was shooting at me, friend or foe, and I relaxed for a second and lowered the gear, forgetting about my extensive tail damage. The nose pitched violently downward, and with my bloody hand I jammed the throttle forward. I had the stick full back, but it was the massive power of the engine that lifted me skyward. I was unable to make a tight-enough turn after I'd cleared the runway and flown out over the front lines, where for the second time in one night I was being shot at. But at least it was both the Americans and the Japanese shooting at me, doubling my chances of being shot down!

I made it through the gauntlet of fire and turned on final to the runway. I kept a little more power on and lowered the gear. I was right over the runway and chopped the power and slammed down onto the runway. I inadvertently went into a skid. I skidded along the Marston matting, up and through a ditch onto a taxiway, and that is when my six .50 caliber guns went off, spewing hot lead into the hills in the distance. I had forgotten to safety the guns before I landed and I had such a death grip on

A VMF-312 Corsair COURTESY OF DARRELL SMITH

the stick that I'd inadvertently pulled the trigger. I thought my flying days were over with that mistake.

When I finally came to a stop and all the dust had settled, I found myself in almost one piece. A jeep approached out of the darkness and a junior officer jumped from it, climbing up in my wing and yelling at me for stopping on his taxiway. He started reciting naval rules that I had broken, but as he reached the cockpit his whole face and demeanor changed.

He took one look at me and the interior of the cockpit, turned to the crowd that was beginning to gather, and yelled, "For God's sake, get an ambulance out here!"

I was taken to sick bay and attended to. My CO, Major Day, walked in and said to me, "How are you doing, son?" (He was twenty-four years old and I was twenty-one.)

I replied, "Those were my guns that went off on the runway."

Major Day looked at me, held up his hand, and said, "Let me worry about that."

I never heard about it again.

Tricks of the Trade

During my recovery period from my leg wound, I wandered over to the flight line where the Corsairs were parked for repair and re-arming. I got to thinking (for a short time) that I'd like to learn more about this airplane that I had been flying and find out more about how it flies and what makes it tick.

We had a crusty old Texan who was the head of engineering. He was the "Grandpa" of the squadron at the ripe old age of thirty-four. I stopped and talked to him one day and told him what I wanted to do and what I expected to learn—how the engine and all the inner workings came together in one harmonious rhythm, what kept this bird in the air, and why. I wanted to know all the secrets!

I noticed that "Grandpa's" face was turning a bright red and his eyes were squinting. Must be the sun, I thought, as I glanced skyward into a gray, cloudy day.

He finally spoke to me after the muscles in his jaw had relaxed and the blood retreated from his eyes. "Son," he said, "if you had any idea what was going on under that hood, you'd never come anywhere near one of these crates again!"

And that was the end of that.

I began flying combat missions again. My left leg felt fine, and I tried not to think too much about what was happening under the cowl. I began to fly more close air support missions for the marine ground-pounders. We were just starting to work with forward air controllers. These FACs (Forward Air Controls) were all pilots that had been taken out of the squadrons and assigned to the ground troops. Being pilots, they knew how we could help them and how we couldn't. The ground war, in that thick, dense jungle in and around Okinawa and its surrounding islands, must have been pure hell for those boys. I often felt that I had the easy part in the air, flying in and away from trouble. But these marines on the ground, with the heat and jungle and all the concealed enemy troops fighting to the death—these were the real heroes.

The Corsair carried a wide variety of ordnance. We used napalm and rockets mainly. The napalm was a deadly weapon, a very nasty weapon.

The distinct checkerboard markings adorn a VMF-312 Corsair. COURTESY OF DARRELL SMITH

And to be on the receiving end of it meant certain annihilation. The napalm was carried under the center section of the Corsair and was used quite effectively. The rockets we used weren't too good. These were primitive by today's standards. They were mounted under the outer portion of the wings. We normally carried four under each wing depending on the mission for the day. When we fired the rockets, you just never knew where they were going to go, but they scared the devil out of the Japanese because of the whistling sound they made. We also had six .50 caliber machine guns, which we used on our runs to the target to hold off enemy fire.

But all of these deadly weapons at our disposal still could not prevent losses among the squadron. No one was immune from the ravages of war.

I soon learned this on one of my last missions.

Ultimate Sacrifice

On May 14, 1945, VMF-312 was tasked with a mission to destroy a Japanese radar installation that was monitoring all of our flights to Japan. This meant that Japanese home defense, both air and ground, would be waiting for B-29s as they made their initial bomb runs.

The radar site was on a small island about 30 miles north of Okinawa, defended by all sorts of antiaircraft emplacements. Our CO, Major Day, was to lead this mission. A strike force of twelve Corsairs, all heavily loaded with rockets, 500-pound bombs, and napalm, took off from Okinawa and headed north on a very short flight. Climbing to 10,000 feet, we were vectored to our target.

Major Day began his dive into the target, increasing his angle to 65 degrees and letting loose with rockets. The rest of the flight followed suit and we began our run, one right behind the other. We got into a big tail chase. The Japanese gunners opened up on us with all the antiaircraft gun they could send our way, but we were moving at such high speeds and high angles that they couldn't compensate.

On our second run into the target, Major Day went back into the same position as the first. This was a costly mistake, because by the time he came around for the second dive into the target, the enemy gunners had us bore-sighted as we dove into their position. Major Day began his dive and pushed the nose of his Corsair over for one last time. The anti-aircraft fire erupted in and around our formation, and Major Day was hit immediately! His Corsair burst into flames, spewing thick, black smoke as it continued in its steep dive to the target. The Corsair impacted into the mountainous terrain below. We had just lost our CO.

The executive officer leading the second flight took over, and we all went back up to make a third pass on the target, but this time we came in from different angles.

It was a costly lesson.

Shortly after this mission I was sent back home to the States for thirty days' rotation. I was placed into a ferry squadron, flying TBMs, F3Fs, SBDs, and Corsairs out of Long Beach, California, to reserve squadrons all over the United States.

I was about to return to combat in the South Pacific, for the invasion of Japan. All this changed when the bomb was dropped.

I stayed in the Marine Corps Reserve–Minneapolis and soon found myself back in VMF-312, flying F4U-4 Corsairs in a combat situation in a far-off place at the end of the world called Korea.

But that's a whole other story to be told later by this "Old Day's Knight."

26

Wolfpack Warrior: P-47

BEHEMOTH BEAUTY
Capt. Russell S. Kyler
56th Fighter Group, 61st Fighter Squadron, 8th Air Force

I graduated from flight training on February 8, 1944, at Camp Eagle Pass, Texas. After ten hours of fighter transition training in the P-40, I was transferred to a field at Baton Rouge, Louisiana, where I came face-to-face with the P-47 Thunderbolt. I'd been flying the little T-6 Texan and the P-40, both small aircraft compared to the P-47. It was a huge machine.

Our instructor introduced us to the razorback C model. I looked at it in utter amazement and then turned slowly to my instructor, a captain just back from combat duty. "Captain, that's not a fighter," I said. "That's a single-engine bomber."

He laughed a little bit and said, "Well, Lieutenant, when you get well trained in that aircraft and get into combat with it, you'll think it's the finest aircraft that was ever made."

No truer words were ever spoken.

I wasn't very impressed with it at first. It was just a big clumsy machine as far as I was concerned, with its beer-barrel-like fuselage and huge radial engine. I didn't know what it would really do, but the more I flew it, the better I liked it. By the time I finished my transition training I was pretty confident in my ability to fly and fight in it.

Russell S. Kyler of the 56th Fighter Group was assigned this P-47 Thunderbolt. COURTESY OF RUSSELL KYLER

My fighting days would soon arrive, as I was sent to England in mid-August of 1944. We went to a transition training base in central England and trained a couple of weeks, practicing formation flying, and getting better acquainted with the English weather and the different combat tactics we were to use against the Luftwaffe. Satisfied that we wouldn't get lost over England, I was shipped out, and was fortunate enough to be sent to the 56th Fighter Group.

Flak Magnet

Based at Boxted, just north of Colchester, England, I was assigned to the 61st Fighter Squadron. I had no idea who they were, who flew with them, or how well they did in combat against the Luftwaffe. I was given after-mission reports and combat reports to read, and it became a real eye-opening experience for me. I read reports by guys like Christenson,

Zemke, Shilling, Klibbe, and Gabreski, to name just a few. As a pilot with Zemke's Wolfpack, I had big shoes to fill and a lot to learn, and was thankful when I was selected to fly wing with another legend.

There were six of us that reported to the 61st Squadron, and during our briefing by the commander, we were being sized up by the other pilots in the room. I was assigned to fly wing on a Polish major who had been with the group at that time. Squadron leader Mike Gladych chose me for whatever reason, and I honestly didn't know what to think of him. He was wearing a Polish cap, a British flight jacket, and US Army OD (olive drab) pants. I had no idea who or what he was until we went off by ourselves.

He took a pencil out of his pocket and marked a piece of paper he had, saying, "This is me, and this is you. Either on this side of me or on this side of me, on the left, or the right."

I nodded, and he said, "If you'll fly in that position, I'll always bring you home."

He kept his promise and always did.

On my fifth mission, September 21, we were on a bomber escort. When we completed the escort mission and started back out, our field order said to search for targets of opportunity. We were flying above an overcast so we let down through it so we could see what was on the ground. We broke out about 2,000 feet above the ground, right in the middle of a bunch of enemy fighters—fourteen to sixteen of them. It was as much of a surprise for us as it was for them.

We had the advantage of the attack, and it only lasted about two to three minutes. It was also my baptism of fire, and I obtained my first victory.

Encounter Report
21st September, 1944.
61st Fighter Squadron, 56th Fighter Group
1515 hours
East of Arnhem, North of Gorinchen
8/10 at 2,000 ft.

I was leading Whippet squadron as top cover for the group. We patrolled the assigned area uneventfully, being vectored by Tackline. As we flew over Arnhem Fairbanks went down through the overcast. I followed as the last squadron. Apparently Fairbanks had engaged some E/A flying on the deck as I saw the Lufbery about a mile in front of me. I shoved the throttle forward and soon saw Fw 190s trying to get away from the scrap. I, with my wingman, picked the leading E/A while my second element pursued the second one. As I closed to approximately 300 yds., I pulled up and to the right and signaled my wingman to get the E/A. He promptly closed and fired a short burst. I observed strikes on the cockpit and saw the E/A nose down out of control at about 50 feet. We broke to the right and I didn't see the crash, but as I looked there a couple of seconds later I saw fire and a pile of smoke.

We climbed to 1,000 feet and I set a wide orbit looking for some targets. I saw an A/C, which I thought was my number 3 man, approach us from 60 degrees and behind. A split second later I realized my mistake; it was an Fw 190. The radio was jammed and I couldn't tell my wingman to break, but I broke myself, switching the water on, and fired as the E/A opened up on my wingman. I saw strikes and the pilot bailed out. I didn't see the chute so after one full orbit I set course west.

By that time, the fight was over and I saw the group forming up ahead of me. I climbed above the cloud. North of Gorinchem I spotted two bogeys flying north. I went down on them and caught them just before they went into the cloud. They were Fw 190s. I fired at the tail aircraft and saw it burst into flames. I then climbed back and resumed course for base.

I confirm one E/A destroyed by my wingman, Lt. Kyler. I claim two Fw 190s destroyed [in the air].
Michael Gladych,
Major, P.A.F.

During the fight, Major Gladych called me and told me to break right. As I broke hard to the right, I looked behind me and up top there was an airplane behind me that was on fire, an Fw 190 that had been firing at me. I was flying the squadron commander Don Smith's airplane on that mission, and wanted to make sure I brought it home in one piece. Unfortunately, that idea didn't work out too good. A couple of gunners on the ground hit me with small-arms machine-gun fire, along with one 20mm cannon round that hit me in the right wing. I was only 400 feet off the ground, and the impact of that 20mm felt like someone hit me with a 12-pound sledgehammer.

But the damage that caused most of my problems was from the 30mm machine-gun rounds that began in the engine accessory section, clear back to the turbo pocket in the tail. It knocked out my turbo supercharger. I didn't have any boost and was probably forty-five minutes away from home, on the wrong side of the English Channel.

I staggered up to 10,000 feet, but at that altitude I'd lost too much manifold pressure, and that was about as high as I could go. I kept falling slowly back, farther and farther behind my leader, and he finally called me and said, "Did you get hit back there?"

And I said, "Yeah, I got hit in the right wing, and I don't know where else, but I don't have any supercharger."

So, he said, "Okay, stay on course and I'll look you over." So, he slowed down and came up beside me and went down under me and came up on my right wing, and just shook his head "No." He said, "Stay on course—I'll fly your wing."

We landed at the emergency landing field called Manston and taxied in, and I couldn't get my flaps back up. That 20mm had knocked out my hydraulic line, and it looked like someone had punched the wing full of little holes with an ice pick, as hydraulic fluid was squirting up about 3 or 4 feet above the surface of the wing.

We looked the airplanes over pretty good, and Mike said, "You take my airplane and we'll run back to Boxted; I'll take yours, and come in behind you."

I said, "No, I can get it home all right."

"No, you fly my airplane," he said. "I'll fly yours."

"Yes, sir," I replied.

So I took his and went on back home, knowing that he wouldn't be able to retract his landing gear, nor his flaps, so he'd be quite a bit slower than I was.

I arrived first and went in and landed and taxied into his parking area.

His crew chief jumped up on the wing and by the time I had the engine shut down, he had the canopy open. He looked at me and said, "Well, where's Mike at? How'd you get in his airplane?" I said, "Well, we changed planes on the way home."

He just kind of let it go at that.

A few minutes later Mike taxied in on my airplane with the flaps still hanging down.

When we got to the pilots' ready room to give our after-action reports, the CO was in there. We were talking about the mission, and I said, "Well, I'm sorry, sir, but I think your airplane is going to need a wing change. I

Named after his wife back home, *Lorene* carried an impressive scoreboard. COURTESY OF RUSSELL KYLER

took a direct hit in the main part of the right wing with a 20mm." And I added, "It's pretty well damaged."

He never said a word and just headed out the door.

About ten minutes later I heard him hollering my name.

I went to see what he wanted, and he said, "You come back out here! I want you to count every hole that's down the belly of that airplane, and you better not miss any, understood?!'"

"Yes, sir."

That's when I found, and I'll never forget it, thirty-two holes in the belly of his airplane. He was a pretty angry old boy, because when you have to change the wing on a fighter, it never does fly good after that for some reason. You get a little bit wing-heavy or out of trim a bit or something. It just doesn't make for a good flying aircraft.

But with a war on, replacements were always around the corner.

Snapshots

During mid-November, we were on a strafing mission in south central Germany and assigned to strafe oil tanks. After our group hit the tanks, we found a train and pounced all over it before climbing back up as a flight to re-form as a group. I was flying wing to Lieutenant Baughman, and as we were climbing up we got bounced by sixteen Fw 190s who dove at us from 10,000 feet.

Encounter Report
18th November, 1944
61st Fighter Squadron, 56th Fighter Group
1230 hours
4 miles East of Hanau
7/10–8/10 stratus at 12–14,000 ft.
One Fw 190 destroyed (air)

I was Whippet Red 4 and we were just re-forming after strafing our assigned target. Approximately 16 Fw 190s bounced us from an altitude advantage of 3–4,000 ft. A break was called and we engaged the E/A. About the middle of the scrap my element leader (Whippet Red 3,

*Lt. Baughman) got on the tail of a 190. Many hits were observed in
the area of the cockpit and the pilot bailed out. About 10 seconds later
I spotted a 190 diving down in front of us at about 2 o'clock. I pushed
my nose down and fired a burst. I didn't see any hits on the E/A, but
the pilot bailed out. I also saw three Me 109s in the target area and
approximately 8–10 crashed E/A burning on the ground. I claim one
Fw 190 destroyed and confirm Lt. Baughman's claim for one Fw 190
destroyed.*

Russell S. Kyler
2nd Lt., Air Corps.

Supporting Statement
*Immediately after we broke combat with this E/A, an Fw 190 came
down from high at about two o'clock in front of Red 4 (Lt. Kyler). He
fired at it. As we turned on around to the left I observed a parachute
from this aircraft and the E/A going down in a spin. I confirm one Fw
190 destroyed by Lt. Kyler.*

Robert A. Baughman
1st Lt., Air Corps.

The group stayed busy with support missions during the Battle of the
Bulge when weather allowed, and in early January of 1945 we received
brand-new P-47M models. Basically the same airplane, the M model had
the wings of a D, the fuselage of an N, and had a bigger R-2800C engine
with a different turbo supercharger. The N model at altitude, pulling full
power, could develop 2,800 rpms and 70 to 72 inches of manifold pressure with water injection. The D models could only develop 2,400 rpm.

You couldn't really tell much difference in flying it except they'd get
off the ground just a little bit faster on takeoff, and they'd climb out a
little bit better. But we always climbed up with fairly low rpm and low
manifold pressure in order to save gas, climbing out at about 170 or 180
miles an hour. The top speed of the D model was 430, and the top speed
of the M model was 470.

I got to see just what a hot rod this new Thunderbolt was in mid-
January of 1945.

I was flying wing to a pilot named Walker and he bounced an Me 109, so I kind of stayed back and above him to give him cover. Walker went down and pulled up to just under my nose and I rolled over to see how he was doing, and I saw the 109 he was chasing crash. I rolled back and tried to level out when I spotted an Me 109, 1,000 yards out in front of me. I lined up on him and fired. We had just received the British Mk 14 computing gunsight and, man, I'll tell you, that was one awesome gunsight! I set the Me 109 wingspan on it and twisted the throttle. The throttle had a twist grip like a motorcycle throttle, and when manipulated you saw a fixed-rate diamond that formed a circle. I cranked it down and I was able to span him and fire that first burst, and it was dead on.

The first burst was about 800 yards, and the second burst, about 600, and the last burst, about 400. Just as I fired the second burst, my first burst hit him. His landing gear came down. I was firing armor-piercing incendiary bullets and when they hit, they make a little flash. When that incendiary gets hot, it explodes. When I let go with the third burst, the second burst hit him really good, and he exploded. And then the third burst got there and it was hitting pieces of airplane flying around all over the air. It just disintegrated there at 9,000 feet. I don't think he ever saw us, and he never realized I was behind him. There wasn't much left of the Luftwaffe, as they were running out of pilots and gas, and the little that was left were mainly targets on the ground.

Total Destruction
In March of 1945 our group was escorting bombers and I saw two airplanes off to my left, quite a ways out, and I thought they were German Me 262s. I called them in, and the squadron commander said, "Take your wingman and try to intercept them."

We peeled off and went after them, and by the time I recognized them, I was able to identify them as P-51s with wing tanks. I was too far below and behind the group to catch up with them so I thought I'd take my wingman and go home.

I saw an airfield below that the bombers were bombing on the way out. I checked them and figured they were bombing two minutes apart between boxes. So, I told my wingman, "When the next box of bombers' bombs explode, I want to start a strafing pass across the airfield." He said, "Okay."

So, the bombs exploded, and I made a run and started my actual firing at about 500 feet off the ground. My rounds found their mark as I destroyed two airplanes, a Ju 88 and an Me 210. When I went zooming in across the target I thought, "Well, this doesn't take any time at all. I'll just pull up, do a pedal turn, and come back and make another run before that other box of bombers bomb."

Just as I pulled up, a guy on the ground hit me with two 20 millimeters. I pushed over and went back down below the treetops. Those hits took out two cylinders on the left side of the engine. Running like a scared rabbit, I stayed down right on the deck and got about 4 or 5 miles north of the airfield before I turned back toward home and started climbing out.

My wingman didn't fare any better, as he went down into the trees when I went down behind him, damaging the leading edge of his airplane and his prop pretty bad as he gave the tops of the trees a buzz cut for 50 yards. I got him back into France, and he said that he needed to get the P-47 on the ground, as it was shaking really bad. I got him back to a 9th Air Force base, and as he was going in to land, his engine quit on final approach and he bellied it in. I circled, fearing the worst, and he waved at me that he was okay.

I started out across the English Channel at about 12,000 feet, wondering if I would even make it back myself. My alternative was a freezing swim in the Channel. With zero oil pressure indicated at the time, it looked like someone had poured a 55-gallon drum of oil over the front of it. The one saving grace was that I was flying the Thunderbolt, and I knew from firsthand experience that it could take repeated punishing blows and keep on ticking, like it was just a small chip in the paint. I had two holes in the cowling that were the size of a 20mm shell, but on the inside, there was one cylinder on the front bank and one on the back bank that were shot completely off the airplane.

(Russ Kyler continued to fly with the 56th Fighter Group until the end of the war in Europe, and flew 57 combat missions in 300 hours. He received credit for three aerial victories and seven ground victories.)

27

Right to the Bitter End: P-51 and F6F

Final Combat Missions over Germany and Japan

JET ASSASSIN
Lt. Hilton O. Thompson
434th Fighter Squadron, 479th Fighter Group

Encounter Report
25th April, 1945.
Vicinity Traunstein, Germany, 24,000 feet.

I was operating in the area east south east of Traunstein, Germany, and was flying as Newcross Blue Three position on a bomber escort mission to Traunstein, Germany. At the target we started a 360-degree turn in our P-51 Mustangs and during the first quarter on the turn I sighted a "bogey" flying in an easterly direction about 2,000 feet above and almost directly over me. We were flying at 24,000 feet at this time. I broke from the turn, with my wingman and a spare, and started climbing beneath the "bogey," trying to identify it. I recognized the aircraft as an enemy Ar 234 and my identification was confirmed by Newcross Blue Four and one Newcross Spare that had followed me from the group.

The jet turned to a southeasterly direction and I closed to 800 yards at his level. Ranging with my K-14 sight I fired two short bursts and observed hits around his left engine. Then I began closing rapidly from

As a recce photo pilot, Clyde East and his P-51 Mustang racked up fourteen aerial victories. COURTESY OF CLYDE EAST

seven o'clock astern and fired several bursts from 600 to 300 yards, observing strikes along the entire left side of the fuselage which caused many pieces to fall off. At 200 yards I pulled to the right and watched him spiral down at 40 degrees angle. Lt. Harold L. Stotts, who was Newcross Spare with me, then fired on the enemy aircraft, getting repeated strikes. The jet pilot bailed out between 10,000 and 6,000 feet. The jet, I believe, crashed in the vicinity of Berchtesgaden.

I claim one Ar 234 destroyed in the air.

POKING A TIGER
Lt. Col. Clyde B. East
15th Tactical Reconnaissance Squadron (TRS)

In early April of 1945 I had racked up my score to thirteen victories, shooting down some Stukas that were attacking our troops—and got my butt chewed in the process—because as my boss, Maj. Gen. Otto Weyland, commander of 9th Tactical Air Command, put it, "As recce pilots your primary role is to gather information and not to attack enemy aircraft!" The general told us in no uncertain terms that, "Unless they attack you first, leave them alone and bring your photographic information home. That's an order!"

With all due respect to the general, we were the ones on the front lines day in and day out, risking our necks, operating alone or with one other Mustang, taking photos of the ever-changing battle lines. At the time, I was young, and didn't really worry about things that didn't make sense to me. As recce pilots we understood what needed to be done, and certainly knew firsthand the business of shooting down enemy airplanes.

Personally I think some of the complaints came from some of the other fighter units. At that time our recce squadron was raking up the victories compared to many of the outfits in the 9th Air Force. They had been relegated to close air support and didn't have the same opportunities to tangle or even see other enemy airplanes. I just knew that if I got into another scrape with a German airplane I would have to claim it was in self-defense.

On May 8, 1945, I was flying my final mission of the war with another P-51. We had been out on a recce, watching for German movements at a marshaling yard near Austria, just prior to their surrender. I looked below and saw this little Fieseler Storch kicking along and really didn't pay too much attention to him. I made up my mind that I wasn't even going to mess with it because I certainly didn't need the added headaches from General Weyland's wrath. Just as the Storch passed behind us, it seemed like the whole town below erupted in a heavy concentration of flak. I guess it was their last salute in trying to knock us down!

It took a lot for me to get angry, and now I was steaming mad! I whipped my Mustang around, pulled the throttle back, and dropped a notch of flaps. I lined up the Storch and gave him a half-second squirt from my six .50 calibers. He began to burn right away and folded up like a piece of paper. As I circled the wreckage I knew that if I had tried to claim this victory I might end up being permanently assigned to a ground unit, developing photos instead of up here taking them. I could just imagine the general's anger if he read a combat encounter report that stated, "While on a recce flight I was attacked by a light observation airplane that dove at me from out of the sun with its guns blazing!"

Shoot, everyone knew that a Storch has a gun that fired rearward! Although that victory would have raised my final score to 14 aerial victories, I knew better than to poke a tiger; unfortunately, the Germans did not understand that philosophy and threw the first punch.

STING OF THE WASP: STRIKING BACK AT THE EMPIRE
Cdr. Robert H. Turnell
VF-81, USN

I am a United States Navy flyer. My countrymen built the best airplane in the world and entrusted it to me. They trained me to fly it. I will use it to the absolute limit of my power. With my fellow pilots, air crews, and deck crews, my plane and I will do anything necessary to carry out our tremendous responsibilities. I will always remember we are part of an unbeatable combat team—the United States Navy. When the going is fast and rough, I will not falter. I will be uncompromising in every blow I strike. I will be humble in victory. I am a United States Navy flyer. I have dedicated myself to my country with its millions of all races, colors, and creeds. They and their way of life are worthy of my greatest protective effort. I ask the help of God in making that effort great enough.

—"A NAVY FLYER'S CREED"

Flying the Navy Way
When I graduated high school in 1941, I was still seventeen years old as I listened on the radio and read about a world war building all around us. When I received my draft card it had a big "1-A" on it, which meant I could be selected for any branch of the service. I really didn't want to carry a rifle or live in a foxhole, and thought that I might like to give flying a chance. When the Japanese attacked Pearl Harbor on December 7, 1941, I visited the first naval recruiter I could find in the State of Washington and enlisted, hoping I could earn my wings of gold.

The navy sent me to a civilian pilot training program (CPTP), where I cut my teeth on aviating in a 65hp Piper J-3 Cub. I quickly fell in love with flying, hoping this was my path to fighters as I eventually earned my private license after 35 hours of flight time.

In early 1943 I learned how to fly the navy way as I progressed through N2S Stearmans and N3N "Yellow Perils" and even some stick time in the mono-wing N2T Timm trainers. From there it was on to the more powerful Vultee SNBs before being selected to proceed to fighter training in Texas in the SNJ. After surviving the rigors of navy pilot training, I earned the coveted wings of gold in October of 1943. I was itching to join my fellow naval aviators over the skies of the Pacific Theater.

F6F Hellcat pilot Robert H. Turnell rests on the tire of his airplane. COURTESY OF ROBERT TURNELL

When I got word that I would be shipped to Miami for Advanced fighter training, I was ecstatic. That was until I arrived and learned that the Brewster Buffalos we were supposed to learn fighter tactics in had all been damaged or crashed by previous students, so it was back in the SNJ to hone our skills. Two months later my dream finally came true when I got checked out in the F4F Wildcat.

I really enjoyed the stubby-winged Grumman fighter. Although the cockpit was kind of cramped, it was maneuverable in the air and a delight to fly and fight with. Our instructors showed us tactics that had been learned in earlier combat against the Japanese by some of the top guns of the Pacific, like Butch O'Hare and Jimmy Thach. The only thing I didn't much care for while flying the Wildcat was the fact that you really had to be an athlete; the only way to lower or raise the gear was by use of the "Armstrong method" of cranking it up or down by hand!

After learning the tips and tricks of Wildcat flying and gunnery work, the navy thought it was finally time for us to earn our keep and teach us how to land our fighters aboard a carrier. In late January of 1944, I left the warm Florida sun and headed to the frozen north for my first attempt at carrier traps.

Arriving at Naval Air Station Glenview, just north of Chicago, Illinois, we were informed once again that there was a shortage of fighters, and we would have to use SNJs. After some field carrier landings at a nearby airfield, I was sent out over the icy cold waters of Lake Michigan to find my ship—the USS *Wolverine*. I had heard wild stories from several other pilots about guys going off the side and ditching in the water, but for me it was a relatively uneventful process, as I made my mandatory eight landings with no problems at all.

With the final phase of my training complete, I was finally being sent to a fighter squadron.

Grumman's Aerial Assassin
In March of 1944 I joined a group of like-minded men and equally trained navy pilots in Atlantic City and became part of VF-81, "The Freelancers." Our commander was Frank Upham, a US Naval Academy graduate with no prior combat history. Although green to the combat world, he did have one old hand serving under him, our executive officer, Lt. Cdr. Tom Provost, who had five years of navy flying to his credit, along with a distinguished record in his F4F Wildcat at the Battle of Midway. Not only did I meet my new squadron mates, but I was also introduced to the world's best fighter, as far as I was concerned: the Grumman F6F-3 Hellcat.

Compared to the Wildcat I had cut my teeth in, the Hellcat was leaps and bounds ahead. For one, it was much heavier and more powerful, with its R-2800 engine that could crank out 2,200hp with its two-speed, two-stage supercharger. With the added power came better time to climb and better maneuverability. The Hellcat also employed six .50 caliber machine guns, three in each wing, and a very well-laid-out, pilot-friendly instrument panel inside a spacious cockpit. But what I liked most about the Hellcat was the fact that it came from the Grumman Iron Works factory and was built tank-tough.

The Hellcat also reminded me of my earlier Piper Cub flying days, because it didn't react like other fighters would when you put it into a stall. While other fighters might snap over on a wing once they quit flying, the

Hellcats prowl the sky. COURTESY OF ROBERT TURNELL

Hellcat had a very gentle tendency, like that of a Cub. It was extremely stable, and I could see how this attribute could work in my favor against a tight-turning Zero.

As a fighter, a la air-to-air, it could hold its own with the best of them, in fact earning top honors with a nineteen-to-one kill ratio. But when Grumman designed this airplane, they knew that it also needed to carry a load and strike the enemy with a one-two punch. Our later model F6F-5 Hellcats had the ability to carry six 5-inch HVAR rockets on wing rails; two 500-pound bombs or one 1,000-pound on the centerline; and 2,400 rounds of .50 caliber ammunition. At close to 14,000 pounds fully loaded, the Hellcat was the ultimate fighter-bomber.

For the next several months we were shown exactly how to employ these strengths as we fired our guns and rockets and dropped practice bombs on targets up and down the East Coast. The trick with dive-bombing was to climb to about 18,000 feet, push the big nose over, and after releasing the bombs, pull out around 3,500 feet, pulling as hard as you could on that stick while converting the rapidly building airspeed for altitude as you zoomed away from the target.

Our training was intense, and we flew almost every day, sometimes twice a day, as we sharpened our skills for our eventual move onto a carrier and into combat.

Joining the Fight aboard USS Wasp

Inching ever so closer to the combat zone, we continued our training in Hawaii before getting orders to shove off for Guam. Before doing so, however, we were required to make some night carrier landings to qualify. The USS *Ranger* was steaming nearby and invited us aboard. The Hellcat was a great airplane both in the air and when catching a wire, and I had no problems with the landings.

In early November, Fighting 81 (VF-81) finally caught up with USS *Wasp* near Guam. The new *Wasp* carried over seventy-two aircraft, which included fighters, bombers, and torpedo planes. When our squadron came aboard we were replacing Air Group 14, which held its own in June of 1944 as it joined the navy air armada in searching out and destroying the Japanese navy near the Marianas. From there it continued on with the incredible fierce fighting in and around the Philippines, Luzon, Formosa, and Okinawa.

When we arrived, we knew there were still a lot of tough battles ahead of us.

We barely had time to get acclimated to the ship before we began flying combat missions. My first one occurred on November 11 as a combat air patrol over Manila Bay. I was assigned to the skipper's flight as the No. 4 man, so our flight was always the first one off the deck and out front of the rest of the pack of Hellcats. During one of those early missions, an attack of Cabanatuan and Tarlac airfields on central Luzon, Philippines, there were eleven of us orbiting, looking for trouble, and it didn't take long to find it. As if on a leisurely cross-country, the skipper spotted a lone Tony fighter, an in-line, single-engine airplane, cruising along at 3,000 feet below us. It sure was a sight to see as eleven Hellcats pushed their noses over and jammed the throttles forward to see who could get this guy first.

By the time I got close, that Tony's right wing was already on fire as hundreds of .50 caliber rounds poured into him. He never knew what hit him. The Tony rolled over as his canopy came off and the guy bailed out.

Other Japanese airplanes were few and far between as we continued our aerial assaults on Japanese-held islands and shipping. But there were still lots of targets of opportunity. One of our typical tactics was to send

An F6F Hellcat pilot looks good to the landing signal officer (LSO) as he makes his approach to land. COURTESY OF ROBERT TURNELL

the first wave of twelve Hellcats in to suppress antiaircraft fire around heavily defended targets like airfields and other military installations. The enemy flak guns were easy to spot and silence; we just looked for the muzzle flashes, dove toward them, and fired our rockets and machine guns. Most of the time they were suppressed quickly.

We seemed to roam all over the Pacific as we hit targets on Formosa, oil storage tanks and refineries on Indochina near Saigon, and shipping in Hong Kong, Manila Bay, and off Okinawa. Whatever the target, the Hellcat could easily adapt and destroy with a mixture of weaponry.

Some of my most memorable uses of the rockets were during the first strike on Tokyo and the invasion of Iwo Jima. About the only enemy the Hellcat could not defeat was the typhoon we encountered; we rode that storm out, hoping to survive and see another day.

We did, and we prepared to attack Japan.

Striking the Homeland

On February 16, 1945, we were practically within spitting distance of Tokyo Bay. Positioned less than 100 miles away from the Japanese Empire, our Hellcats were loaded for bear, carrying a combination of bombs and rockets. Although our target was another Japanese army airfield, this one was special because it was near the capital of Japan. It was also one of the very first missions to strike the Empire.

Over fifty-five Hellcats launched and climbed to 18,000 feet, and I am sure we all thought about what was waiting up ahead for us on the relatively short flight inland. On this mission I followed the first wave of Hellcats that had been sent ahead as flak suppressors. Nearing the target, there was still plenty of sporadic flak to welcome us as we pushed over and made our bomb and rocket runs on the airfield. I was somewhat dismayed that there was not a single enemy fighter up trying to protect the homeland. But that all changed after our bombs exploded and our rockets found their mark. For a few seconds I was able to watch one of my 500-pound bombs hit dead center on a hangar before pulling up.

But as I pulled off the target and climbed back up to join the other Hellcats at our rendezvous point, so we could head back to the ship en masse, we spotted them turning above us.

There must have been eight of them, a combination of Zeros and Zekes circling above us like angry bees. They had the drop on us with their altitude advantage, and had this been back in 1943 or mid-1944, those Japanese pilots certainly would have given us a run for our money. But now things were different and their pilots were much less experienced. For whatever reason, they came down on us one at a time. There were so many Hellcats and Corsairs all locked and cocked, swirling around on that mission, it was like shooting fish in a barrel as all eight enemy fighters were shot down one by one.

Four days later, on February 20, I had a front-row seat for the invasion of Iwo Jima. On that mission we worked with ground controllers as they called out targets of opportunity for our orbiting flights. With grid maps in hand the controllers gave us coordinates to the target.

One controller came on the radio with the location of a Japanese tank. I checked in with him and after confirming it was in fact enemy armor, I began my rocket run in on him. He was obviously moving much slower than I was as I lined him up and began unleashing the 5-inch HVAR rockets. As I pulled up I could already see he was burning and received confirmation from the ground controller that he was dead in his tracks.

Our squadron continued to pound the enemy homeland with repeated trips to Tokyo, Iwo Jima, Okinawa, and Chichi Jima. On every one of these missions, I encountered flak or small-arms fire, and never once did my Hellcat miss a beat. By the time my tour was done, I had flown thirty-eight combat missions off of USS *Wasp* and never received a nick in combat.

Our group departed USS *Wasp* in March of 1945, sent home to retrain in the F4U Corsair before a planned return to participate in the invasion of Japan. A week after we left, the *Wasp* took several 500-pound bombs from Japanese dive-bombers. It was knocked out of the war, limping back to Washington for repairs.

By the time VF-81 was ready to return to the fight, two B-29s sealed the deal as the Japanese surrendered.

As far as I was concerned, the Hellcat not only played a major role in the Pacific, but because of its toughness, it kept me alive throughout my cruise.

Part IV

Props to Jets

28

Meteor Show: Gloster Meteor I

FIRST ENCOUNTER
Flt. Cdr. Robert "Bob" Large
RAF 504 Squadron and RAF 245 Squadron

I began my combat flying in Spitfires for the RAF in early 1941 and did so through 1943. The Spitfires were a delight to fly and I loved to do aerobatics with them, enjoying it immensely.

But it was during this time frame, in the early summer of 1942, that I had been obliged to leave my bullet-riddled Spitfire Mk VI in the English Channel, about 12 miles out from the White Cliffs of Dover. I had been up at high altitudes over France on a fighter sweep, but the German Bf 109Gs were up even higher and dove onto me, spraying my Spit with cannon and machine-gun rounds. Needless to say, I was out of luck and ended up taking a summer swim in the Channel.

In late 1943 I was assigned to a Lysander squadron, 161 Squadron Special Duties. Although flying the Lysander was a break, and quite different, I was very much interested in this cloak-and-dagger business, which involved flying at night into occupied France in a single-engine, unarmed, relatively slow aircraft, dropping off and picking up spies.

I did this for a period of time and rather enjoyed the work, but I must confess I did miss the "fast aeroplanes" like the Spitfire.

In March of 1945 I got another chance to fly something fast again, and was somewhat surprised to learn that my next airplane had no propeller attached to it.

Flt. Cdr. Robert "Bob" Large along with fellow 245 Squadron pilots pose with their dogs in front of one of their Meteor jets. COURTESY OF ROBERT LARGE

I joined 504 Squadron at Colerne where I came face-to-face with the Allies' first operational jet fighter of the war, the Gloster Meteor I. My first impression of the Meteor was that it looked absolutely wonderful—completely different from anything else I had ever seen. It was beautiful and clean, sleek and fast-looking, even on the ground, where it squatted down low, supported by a tricycle undercarriage. I relished the opportunity to fly fast again and likened it to going from a tortoise to a hare.

A Brief History of the Meteor at War

My old Spitfire Squadron (616 Squadron) was the first to be equipped with Meteors during the war in 1944, and those chaps used them quite successfully against the V-1 flying bombs as they made their murderous attacks on England. Although the V-1s were a menace to our homeland, my old squadron mates really wanted to tangle with the Luftwaffe's Me

262 Swallow jet. Although both jets were similar-looking—a jet engine and nacelle attached to each wing, with tricycle landing gear and guns in the nose—most of us felt that the Me 262 was superior to the Meteor, especially in the airspeed arena.

The original Meteor Is we flew were powered by a pair of Sir Frank Whittle–influenced turbojet engines. The ones installed in the Meteor I were called B.23 turbojets, built by Rolls-Royce. They produced 1,700 pounds of force (lbf) of thrust each. By the time I got into the jet game in early 1945, the much-improved Meteor III was on line. The improvements included longer jet nacelles, a sliding bubble-type hood instead of a hinged one, a sturdier airframe, and larger internal fuel capabilities, along with some engine refinements.

Even with all of these enhancements, the Meteor III, by all accounts, was still a short-range single-seat interceptor fighter. The early turbojet engines were big fuel hogs, gulping fuel at an alarming rate. They carried 330 gallons internally in one main fuselage tank, and I will never forget the sight of watching my fuel gauge moving from full to empty as I pushed the throttle forward. Without drop tanks we could only get about forty minutes of flying time, with enough reserve to get us back to base safely.

The Meteor airframe was obviously constructed from all metal, with a very unique tail plane mounted on the fin. This was designed so that all moving parts—the rudder and the elevator—would be well clear of the jet blast from the twin turbojets. A wingspan of 43 feet with a turbojet mounted in each mid-wing also incorporated the use of split flaps. The wing supported a fuselage that was over 41 feet long, and both rested on a hydraulically operated tricycle undercarriage. A single pilot seat offered outstanding visibility, especially sitting under the large bubble hood. For armament we carried four Mk II 20mm Hispano guns—two on each side of the cabin, imbedded in the nose, right in front of the pilot—with 150 rounds allotted for each gun. Our full loaded weight was over 12,000 pounds, and that number increased to over 14,000 pounds when a 180-gallon ventral tank was later added.

A few of 616 Squadron Meteors were stationed on the Continent near Brussels, and these were used sparingly in a ground attack role. Sadly, none of the chaps ever got to tangle with the 262s, as the Luftwaffe was rapidly running out of fuel near war's end. That must have been a god-send for RAF Fighter Command, because they certainly did not want the Germans to get their hands on one of our Meteors, either.

After familiarizing myself with the proper instruments and cockpit layout, along with the emergency procedures, I was ready to make my first flight in a jet.

Jet Jockey

On April 5, 1945, I finally got my chance to see what a propeller-less aircraft could do. Because we had no two-seater Meteor trainers in which to acquire dual in, it was more or less jumping in and going.

The engine start-up was simple and smooth. I was most amazed by the fact that there was no clanging and banging from under the hood like I had been accustomed to in my propeller days.

As I taxied out for the first time, it felt as though I was driving an automobile. With the tricycle undercarriage, the forward visibility was quite remarkable. With the elevator and rudder trimming tabs set at neutral and the engine run-up complete, I was all set to go.

As I advanced the throttle lever forward, I immediately noticed that there was no "swing" or torque like I would have encountered in a Spitfire. It stayed true to its heading as it trundled down the runway. Conversely, I did not get that kick in the back that I thought I would as we accelerated slowly down the runway. As you might imagine, the early Meteors were quite sluggish in those days, as it took some time to get up to flying speed. Relatively speaking, some of that was due in part to the shape of the wing, which had been designed to combat compressibility at altitude—something I would encounter soon enough!

As flying speed was reached and the undercarriage tucked away, it was very smooth and relatively quiet. There were no noises from rattling winds or shaking hoods because I was sealed up hermetically inside the very comfortable pressurized cabin. The climb out was at a reasonable rate—not outstanding by today's standards, but acceptable once you established a high rate of speed and a suitable angle of climb. The one noticeable item while flying the Meteor was that the ailerons seemed a bit heavy at all speeds. All in all, I was quite pleased with the flying qualities of the Meteor and was delighted to once again fly something fast.

One particular fact that was stressed early on in training was that bailing out of a Meteor was more or less a death sentence. With that tall tail plane behind you it was almost a certainty that you would hit it on the way out, even if you tried to slow it down before jumping. Slowing it down made the attitude of the Meteor become tail low, and, unfortunately, you would end up hitting it anyway. But for all those naysayers, I did know a chap who was able to jump from his stricken Meteor and live to tell about it.

This chap was a wing commander, and he was leading his whole squadron down on the deck, making a low pass and beating up the airfield. As he pulled up very quickly he heard a loud bang as the Meteor's nose shot up even higher above the horizon. The wing commander lost all control of his stick as the energy from the once rapidly moving Meteor began to recede quickly. As the Meteor leveled off for a second or two, with only one solution left, the wing commander knew his only alternative was to get out before gravity took over.

A Gloster Meteor taxis in after arriving at EAA AirVenture in Oshkosh, Wisconsin. COURTESY OF EAA

Quickly popping his hood, he knew he had to risk hitting the tail; unfortunately, he had no other viable options. As he went whizzing backward down the fuselage, expecting to hit the tail at any millisecond, he realized what that bang was that he had heard earlier. His entire tail had snapped completely off! The wing commander was one of the lucky ones; regrettably there were others who were not as fortunate. Thankfully the odds became better for us once ejection seats were installed on newer Meteors.

With my Meteor checkout complete, I experimented on my own and found that the Meteor was a delightful aerobatic machine, one I hoped to use in combat. Unfortunately, the war came to an end before our squadron could test our newfound tactics out on the Luftwaffe.

But it certainly didn't stop us from mixing it up with the Yanks!

Tally-ho! Flying Fortresses Below!

Although the war in Europe was over, we were thankful for some brilliant chaps within both the RAF and US Army Air Force (USAAF) who decided that the best thing for all of us Allied pilots to do was to continue to fly and develop combat tactics with our jets. There was just too much at stake to let both pilots and airplanes sit for too long, lest both become rusty in no time.

It had been decided that aerial combat between fighters and bombers would continue, and instead of shooting with machine guns and cannons, we would shoot at one another with cameras. By this stage in my flying career, I had obtained the rank of flight commander, and rather enjoyed leading five other Meteors around the skies of England and parts of Europe.

These big practice flights—or "mock raids," as we called them—consisted of large formations with hundreds of B-17 Flying Fortresses being shepherded by their P-51 Mustang fighter escorts launching from the Continent and making their way to targets in England, such as London and other industrial cities, just like the Battle of Britain days. It was tremendously good practice for everyone involved, and we enjoyed it immensely. You had the thrill of combat without having to worry about all the "hot lead" being thrown at you!

I had briefed the five other chaps in my flight that we would utilize the same tactics as the Me 262 pilots had used on the B-17 formations during the war; in other words, we would avoid the Mustangs at all costs and concentrate on the Fortresses. It was certainly a sight to see as we climbed well above the bombers and fighters in our Meteors and waited to pounce on them.

As we broke we did split-off attacks and dove down toward the bomber formations as quick as we could. As soon as the Mustangs saw us turn over on our backs and begin our dive, they tried to break into us. The six of us ignored the P-51s and kept on going straight down. We knew we had a higher speed advantage and that there would be no way the Mustangs could catch us. But if we tried to stick around and turn with them, then the tables would have certainly been turned on us.

A box of B-17 Flying Fortresses and a lone B-24 Liberator on the way to an Axis target. COURTESY OF EAA

I wasn't paying attention to my airspeed, to be honest with you, as I broke through the Mustang gauntlet and looked back to see their "tongues hanging out" as they tried to catch us. Nearing the Fortresses from high right, I locked into one of them with my G.45 camera that was mounted in the Meteor's nose fairing, and "fired away."

As I broke away I dove to the lower right, giving the rear gunner the most difficult target to follow. The difficulty for me, however, occurred seconds later. As I pushed the Meteor's nose farther down, my speed increased to the point that I hit compressibility. It was one of the most terrifying experiences I have ever had at the controls of an airplane!

The entire airplane went from being very, very smooth and easy to maneuver to one that became like a "rope snake," fluttering up and down. The controls became useless as my nose dropped. I could waggle my stick around and it produced no response from the ailerons or elevator; it was as if the entire tail had come off!

What was happening was that the lifting surfaces were reaching near the speed of sound and the airflow over the main plane was breaking away and not adhering to the shape of the airfoil. Ironically, I wasn't the only one in trouble with compressibility, as all the other chaps next to me in their Meteors hit it at almost the exact same time as I did. I immediately throttled back and so did the other chaps. Thankfully none of us tried to trim the Meteor out of compressibility, like some other poor chaps had done. (They didn't make it.)

Although all six of us in our Meteors were petrified as we hurtled earthward, not a word was said over the radio. For a long moment it felt as though the Meteor was on the verge of disintegrating. As we passed through 5,000 feet with the bloody awful buffeting, we finally reached denser air and it suddenly became beautifully smooth once again. The lifting surfaces reverted back to what they were designed to do—lift us away!

I re-formed my flight as we very gently flew back to our base, all of us reciting our own little prayers of thanks.

Although I had encountered compressibility by complete accident and endured the subsequent terror that followed, I didn't completely shy away from it, as I began to experiment with it quite a bit on future flights.

I filed reports with the lessons I had learned, and these were later analyzed in hopes of keeping other chaps out of trouble.

Mustang Melee

After the war, while I was stationed at Horsham St. Faith, our 504 Squadron was renamed 245 Squadron. There was a Polish P-51 Mustang Squadron, No. 303 Polish Fighter Squadron, stationed nearby at Hethel, and I became acquainted with one of their pilots. His name was Jan "Johnny" Zumbach, and he was quite famous in his own right, having scored eight victories during the Battle of Britain and ending the war with thirteen total. He had a chest full of medals, including a DFC with bar and an assortment of others, but none of that seemed to matter when we met socially at a local pub, quite frequently.

Johnny and I were talking over a pint one day about the merits of our various aircraft and I brought up the fact that while the Me 109G was faster than the Spitfire, if you saw it in time there should be no reason to get shot down by it, because the Spitfire could always out-turn them. Now with the Meteor, I reckoned the tactics I used during the "mock battles" were similar to those of the 109G during the war. As I described these facts in great detail to Johnny—that these hit-and-run tactics worked very well for the Germans against the Flying Fortresses—I said that I wouldn't under any circumstances go into combat against the Mustangs for fear that they could out-turn me. But then again, I reminded him, it wasn't the Mustangs that the fighters were after, it was the bombers.

I must have piqued Johnny's interest because he looked at me, rubbed his jaw vigorously, and said, "Why don't we have a little prearranged battle of our own and see who can shoot down who first?"

The following day I took off with six Meteors and met Johnny and his six Mustangs at 25,000 feet. We had previously briefed that we would circle around one another, straighten out, and then fly past one another, straight and level, with our flights going in opposite directions. As soon as our Meteor wing tips flashed by the Mustangs, the fight would be on, and we were free to use whatever tactics we wanted to.

I had briefed my chaps earlier that we would not mix it up with the Mustangs, and to not even think about trying to turn with them. Instead we would act as if we were 109Gs, just like the painful encounter I had experienced with them earlier in the war.

As soon as we passed by the Mustangs we opened up our throttles and climbed. Our Meteor IIIs were significantly faster in a climb than the Mustangs as we sat up high on our perch, circled above Johnny's P-51s, and took advantage of our height. We pushed our noses over and dove down onto the Mustangs. As we drew closer each of us picked out a target and began to fire with our cameras. We hit them hard and then continued to zoom right through them. We had a higher mach number than the Mustangs, and there was no way they could catch us in a dive.

Back at the pub each of us, with a pint in hand, claimed we had shot each other down. Broadly speaking we held the edge with our Meteors because we didn't allow ourselves to engage them in a turning battle. To do that would have been quite absurd—like a 109G trying to out-turn a Spitfire.

Dog Flight

It was quite common for pilots in RAF squadrons to have dogs living with them while at the airfield. I was no exception, and owned a young Labrador mix named Patrick. For whatever foolish reason I really wanted Patrick to fly with me in the Meteor but knew I couldn't carry him on my lap, especially with the control stick between my legs. I couldn't put him on the floor, either, because there was none; your feet rested in rudder pedal stirrups.

I scratched my head for a while, trying to figure out a way to carry him aboard the Meteor, and realized I could put him right behind my head. Because the hood flared down into the fuselage behind the pilot's head, there were transparent armor plates installed, made of heavy thick plastic to protect us from rear attacks. I decided to take one of these panels off from the left side and pushed old Patrick in stern first. As he lay in that position, he was held in place quite nicely and his head was just about level with mine.

As we took off on May 11, 1946, I received a lot of nervous licks from Patrick, but I could see he was not in any distress. As I climbed I did a beautiful roll with him and he didn't seem to mind in the least. I pushed the throttle forward and did 500 mph, and I smiled as I looked at Patrick watching the world go by. I didn't go very high or do a loop for that matter because I didn't want to hurt his ears. All the flying we did was down low and Patrick seemed to enjoy flying in the Meteor as much as I did—although his tongue hung out more than mine did! After I landed I quickly removed my stowaway before anyone reported me, as it was all quite illegal!

I included Patrick's name in my logbook as a copilot and took him up on several more flights until he outgrew his window seat. Years later, word of Patrick's flight in the Meteor leaked out and he and I were eventually listed in the *Guinness Book of World Records* as the first Allied dog to ever fly in a jet. I had no way of confirming that the Luftwaffe chaps flying jets during the war didn't pack one of their dogs inside and take it out on a combat mission. If the German pilot had mixed it up with some Allied fighters, that would have been one cracking dogfight!

In my mind the Meteor jet-propelled the RAF into a new realm of flight. It seemed that new technology brought higher speeds and altitudes—and with it, revised fighter tactics. Unfortunately, you could not turn as tight a lovely circle as you could with a Spitfire. As a fighter pilot you had to now think miles and miles ahead of the airplane, with the one constant worry about how many pounds of fuel one had left. But with all of its shortcomings, the Meteor was truly a delight to fly, and thankfully I never had to leave one in the Channel!

29

Jets Are for Kids: P-80 Shooting Star

TEACHING LUCKY LINDY HOW TO FLY A SHOOTING STAR
Maj. Roy C. Ihde
4th Fighter Group, 336th Fighter Squadron

Props to Jets
In the early summer of 1948, I was nineteen years old and had just survived the rigors of AT-6 Texan and P-51 Mustang flight training with the rest of single-engine pilot school Class 48B. We were told by our graduating class guest speaker, Brigadier General Darcy of the air force, to look around the room, because, he said, "In less than a year's time, over 10 percent of you will be missing from your ranks due to aircraft accidents." To encourage us even more, the general added that very few of us would reach retirement age.

Although retirement age for me was a whole world away, I took what the general had to say and tucked it into the back of my brain as I prepared to enter the air force's jet age as a green second lieutenant.

I joined World War II's famed 4th Fighter Group, 336th Fighter Squadron (Rocket) at Andrews AFB, Camp Springs, Maryland, and was introduced to the Lockheed P-80 Shooting Star. It was the first operational jet fighter of the US Army Air Forces and would become my front office for the next year.

The single-seat P-80 was sleek and fast-looking even as it sat on the ramp. Compared to the slower speed of the P-51 Mustang that I had flown in Advanced, the P-80 was like a rocket. So much so, I likened it to

The jet age comes to America—Lockheed P-80 Shooting Stars lined up. COUR-
TESY OF EAA

riding on the tip of a bullet! I wasn't flying behind a propeller anymore, and as a wet-behind-the-ears "jet jockey," I learned the hard way just how fast a Shooting Star could fly—especially going straight down!

I was up flying one day with an experienced World War II pilot in another P-80 parked just off my wing. I was practicing instrument flight condition training while the guy flying next to me was my extra set of eyes, looking for other traffic. I found this training to be too tame, so I caged my gyro instruments and placed a local area flight map over my head to make it more realistic. I began to get bored with straight and level partial panel flight and started to do turns to the right, when suddenly all the instruments went wild.

A classic case of spatial distortion was taking place inside my cockpit as I tried to figure out what was happening. I watched as my airspeed began to build and my altimeter unwound from 10,000 feet. I ripped the map off my head and looked out at a very strange sight: There, right above my canopy, was a ship slicing through the water up in the sky above me. I suddenly woke up and realized that I was upside down, screaming earthward toward the Chesapeake Bay!

A P-80 Shooting Star COURTESY OF EAA

As I hung on for dear life, I throttled back and popped the speed brake as I watched the P-80's speed climb over the 580 mph (Mach .80) mark. As the ship grew larger in front of me, the nose of the P-80 began to rise as I regained control of the runaway rocket. I managed to complete a split-S right above the ship just as my wingman called, "You okay, Ihde?" To him I had simply slipped away, and he was wondering if I was still among the living. I weakly replied that I was fine; that is, until I met my crew chief back on the ground. The crew chief snarled at me and said, "What are you trying to do, Lieutenant, set a new speed record?" as he pounded the outside of the fuselage with his fists, popping the fillets back into place that had worked their way loose.

I quickly realized that I had almost become one of General Darcy's statistics, and gave the P-80 newfound respect.

Frozen Star

In the late fall and early winter of 1948, our group was sent to Ladd Field in Alaska for cold weather operational training in the P-80. The air force was having problems with the Shooting Stars at extreme cold temperatures due to ice crystals forming in the low-pressure fuel filter. When the ice formed, it caused oscillation in the engine rpms, and this led not only to flameout but lack of forward thrust as well.

Needless to say, the P-80 flew like a brick when the flame blew out. To remedy the situation, an alcohol system that removed ice from the fuel system was installed that could be turned on manually before a flameout occurred. We had plenty of opportunities to test the new equipment, especially on balmy -43 degree days out in the frozen tundra!

In my spare time I had volunteered to create and build a squadron mission briefing board. For whatever reason, the squadron operations officer, Captain

Roy C. Ihde COURTESY OF ROY IHDE

Melancon, liked my handiwork and asked me if I would "volunteer" for another assignment, which he called a "special project." Although I had been warned to never volunteer for anything in the service, I also knew there was not much to do in the Alaskan wintertime.

The following Monday Captain Melancon called me into his office to meet someone. As I entered the room, there standing in front of me, larger than life and legend, was Col. Charles Lindbergh. My jaw just about hit the floor as I was introduced to one of my childhood heroes. I was still two years away from entering this world when "Lucky Lindy" and the *Spirit of St Louis* made their historic flight together over the Atlantic in May of 1927.

On Lindy's Wing

Captain Melancon explained to me that Colonel Lindbergh was a special advisor to the air force and would be spending two weeks with our group, evaluating our capabilities and other things. One of the "other things" was that Lindbergh wanted to be checked out in the P-80. I thought I was dreaming when Captain Melancon explained to Colonel Lindbergh that I would take him through a refresher course on the P-80's flight manual in its entirety. I was told to give Colonel Lindbergh cockpit time, a blind-fold checkout on instrument and control locations, start-up and run-up procedures, taxi and radio checkout, along with fuel-purging techniques in the event of low-pressure fuel system ice. I was told to teach Colonel Lindbergh everything I knew about flying the Shooting Star.

To me Lindbergh was the greatest pilot that ever flew, and here he was mere feet away from me as we went over the P-80 flight manual. I tried to make small talk with him, but he was rather quiet and didn't say much, especially if I asked him a question about his historic flight from New York to Paris. I asked him about the difficulties of staying focused and awake while flying for almost a day and a half. Colonel Lindbergh quietly responded, "Yes, that was a problem," and then quickly countered with a question for me: "Lieutenant, how did you enjoy your cadet training?"

I soon learned that Colonel Lindbergh did not want to talk about himself or his accomplishments. I felt sorry for him in a way because he had been asked the same questions over and over again and had been publicized to death about his famous flight.

It was extremely easy to teach Colonel Lindbergh on P-80 flight operations. It seemed that I had to just merely give him the idea and he not only took it from there but he explained it back to me with much more detail. I also stopped pestering him with questions about the Atlantic crossing and let him talk about what he wanted to talk about. Colonel Lindbergh shared some of his experiences with me while flying F4U Corsairs and P-38 Lightnings in the Pacific Theater during World War II, teaching fighter pilots how to lean out their fuel mixture to maximize their range.

I think the thing that intrigued Colonel Lindbergh the most, however, was when he asked me what I liked to do to pass the time when I wasn't flying. I sheepishly told him that I built and flew gas model airplanes. Colonel Lindbergh's eyes lit up like a child's when I told him that, and he asked me if I had a flyable one. When I told him I did, he asked for a flight demonstration. I couldn't have been any prouder as I stood in the snow with a 50-foot control line attached to my Tiger V-Shark on skis as it zoomed around in a circle at 107 mph in front of a smiling Colonel Lindbergh. It was one of the only times during our two weeks together that I saw him smile.

Although I couldn't see his face under the oxygen mask as our flight of four P-80s took off from Ladd Field, I imagine that Colonel Lindbergh had a small grin across his face and was in awe at the quietness of jet flight. With no propeller whirling up front and the lack of noise from the popping and crackling of cylinders that he had been accustomed to in his early aviation days, it must have been a pleasant surprise for him, as the only noise he heard was the whistling of air that flowed over his canopy.

The four of us flew in a tight finger-four formation out to the gunnery range. Colonel Lindbergh flew that P-80 as if it were on a rail—very tight and crisp. His formation flying was excellent, and as a natural-born pilot, it seemed to me like he had flown the Shooting Star for thousands of hours. We took turns dropping small "blue boy" practice bombs and shooting old barrels that were scattered about in the snow.

As we joined back up I couldn't help but stare into Colonel Lindbergh's cockpit. I could see his eyes peering out from his helmet and oxygen mask, and all I thought was, "Those eyes belong to the most famous pilot in the world." There has never been any greater honor for me in my life than when I flew a Shooting Star with the Lone Eagle off my wing.

INDEX

Abbreviations RAF, RAAF, RCAF, RNZAF, and USAAF stand for Royal Air Force, Royal Australian Air Force, Royal Canadian Air Force, Royal New Zealand Air Force, and U.S. Army Air Force, respectively.

White, Johnny (USAAF), 24
Whittle, Sir Frank, 291
Williams, George (USAAF), 215
Willits [LT] (USAAF), 174
Winters, Theodore Hugh (USN), 148, 150, 152, 154
Wolfe, Roland (USAAF), 193

Z

Zemke, Hub (USAAF), 117–18, 122, 176, 267
Zemke's Wolfpack, 117–19, 177, 234, 265–67
Zeola, Leo (USN), 163, 166–67